The AutoCAD® Textbook

James M. Kirkpatrick
Eastfield College

Merrill Publishing Company
A Bell & Howell Information Company
Columbus   Toronto   London   Melbourne

To Bev

Cover Photo: Courtesy of Autodesk, Inc.

Published by Merrill Publishing Company
A Bell & Howell Information Company
Columbus, Ohio 43216

This book was set in Century.

Administrative Editor: John Yarley
Production Coordinator: Mary Harlan
Art Coordinator: Ruth Kimpel
Cover Designer: Brian Deep

Figures 1-7 (right), 2-5, 11-1, 11-2, 11-3, 11-4, 11-5, and 11-6 are reproduced courtesy of Autodesk, Inc.

AutoCAD is a registered trademark of Autodesk, Inc.

Library of Congress Catalog Card Number: 88-63524
International Standard Book Number: 0-675-20882-3
Printed in the United States of America
1 2 3 4 5 6 7 8 9—93 92 91 90 89

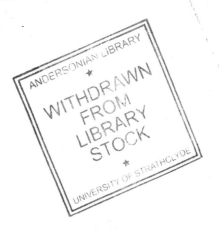
The AutoCAD® Textbook

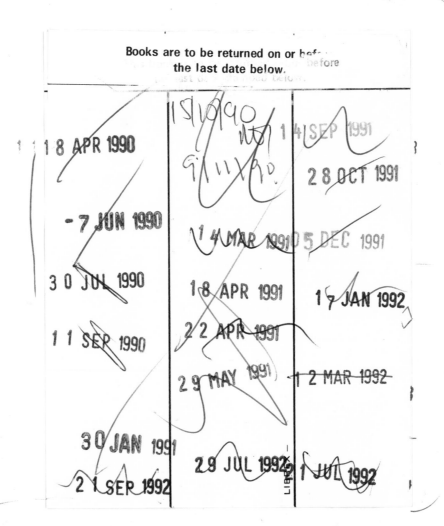

MERRILL SERIES IN MECHANICAL, INDUSTRIAL, AND CIVIL TECHNOLOGY

Preface

The versatility and economy of the AutoCAD system have made it the leading tool for computer-aided drafting in a wide variety of industrial applications. Few companies that produce graphics in this country have not considered AutoCAD; many have adopted it as their primary drawing program.

The popularity of AutoCAD has generated numerous books and manuals, most of the reference variety, similar to the reference manual that accompanies the AutoCAD software. AutoCAD is difficult to learn using just a reference manual or a book structured very much like one. *The AutoCAD Textbook* was written in response to the need for a textbook with an easy-to-follow format designed for students with various educational backgrounds and at differing levels of computer experience. It was developed by people who use AutoCAD to produce drawings for manufacturing and construction. In addition, the author and contributors teach AutoCAD in the classroom setting.

All of the material has been carefully class-tested. People who have used the book have learned quickly to become productive with AutoCAD. Many have been inspired to create menus and customize AutoCAD for their specific situations. Students are pleased with the clarity of the presentation and the fact that it assumes no familiarity with computers. Those who have had some drafting background, however, have benefited more quickly from this text than those who have not.

The purpose of this book is to prepare students to produce drawings that can be used effectively in industry to manufacture, construct and assemble buildings and products. It begins with two chapters explaining the types of drawings to be covered and the structure of AutoCAD. Chapter 2 also discusses the equipment necessary to use AutoCAD to its fullest extent.

Chapters 3 through 10 are drawing chapters showing students step-by-step how to produce several different types of drawings, including orthographic, sectional, isometric, and plan views. The topics of dimensioning, tolerancing, geometric constructions, space planning, block diagrams, and drawing formats are also covered in these chapters.

Chapter 11 explains how to customize the standard AutoCAD menu for both tablet and the screen. The use of "macros" and "icons" to combine commands and create pictures for screen menus to make drawing more efficient is discussed in detail in Chapter 11.

The final chapter is devoted to solving common problems associated with AutoCAD. Many of the most perplexing problems often have simple solutions. This chapter is a joy to someone who has one of these problems and is at a loss as to how to fix it.

At the back of the text is an appendix devoted to DOS. It describes the most common DOS commands and how to use them. The creation and use of directories is also covered in this appendix. It employs the same step-by-step format as the drawing chapters.

Each chapter in *The AutoCAD Textbook* features

- objectives listing commands used in the chapter;
- clear, concise definitions for new terms when they are first introduced;
- examples of drawings relating to the chapter topic;
- step-by-step listings of all commands used in examples and an illustration of each command or series of commands; and
- assignments of varying difficulty, similar to the examples.

The AutoCAD Textbook allows the student to learn AutoCAD by drawing with it. Commands are presented and repeated as they are needed. Using the "hands on" approach to the AutoCAD computer package is the fastest and most effective method of learning to use this powerful and exciting drawing tool.

I wish to acknowledge the contribution of several people in the preparation of this text: Bill Sorrells, for his well researched and thorough contribution to Chapter 11, Customizing Menus; Michael Smith, for his contribution to Chapters 5 and 6; Bruce Smith and Chad Savage, for their patience and expert knowledge of computer systems.

I would also like to thank the following prepublication reviewers for their helpful comments and suggestions: Dennis Short, Purdue University; Jack Swearman, Montgomery College; Jack North, Golden West College; Felicitas Czierba, Texas State Technical Institute-Amarillo; and Tom Schoellen, Hawkeye Institute of Technology.

Contents

1
Introduction

Objectives

The student will acquire the skills and knowledge to:

- describe the purpose of the textbook
- identify the types of drawings to be drawn in this textbook
- describe how the textbook is organized
- describe how the textbook is to be used

Purpose

This textbook is intended to present information in such a manner that the student can learn AutoCAD by drawing with it. A minimum number of pages is devoted to subjects that do not involve hands-on use of AutoCAD commands. A command is an operator response that tells the computer to do something. Step-by-step listings are used to show students how to draw each type of drawing described in the following paragraphs.

References to specific versions of AutoCAD have been avoided in this text. Users of the earlier versions may find a few commands that are not available to them. When this is the case, other commands can easily be substituted, although they may be slower than version 2.62 or Release 9 with its pull-down menus and handy icons. The uneasiness felt by some who have worked with earlier versions is unnecessary. Students who have learned earlier versions well will have no trouble with later versions. The later versions just make drawing with AutoCAD a little easier and faster.

1

Types of Drawings

These are the types of drawings, dimensions, and constructions that will be produced by the student who completes this textbook:

- block diagrams
- geometric constructions
- orthographic drawings (including floor plans)
- dimensioned drawings
- toleranced drawings
- drawing formats
- sectional drawings
- three-dimensional drawings

These drawings are described briefly in the following paragraphs. Later chapters describe them in greater detail.

Block Diagrams

Figure 1-1 shows examples of block diagrams drawn on a computer. These diagrams are used to show as simply as possible how a company or other group is organized, and how equipment or groups function. Some of these diagrams have specific symbols and uses not shown in this figure, but they are all similar in construction. Most of them have blocks, lines connecting the blocks, and arrows showing the directional flow.

Figure 1-1
Block Diagrams

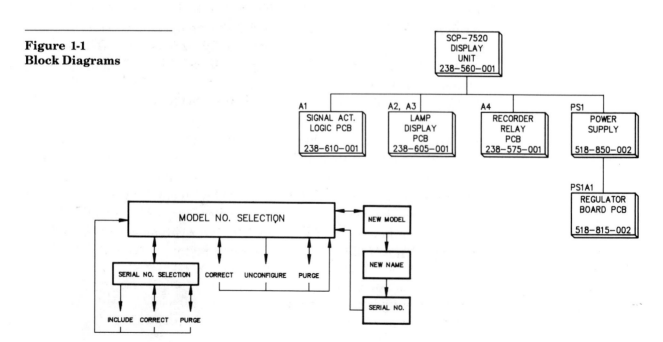

**Figure 1-2
Geometric
Constructions**

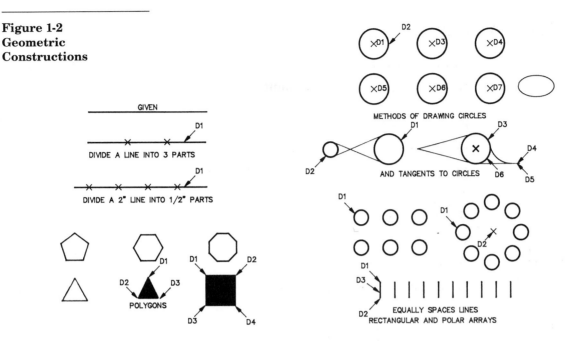

Geometric Constructions

Although geometric constructions are not a drawing type, they are placed as the next subject in this list. These constructions are the building blocks of all types of drawings. Terms such as parallel, perpendicular, horizontal, vertical, and tangent, are defined and are used to create these constructions. The term *geometric* may sound as if higher-level math will be required; not so in computer drafting. If you can add, subtract, multiply, and divide on a calculator, you can do all of the drawing problems in this book.

Figure 1-2 shows several of the geometric constructions covered in Chapter 4. These constructions are often very difficult to draw manually in pencil or ink, but with the computer they are very easy. If the correct commands are used to draw them, they can be extremely accurate and beautifully drawn. As one who has labored for years on the drawing board, I find AutoCAD drawing a delight.

Orthographic Drawings

Two-dimensional drawings are called orthographic drawings in the drafting business. These drawings are the universal language of technical drawing. Only two dimensions are seen in any one view. Those dimensions may be height and width, height and depth, or width and depth. Figure 1-3 shows some examples of orthographic drawings. The top drawing shows three views of a single object. The bottom drawing is a floor plan showing a single view of a structure. Further details will be presented in a later chapter.

Figure 1-3
Orthographic Drawings

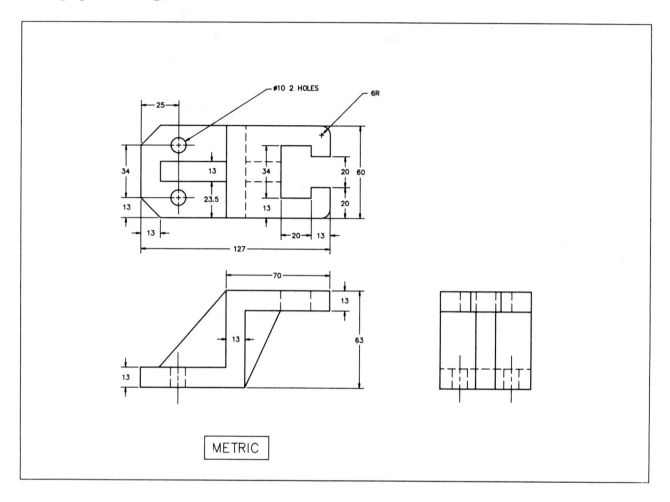

METRIC

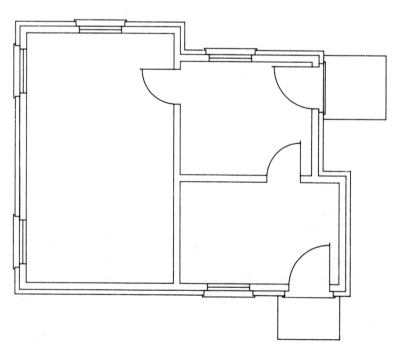

Dimensioned Drawings

A dimensioned drawing is a type of orthographic drawing that gives the size and location of features. AutoCAD is very useful in dimensioning because it can become almost automatic when drawings are made full-size. Figure 1-4 shows two drawings that have been drawn to scale and dimensioned using AutoCAD.

Figure 1-4
Dimensioned Drawings

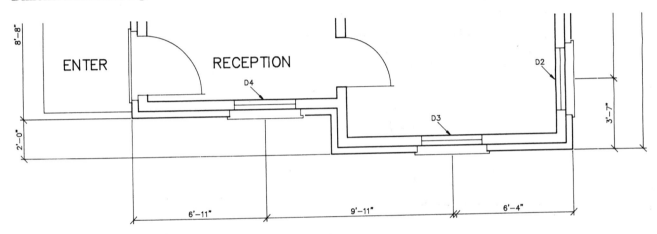

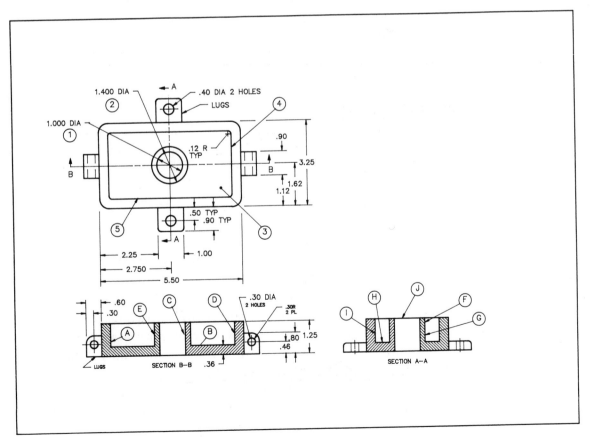

Figure 1-5
Toleranced Drawings

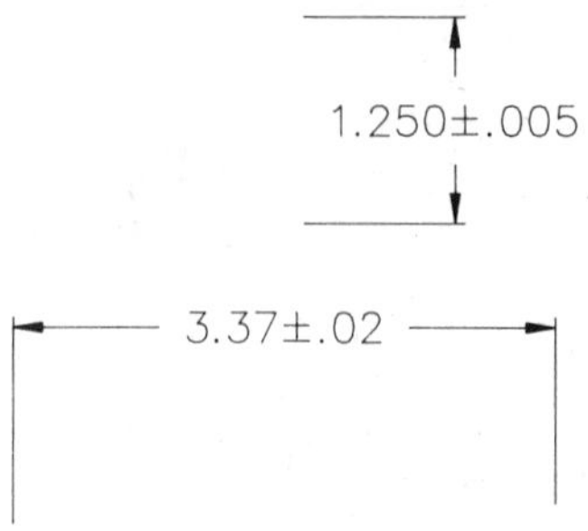

1.250±.005

3.37±.02

Figure 1-6
Sectional Drawings

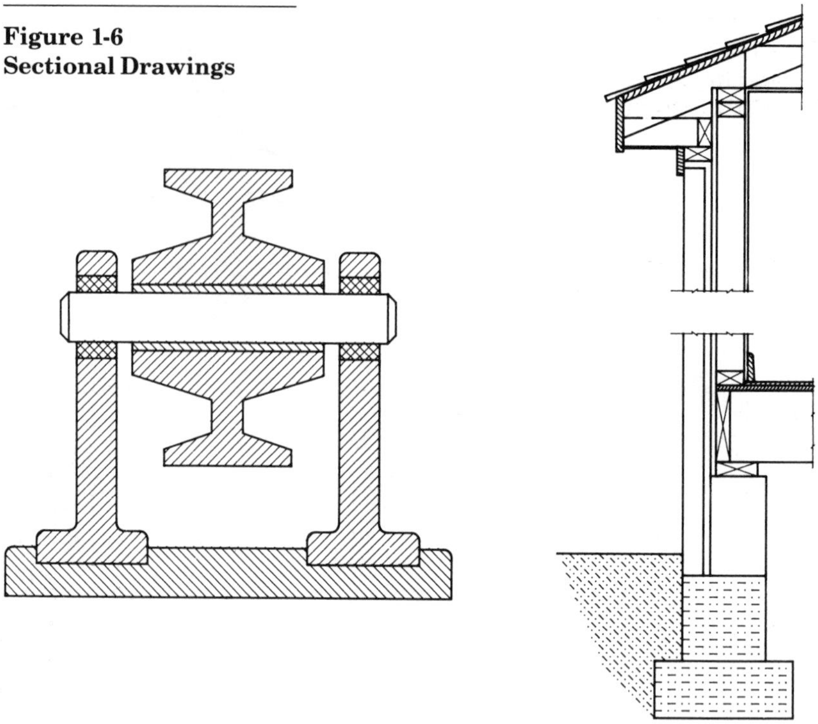

Toleranced Drawings

All drawings used to build parts or structures have tolerances (limits) that are placed on all dimensions. These tolerances may be very specific as shown in Figure 1-5. For example, an understood tolerance of ±¼″ on a 3″ dimension means that the part, when inspected, must measure 3¼″ or 2¾″ or any dimension between those two to pass. A more accurate tolerance for the same 3″ dimension could be ±.005″. The upper limit for this dimension would be 3.005″. The lower limit for this dimension would be 2.995″. AutoCAD allows parts to be drawn with extreme accuracy using certain commands. It also allows parts that do not require accuracy to be drawn faster but with less accuracy.

Sectional Drawings

Sectional drawings are used in many different industries to clarify internal or hidden external construction. AutoCAD allows the spacing of shading lines to be very accurate and eliminates the tedious task of drawing those lines or using stick-on or rub-on shading lines. Figure 1-6 shows two sectional drawings drawn using AutoCAD. This type of drawing can often be drawn with more consistent lines and with much less effort with AutoCAD than manually. Shading lines are often drawn with a thinner pen by using a "Layer" command, which is presented in Chapter 3. Layers are used to separate line types or other features that allow the drawing to be used more efficiently.

Figure 1-7
Three-dimensional
AutoCAD Drawings

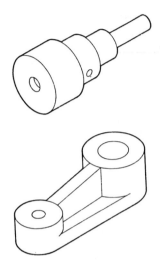

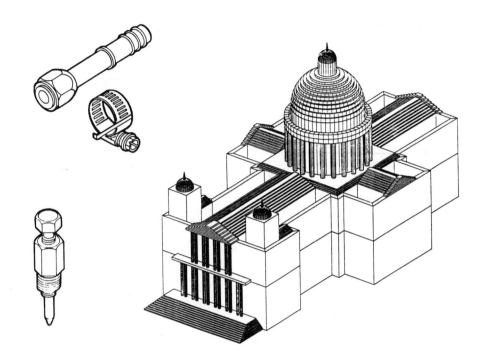

Three-dimensional Drawings

3-D is a feature of AutoCAD that may be used to show pictorial views of objects. If drawings have similar shapes and parts, such as screws, nuts, and washers, this form can become a valuable tool in identifying parts. Figure 1-7 shows examples of three-dimensional and isometric objects drawn using AutoCAD.

Additional Topics

In addition to chapters concerning the drawing types listed above, one chapter is devoted to customizing menus and creating Release 9 icons, which is a way to tailor AutoCAD so that it may be used more effectively for specific situations. Another chapter deals with the common problems associated with using AutoCAD, and with their solutions.

Textbook Organization

Two short preliminary chapters introduce drawing types, AutoCAD, and tell you how to get started. After these chapters, the textbook is arranged so that each of the drawing types listed can be drawn using a set of AutoCAD commands given for that particular drawing type. Although commands are often repeated in later drawings, each drawing has new commands, and familiar commands are often used in a manner other than the one first introduced. The complete AutoCAD Menu or list of commands is used in this textbook. Each chapter begins with objectives, and the drawing chapters have an initial list of the commands to be introduced. Next, a drawing is presented with a step-by-step explanation of how it was constructed. Each drawing chapter ends with exercises similar to the one presented in the chapter and quizzes based on the objectives.

Test on Objectives—Chapter 1

Circle the correct answer.

1. How many chapters of this book do not require the student to make, dimension, or change a drawing? (Look at the Table of Contents)

   a. 1
   b. 3
   c. 4
   d. 7
   e. 9

2. Which of the following is *not* a type of drawing covered by this book?

   a. sectional
   b. block diagrams
   c. auxiliary
   d. orthographic
   e. isometricb

3. Which of the following is used to show how a company is organized?

   a. block diagram
   b. isometric drawing
   c. orthographic drawing
   d. auxiliary drawings
   e. assembly drawings

4. Which of the following is a three-dimensional drawing?

   a. orthographic
   b. sectional
   c. isometric
   d. auxiliary
   e. floor plan

5. Dimensioning with AutoCAD can be nearly automatic.

   a. true
   b. false

6. List the seven drawing types covered by this book.

   a. _____

   b. _____

   c. _____

   d. _____

   e. _____

   f. _____

   g. _____

7. Describe how each chapter is organized.

   _____

   _____

   _____

8. List three chapters that do *not* require the student to draw or dimension something.

   a. _____

   b. _____

   c. _____

9. Define the term "customized menu."

   _____

   _____

   _____

10. Define the word "command" as used in AutoCAD.

    _____

    _____

    _____

2

The Uses and Structure of AutoCAD and Its Equipment

Objectives

The student will:

■ identify the parts of a hardware system (the physical parts of the system) that will operate AutoCAD software (a computer program that instructs the computer to do something)

■ identify Main Menu, Root Menu, and submenus

■ describe the uses of each menu

Before learning to use the AutoCAD system, it is helpful to know something about the equipment which allows AutoCAD to be used. A description of the parts of the system will provide that introduction.

Parts of the AutoCAD Hardware System

The parts of a typical personal computer system (Figure 2-1) on which AutoCAD software can be used are:

■ the computer
■ a video monitor
■ a floppy disk drive
■ a hard disk drive
■ a keyboard
■ a mouse; tablet and stylus or puck; or light pen
■ plotter

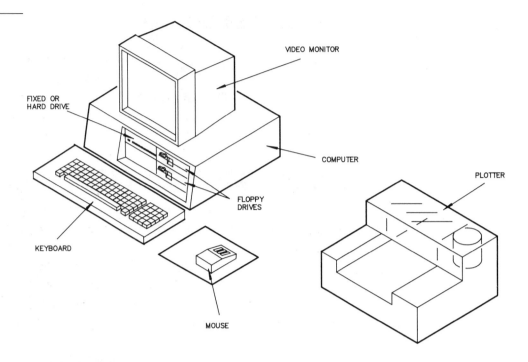

Figure 2-1
AutoCAD Hardware

VIDEO MONITOR

FIXED OR
HARD DRIVE

COMPUTER

PLOTTER

FLOPPY
DRIVES

KEYBOARD

MOUSE

The Computer

The computer should be of sufficient capacity to run AutoCAD
easily. The "AutoCAD Installation Guide" recommends a minimum
of 512K (512,000 bytes) of operating memory. (Release 10 requires
1M—1 million.) It should also have a graphics card (a printed circuit
board that allows a high-quality display of graphic data) and other
features that will allow the display (the screen) to be easily read and
quickly generated. In addition, later versions (Release 9 and later)
require a math-coprocessor chip. A slow response to commands or a
poor display will defeat the advantages of this valuable drawing tool.

A Video Monitor

The video monitor (similar to a television screen) may be either
monochromatic (black and white) or color. A color monitor is a
necessity for some drawings, but a monochrome monitor can be
used for many drawings if color is not available. The resolution of
the display is important. The resolution of the display is stated in
pixels, which is the number of dots arranged in rows and columns
to make the visual display on the screen. The finer the better. The
minimum resolution display listed in the "AutoCAD Installation
Guide" is 320×200 pixels. The best listed is 2048×1280. A common
resolution that balances price and quality is 640×350.

A Floppy Disk Drive

At least one floppy disk drive (the device that reads and writes to the floppy disk) is needed to move large blocks of information into and out of the computer. The floppy disk (a thin plastic disk packaged in a square envelope) is also used to store copies of drawings as insurance against failure of the hard drive. Currently, there are two types of 5¼″-diameter floppy drives. They are the *high-density drive* and the *double-density drive.* The high-density drive uses a 5¼″ high-density floppy disk. This disk stores approximately 1.2 million (1,200,000) bytes of information. (A byte is approximately one character such as one letter or number.) The double-density drive uses a 5¼″ double-density floppy disk. This disk stores approximately 360K (360,000) bytes of information. The high-density and double-density floppy disks are sometimes used interchangeably, but high-density and double-density disks sometimes require copying to the hard disk (permanently fixed disk of much larger capacity) for proper operation. Many of the newer computers have 3½″ floppy drives that use a 3½″ disk storing 720K bytes of information.

A Hard Disk Drive

A hard disk drive of adequate storage capacity for your situation is necessary; 20-megabyte (20,000,000) to 40-megabyte (40,000,000) drives are commonly used. AutoCAD can be operated on two floppy drives, but to get full advantage of the time-saving features of AutoCAD, a hard disk drive is needed. The hard disk drive can be used to store the AutoCAD program and drawings. When used for this purpose, no disk swapping is needed to call up AutoCAD and begin drawing. A hard disk drive is highly recommended.

**Three-dimensional
IBM-based system showing
a three-dimensional part
in isometric.
(Courtesy CALCOMP)**

A Keyboard

The keyboard is needed to type the lettering that will appear on your drawings and to occasionally insert commands. Function keys (the keys labeled F1, F2, F3, etc.) on the keyboard are also used to flip screens, operate SNAP and ORTHO modes, escape from commands, display grids, and so forth. All of these functions will be used in the drawing chapters of this book. They will be explained when you use them.

A Mouse or Digitizing Tablet and Stylus or Light Pen

Any of these three input pointing devices can be used to create drawings with AutoCAD. The mouse is used with the menu that appears on the screen. (Menus are lists of commands used to make drawings.) It is moved across a tabletop pad as its action is described on the screen. The digitizing tablet has the menu placed around the outer edges of the drawing area. Commands are selected by picking them from the menu with a stylus. A light pen can be used by pointing directly to the monitor's screen to enter points or to select commands from the screen menu.

The HIPAD digitizer (11 inches × 11 inches) (Courtesy Houston Instrument)

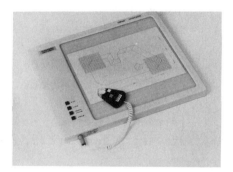

A Plotter

To do high quality, usable drawings (hard copies), a plotter is essential. One type of plotter uses pens similar to technical drawing pens used in manual inking. It also uses felt markers if you choose to use them for multicolor drawings. A good plotter makes drawings with nice, smooth curves, dense lines, and crisp connections. Plotters may have one pen or multiple pens. They may accept only 8½ × 11″ paper or they may accept rolls of paper. Electrostatic plotters (similar to photocopy machines) are also available. Many dot matrix printers (printers that use dots to form letters and lines) may be used to obtain check prints of drawings, but are usually not adequate for final drawings. Laser printers are now available; they will produce hard copies of acceptable quality.

Figure 2-2
Screen Display

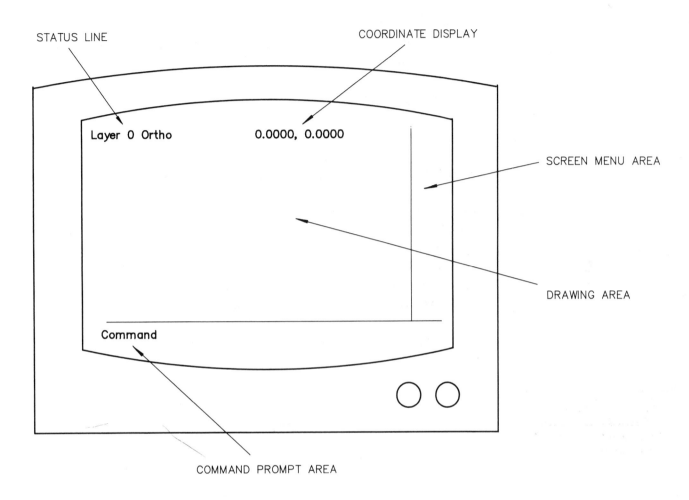

The Basic Structure of AutoCAD

AutoCAD commands are displayed as a menu on the front of the
CRT (the monitor, Figure 2-2) or on a tablet. These commands are
activated by a mouse, a puck, or a stylus. The basic structure of
AutoCAD can be understood most easily by observing the menus as
they appear on the CRT screen. Appearing in the lower left of the
screen is the prompt area. The prompt area tells you what to do next
and the status area, in the upper left, tells you what layer you are on
and whether SNAP or ORTHO are ON or OFF. The coordinate display, to the right of the status area, tells you where the cursor (the
indicator shown on the screen) is in relation to the origin, 0,0. These
areas will be described in detail in a later chapter. Figure 2-3 shows
the Main Menu as it appears after the AutoCAD program is activated.
A brief description of the Main Menu and each of the submenus is
given in the following paragraphs. Each menu and command is
described in detail in later chapters.

Figure 2-3
Main AutoCAD Menu

```
0. Exit AutoCAD
1. Begin a NEW drawing
2. Edit an EXISTing drawing
3. Plot a drawing
4. Printer plot a drawing
5. Configure AutoCAD
6. File Utilities
7. Compile shape/font description file
8. Convert old drawing file
```

The Main Menu

The Main Menu is shown in Figure 2-3. The commands on this menu are activated by pressing the number of the command on the keyboard and then pressing the Enter or (Return) key. The Main Menu is used to:

0. Exit AutoCAD

This command returns the system to DOS or another system controlling software program.

1. Begin a NEW drawing

This command prompts you to name a new drawing (so you can refer to it later) and then gives you a drawing area on the screen and displays the AutoCAD prompts and the AutoCAD Menu (Figure 2-3). The prompts are the information displayed at the bottom of the screen telling you what to do next.

2. Edit an EXISTING drawing

This command allows you to modify an existing drawing. It brings up the drawing you call for and the AutoCAD Menu in the same manner as command No. 1 above.

3. Plot a drawing

This command begins the sequence of steps needed to make a hard copy of your drawing on a plotter. These copies are often of a very high quality. The plotter uses either felt marker pens or technical inking pens similar to those used for manual inking of drawings.

4. Printer plot a drawing

This command sequence allows you to make a copy of your drawing on a printer. This is often a poor quality drawing and is used only for check prints or similar applications where better quality is not needed. Other printers are now available that produce drawings of very high quality.

5. Configure AutoCAD

This set of commands allows you to give the AutoCAD program the information it needs to work with your computer and its accessory hardware.

6. File Utilities

This set of commands allows you to copy, delete, and rename drawings. It also is used to find a drawing or drawings on either the floppy or hard disks.

7. Compile shape/font description file

This set of commands allows you to create your own alphabet that can be used on your drawings.

8. Convert old drawing file

This set of commands allows you to change drawings done on an earlier version of AutoCAD to drawings that will be accepted by a later version. This is usually not necessary, as later versions accept most drawings done on earlier versions, automatically converting them to the newer form. The reverse is not true, however, converting a drawing done on a later version to an earlier form requires the use of conversion commands called DXFIN and DXFOUT.

**Figure 2-4
Root Menu**

```
AutoCAD

* * * *
SET UP
BLOCKS
DIM
DISPLAY
DRAW
EDIT
INQUIRY
LAYER
SETTINGS
PLOT
UTILITY
3-D
SAVE
```

Root Menu or AutoCAD Menu

The next menu in the AutoCAD sequence is the Root Menu (also identified on the screen as the AutoCAD Menu, Figure 2-4). This menu appears on the screen to the right of the drawing area whenever "Begin a NEW Drawing" or "Edit an EXISTing Drawing" is selected from the Main Menu. Most of the commands displayed on the Root Menu flip you to a more detailed submenu. For example, when you select DRAW on the Root Menu, a list of items that can be drawn will appear and the Root Menu will disappear. All submenus have a means of getting out of the submenu and back to the Root Menu. A description of the submenus and other commands on the Root Menu follows:

****   This command leads you to a list of features called OSNAP. They allow you to draw very accurately. Some of the features are: tangent, perpendicular, endpoint, and midpoint.

SET UP   Set up allows you to select the scale of your drawing and the page size of the paper on which you will plot the drawing.

BLOCKS   Blocks is the command sequence used to create drawings of often-used parts or symbols. These blocks are stored in memory. They can be instantly recalled and inserted in the drawing at any point and at any scale. This is a wonderful time-saver.

DIM   This menu is used to dimension drawings. It also is a wonderful timesaving device. It can be set up to do many dimensioning tasks automatically.

DISPLAY   This menu contains the commands having to do with the screen display. The zoom feature of this menu is used to temporarily enlarge a smaller area of the drawing so it may be worked on more easily. It may also be used to make the view of the drawing smaller so other drawings may be added to it. The DISPLAY submenu also contains other display features allowing you to manipulate views, redraw the screen area to clean up areas that have been erased or otherwise edited, or to move from one area of the drawing to another without enlarging or reducing.

DRAW   This menu contains all of the commands used to draw objects and to place lettering on the drawing. The submenu contains such elements as lines, circles, ellipses, arcs, polygons, text, and several other features.

EDIT   This menu contains some very powerful commands. Some can be used to make multiple copies of features such as circles, lines, and other shapes. Others allow you to make a mirror image of an object, to rotate objects, divide, erase, extend, chamfer, fillet, stretch, trim and break objects. It also allows you to correct mistakes by undoing anything you do that does not work out.

INQUIRY This menu allows you to measure exact distances on the drawing, to discover the status of the total drawing, and to discover the status of features. The status of features includes the length of lines, the sizes of circles and arcs, the location of features, the names of blocks and the layer on which these features reside. Time, area, and other features are also included in this menu.

LAYER This menu allows you to create and use layers (similar to transparent overlays) on which parts of the drawing are placed. For example, lines you want to be drawn with a thick pen would be placed on a different layer than those drawn with a thin pen. Often, lettering (text) is placed on a separate layer. Hidden lines also are often placed on a separate layer. The LAYER Menu becomes very useful and is extremely valuable in the hands of a clever drafter.

SETTINGS This menu provides a means of changing many of the commonly used features, such as grids, that may be displayed on the screen as an aid to drawing. Other variable features are the axis, the aperture or size of the selector (called the cursor or pickbox) that appears on the screen, the limits of the drawing, and others that will not mean anything to you until you begin working with the system.

PLOT This single command may be used to begin the sequence of steps needed to plot a drawing. Drawings may also be plotted from the Main Menu. It is usually better to plot from the Main Menu in case a replot is necessary, as replots are done more quickly from the Main Menu.

UTILITY This menu allows drawings to be saved onto floppy or hard disks, to rename drawing files, to exit to the Main Menu, and to perform other tasks needed to keep your drawings neat and orderly.

3D This menu is used to make three-dimensional drawings that can be changed or viewed from different angles.

SAVE This single command is used to save a drawing onto a floppy or a hard disk. The Save command is often used as insurance in case of a catastrophe such as disk failure or a mistake. The most recently saved drawing may be recalled at any time.

Figure 2-5
AutoCAD Primary Menu Hierarchy

AUTOCAD
(PRIMARY MENU HIERARCHY)

AutoCAD — Always causes AutoCAD ROOTMENU to appear.

* * * — OSNAP overrides (same as third mouse/digitizer button).

SETUP — User defined drawing scale and sheet size. Places border lines around drawing limits.

CENter
ENDpoint
INSert
INTersec
MIDpoint
NEArest
NODe
PERpend
QUAdrant
QUICK,
TANgent
NONE
CANCEL:
U:
REDO:
REDRAW:
'SETVAR

BLOCKS
ATTDEF:
BASE:
BLOCK:
INSERT:
MINSERT:
WBLOCK:

DIM:
DIM1:
LINEAR — horizontal
angular — vertical
diameter — aligned
radius — rotated
center — baseline
leader — continued
dim vars
redraw
status
undo
exit

dimalt   dimscale
dimaltd   dimse1
dimaltf   dimse2
dimasz   dimtad
dimblk   dimth
dimcen   dimtm
dimdle   dimtoh
dimdli   dimtol
dimexe   dimtp
dimexo   dimtsz
dimlfac   dimtxt
dimlin   dimzin
dimmd
                next

DISPLAY
ATTDIP:
PAN:
REDRAW:
REGEN:
REGENAUTO:
VIEW:
VIEWRES:
ZOOM:

DRAW
ARC   POINT:
ATTDEF: POLYGON:
CIRCLE   SHAPE:
DONUT: SKETCH:
DTEXT: SOLID
ELLIPSE: TEXT
HATCH:
INSERT:
LINE:
MINSERT:
OFFSET:
PLINE:
        next

EDIT
ARRAY: MIRROR:
ATTEDIT: MOVE:
BREAK: OFFSET:
CHAMFER: PEDIT:
CHANGE: ROTATE:
COPY: SCALE:
DIVIDE: STRETCH:
ERASE: TRIM:
EXPLODE: UNDO:
EXTEND:
FILLET:
MEASURE:
        next

INQUIRY
AREA:
DBLIST:
DIST:
HELP:
ID:
LIST:
STATUS:
TIME:

LAYER:

SETTINGS
APERTUR: SETVAR:
AXIS: SNAP:
BLIPS: STYLE:
COLOR: TABLET:
DRAGMOD: UNITS:
ELEV:
GRID:
LINETYP:
LIMITS:
LTSCALE:
OSNAP:
QTEXT
        next

PLOT
PLOT:
PRPLOT:

UTILITY
ATTEXT: DXFIN: MSLIDE:
DXF/DXB   DXFOUT: VSLIDE:
FILES: DXBIN:
IGES   IGESIN:
MENU: IGESOUT:
PURGE:
RENAME:
SCRIPT:
SLIDES   CATALOG
EXTERNAL   DEL:
COMMANDS   DIR:
END: EDIT:
QUIT: SH:
              SHELL:
              TYPE:

3D
ELEV:
CHANGE:
VPOINT:
HIDE:

SAVE:

Common sub-menu calls

LAST ———— Calls last screen menu.
DRAW ———— Calls DRAW sub-menu.
EDIT ———— Calls EDIT sub-menu.

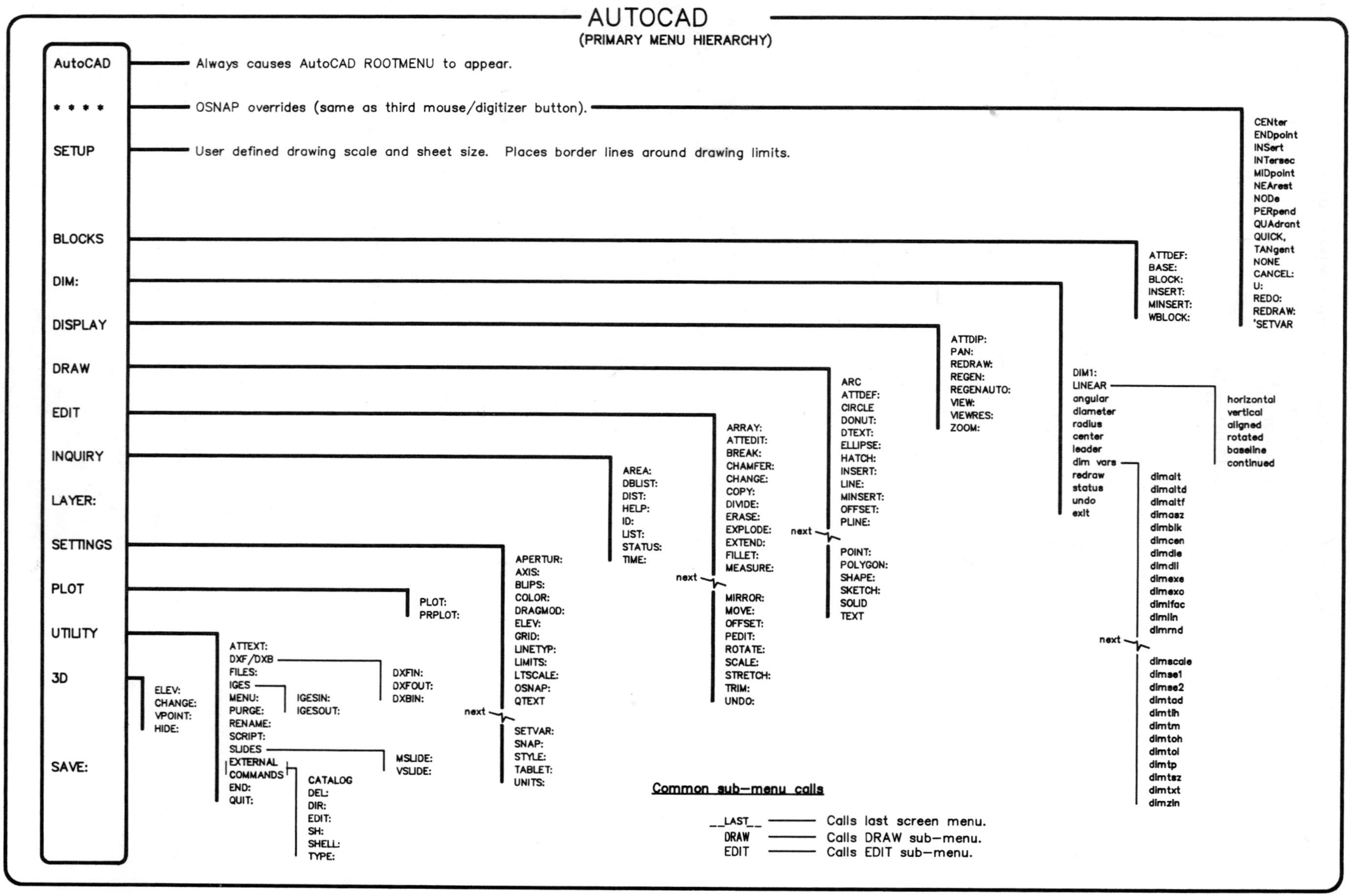

Many submenus contain the commands:

LAST   This calls up the LAST screen menu.

DRAW   Calls up the DRAW Menu.

EDIT   Calls up the EDIT Menu.

NEXT   Calls up the next page of the menu.

Figure 2-5 shows the Root Menu and all of the lower-level menus. Other lists of commands are used in some of the submenus to allow you to select the way you want to draw some features or to operate commands from the menus. These will be examined in detail in later chapters.

Test on Objectives—Chapter 2

Circle the correct answer.

1. Which of the following systems is best for using AutoCAD?
   a. a fast computer, color monitor, keyboard, pointing device (such as a mouse, digitizing tablet and stylus or light pen) and two floppy drives
   b. a fast computer, monochrome monitor, keyboard, pointing device, and two floppy drives
   c. a fast computer, color monitor, keyboard, hard drive, and two floppy drives
   d. a fast computer, color monitor, keyboard, pointing device, hard drive, and a floppy drive
   e. a fast computer, color monitor, keyboard, pointing device, two hard drives

2. Which of the following is used to store information?
   a. hard disk
   b. stylus
   c. mouse
   d. keyboard
   e. plotter

3. Which of the following can be used to move large blocks of information into the computer most quickly?
   a. floppy disk
   b. keyboard
   c. plotter
   d. mouse
   e. digitizing tablet

4. Which of the following has a menu placed around its drawing area?

   a. light pen
   b. digitizing tablet
   c. mouse
   d. keyboard

5. Which of the following is used to obtain high-quality hard copies of drawings?

   a. hard disk
   b. plotter
   c. digitizing tablet
   d. stylus
   e. mouse

6. Which of these menus contains a command used to begin a new drawing?

   a. Main Menu
   b. Root Menu
   c. DISPLAY Menu
   d. DRAW Menu
   e. EDIT Menu

7. Which of these menus contains a command used to temporarily enlarge or reduce a drawing area?

   a. Main Menu
   b. Root Menu
   c. DISPLAY Menu
   d. DRAW Menu
   e. EDIT Menu

8. Which of these menus contains a command used to save a drawing?

   a. Main Menu
   b. Root Menu
   c. DISPLAY Menu
   d. DRAW Menu
   e. EDIT Menu

9. Which of these menus contains a command used to draw a circle?

   a. Main Menu
   b. Root Menu
   c. DISPLAY Menu
   d. DRAW Menu
   e. EDIT Menu

10. Which of these menus contains a command used to plot a drawing?

    a. Main Menu
    b. SETTINGS Menu
    c. DISPLAY Menu
    d. DRAW Menu
    e. EDIT Menu

11. Which of these menus contains a command used to stretch a drawing?

    a. Main Menu
    b. Root Menu
    c. DISPLAY Menu
    d. DRAW Menu
    e. EDIT Menu

12. Which of these menus contains a command used to erase a drawing?

    a. Main Menu
    b. Root Menu
    c. DISPLAY Menu
    d. DRAW Menu
    e. EDIT Menu

13. Which of these menus contains a command used to draw a line perpendicular to another line?

    a. INQUIRY
    b. UTILITIES
    c. ****
    d. LAYER

14. Which of these menus contains a command used to find the exact distance from one point to another?

    a. INQUIRY
    b. UTILITIES
    c. ****
    d. LAYER
    e. BLOCKS

15. Which of these menus contains a command used to keep the lettering separate from the drawing itself?

    a. INQUIRY
    b. UTILITIES
    c. ****
    d. LAYER
    e. BLOCKS

16. Which of these menus contains a command used to store a symbol that may be used repeatedly?
    a. INQUIRY
    b. UTILITIES
    c. ****
    d. LAYER
    e. BLOCKS

17. Which of these menus contains a command used to rename a drawing?
    a. INQUIRY
    b. UTILITIES
    c. ****
    d. LAYER
    e. BLOCKS

18. Which of these menus contains a command used to select the scale for the drawing?
    a. SETUP
    b. DIM
    c. LAYER
    d. 3D
    e. UTILITY

19. Which of these menus contains a command used to select the page size for the drawing?
    a. SET UP
    b. DIM
    c. LAYER
    d. 3D

20. Which of these menus contains a command used to select the grid size for the drawing?
    a. SET UP
    b. DIM
    c. SETTINGS
    d. 3D

21. List the five major items of equipment necessary in a typical personal computer used to operate AutoCAD?
    a. _____
    b. _____
    c. _____
    d. _____
    e. _____

22. The AutoCAD manual (prior to Release 10) suggests a computer with a RAM capacity of _____ bytes to successfully run AutoCAD. (RAM is operating memory, called Random Access Memory.)

23. A video display should have minimum resolution of _____ to successfully operate AutoCAD.

24. What is the purpose of a floppy disk drive?

_____

_____

_____

_____

25. List two means of storing drawings on an AutoCAD system.

    a. _____

    b. _____

26. Which pointing device allows the operators to keep their eyes on the screen at all times?

_____

27. Which piece of equipment is used to plot drawings?

_____

28. List 10 menus found on the AutoCAD Root Menu.

    a. _____   **f.** _____

    b. _____   **g.** _____

    c. _____   **h.** _____

    d. _____   **i.** _____

    e. _____   **j.** _____

29. List 7 commands found on the Main Menu.

    a. _____   **e.** _____

    b. _____   **f.** _____

    c. _____   **g.** _____

    d. _____

30. List 15 commands found on the EDIT Menu.

a. _____   i. _____

b. _____   j. _____

c. _____   k. _____

d. _____   l. _____

e. _____   m. _____

f. _____   n. _____

g. _____   o. _____

h. _____

3

Making a Block Diagram

Objectives

The student will:

■ use the following commands to construct and plot block diagrams using AutoCAD:

SETUP	SNAP
BEGIN A NEW DRAWING	ZOOM
LAYERS	SOLID
MAKE LAYERS	DRAW TEXT
CHANGE LAYERS	SCALE
DRAW LINES	SAVE
GRID	CHANGE
COPY	ROTATE
MOVE	QUIT
ARRAY	ERASE

■ edit an existing drawing
■ correctly answer review questions describing the function of each of the above commands

Drawing Diagrams

Figure 3-1 is a block diagram drawn using the sequence of steps to be presented in this chapter. You will be asked to draw this diagram and a similar diagram to complete this chapter. The method used to make this diagram is not necessarily the best or the only way to do it. It

Figure 3-1
Block Diagram

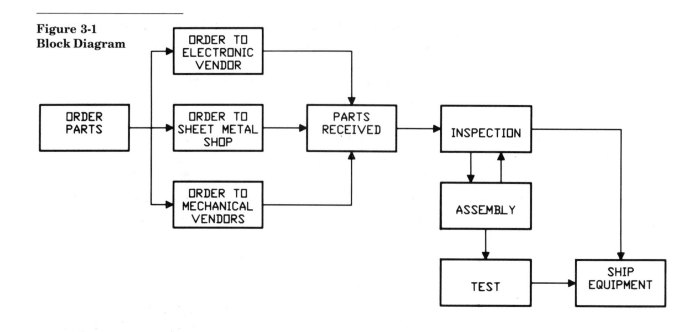

does introduce you to some useful commands, though, which will be more fully developed in later chapters.

Drawing a Block Diagram

Step 1. Load AutoCAD and begin a new drawing.

From the Main Menu:

Response: {Type} 1 {(begin a NEW drawing) and then press Enter}

Prompt: Name of new drawing:

Response: {Type a drawing name of 8 characters or less and then press Enter}

Use the following commands in the order shown.

Step 2. Select a scale and a paper size.

Prompt: Command:

Response: SETUP {digitize the command from the screen menu}

Digitize means to move the lighted bar on the screen so it lies over the chosen command or point, and to pick that feature by pressing the left button on the mouse or other pointing device.

Prompt: Select the units from the screen menu:

Response: {Type} 2 {from the keyboard (decimal) and press Enter}

Note: *If there are three buttons on your mouse, pressing the middle button on the mouse is equivalent to pressing Enter on the keyboard. However, if the middle button on your mouse does not* *activate the command, or if you do not have a mouse with three buttons, then press Enter on the keyboard to activate commands.*

Prompt: Select the scale from the screen menu:

Response: FULL

Prompt: Select the paper size from the screen menu:

Response: A – 8.5 × 11 {paper size}

Note: *If a message indicating insufficient node space appears, skip Step 2 and proceed to Step 3. The default size is 9 × 12".*

Step 3. Select a GRID and a SNAP setting.

Prompt: Command:

Response: SETTINGS–SNAP {you will have to go to the next page of the SETTINGS Menu to find SNAP—after QTEXT digitize "next"}

SNAP is the spacing on the display to which the crosshairs of the pointing device snap when the SNAP function is ON.

Prompt: SNAP spacing or ON/OFF/Aspect/Rotate/Style < >:

Response: {Type} .125 {press Enter or Return, ↵ will now be used to indicate Enter or Return}

You have set the cursor (crosshairs or a box) to snap at every .125 inch. Go back to the Root Menu by digitizing *AutoCAD*.

Prompt: Command:

Response: SETTINGS–GRID (GRID is the pattern of dots displayed on your screen.)

Prompt: GRID spacing (X) or ON/OFF/Snap/Aspect < >:

Response: {Type} .25 ↵

You now have a grid of .25". If GRID is not visible, press the GRID function key F7. Also turn SNAP ON by pressing F9. Turn ORTHO ON by pressing F8. This allows you to draw only horizontal or vertical lines and keeps them very straight.

Prompt: Command:

Response: ZOOM

Prompt: All/Center/Dynamic/Extents/Left/Previous/Window/Scale (X):

Response: {Digitize} ALL

Note: *You must use the ZOOM ALL command periodically to see what your whole drawing looks like.*

Step 4. Make layers on which to draw.

Layers are similar to transparent overlays. You will need separate layers for the following:

- boxes
- connecting lines and arrows
- lettering

To do this, follow this sequence:

Prompt: Command:

Response: {Digitize} LAYER {from the Root Menu}
{Digitize} NEW {from the LAYER Menu or type N from the keyboard}

Prompt: New Layer name(s):

Response: {Type} THICK,LETTER,THIN ↵ {from the keyboard, THICK will be for the boxes, THIN for connecting lines and arrows, and LETTER for the lettering. CAUTION: Do not put any space between the words—just a comma.}

Prompt: ?/Make/Set/New/ON/OFF/Color/Ltype/Freeze/Thaw:

Response: {Digitize or type} COLOR {press ↵ if typed from the keyboard (be sure the LAYER prompt described above is present)}

Prompt: Color:

Response: {Digitize any color, for example:} WHITE {or type W ↵ from the keyboard}

Prompt: Layer name(s) for color? (white) <0>:

Response: {Type} THICK ↵ {now anything drawn on layer THICK will be white}

Prompt: ?/Make/Set/New/ON/OFF/Color/Ltype/Freeze/Thaw:

Response: {Digitize} COLOR {or type C from the keyboard}

Prompt: Color:

Response: {Digitize} GREEN {or type G ↵ from the keyboard}

Prompt: Layer name(s) for color 3 (green) <0>:

Response: {Type} LETTER ↵ {now everything drawn on layer LETTER will be green}

Prompt: ?/Make/Set/New/ON/OFF/Color/Ltype/Freeze/Thaw:

Response: {Digitize} COLOR

Prompt: Color:

Response: {Type or digitize} YELLOW

Prompt: Layer (name(s) for color 2 (yellow) <0>:

Response: {Type} THIN ↵ {now everything drawn on layer THIN will be yellow}

Prompt: ?/Make/Set/New/ON/OFF/Color/Ltype/Freeze/Thaw:

Response: {Digitize or type} ?

This will tell you what layers you have created, what their colors are, their linetypes, and whether they are ON or OFF. If any of the layers are OFF, turn them ON by typing ON, press Enter. Then type the layer(s) you want ON, separate each layer name by a comma, and press Enter. Now press F1 or the flip screen key if the keyboard does not have F1.

Prompt: ?/Make/Set/New/ON/OFF/Color/Ltype/Freeze/Thaw:

Response: {Digitize or type} SET {This will establish the layer on which you are drawing}

Prompt: New current layer <0>:

Response: {Type} THICK {and press Enter}

Prompt: ?/Make/Set/New/ON/OFF/Color/Ltype/Freeze/Thaw:

Response: ↵

You have now completed the setup for your first drawing. *If your computer is equipped with Release 9 or later,* the setup could have been accomplished more quickly using the pull-down MODES Menu located at the top of your screen display. To do this:

a. Digitize MODES from the pull-down menu that appears when you move your cursor to top of screen.
b. Digitize DRAWING AIDS from the MODES Menu.
c. Move your cursor arrow to the area under SNAP that identifies x-spacing. Then, digitize the box containing the value for x-spacing. The area will change to the highlight color. Now type .125 and press Enter or digitize OK. Notice that the Y value also changes to .125 as the default. When a different Y value for the SNAP spacing is needed it may be changed at this time.

Figure 3-2
Digitize the First Block

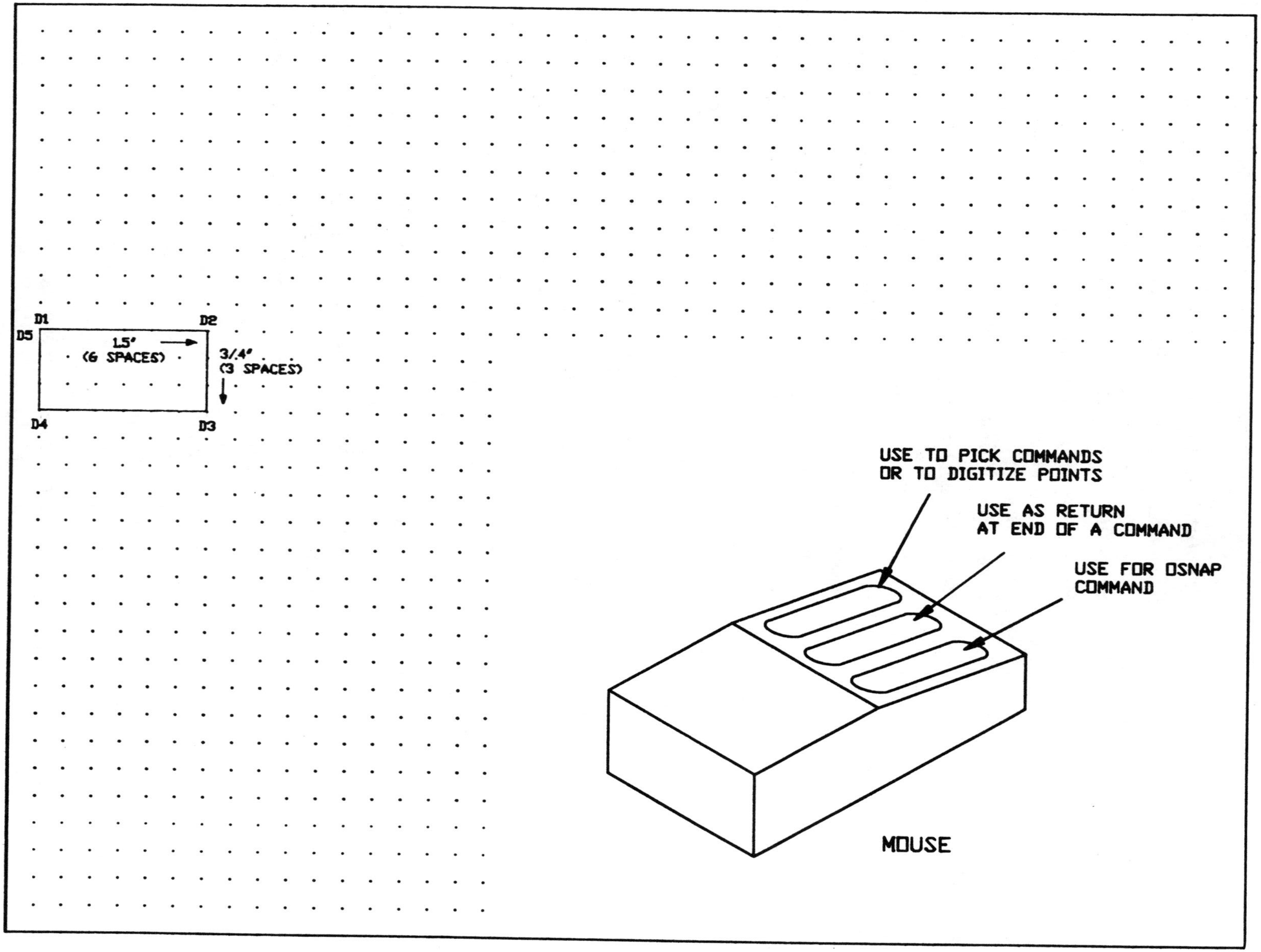

USE TO PICK COMMANDS
OR TO DIGITIZE POINTS

USE AS RETURN
AT END OF A COMMAND

USE FOR OSNAP
COMMAND

MOUSE

3/4"
(3 SPACES)

1.5'
(6 SPACES)

D1   D2   D3   D4   D5

   d. Now set the GRID to .25 in a similar manner. Then find the box labeled "OK" at the bottom of the display and digitize that box.

   e. Digitize MODES Menu, then select MODIFY LAYER from that display.

   f. Digitize the area to the right of the words *New Layer*. (The area will become highlighted.)

   g. Type the name of the new layer *letter* and press Enter. (The new layer appears in the layer name column.)

   h. Now digitize the word *white* under the color column. (The selectable colors chart appears.)

   i. Select the desired color (in this case *green*) by digitizing the blank box between the name of the color and the green bar. Then digitize *OK* at bottom of the color chart. (The Modify layer chart reappears with the layer name and the color in their required columns.)

   j. Create all other layers and select their colors. The linetype for all of the layers used in this drawing will be continuous; therefore, no other linetypes need to be selected. Other linetypes, such as *hidden, center, phantom,* may be chosen after they have been selected from the side menu.

Step 5. Draw the boxes and put lettering in them.

Prompt: Command:

Response: {Type or digitize} LINE {from the DRAW Menu—Release 9 has DRAW Menus on both the right side and the top of the display}

Prompt: LINE from point:

Response: D1 {digitize a block in the location shown in Figure 3-2}

Locate this point with the cursor (the crosshairs and pickbox controlled by the mouse or stylus) and digitize that spot using the left button on the mouse or the digitize button on the puck or stylus.}

Prompt: To point:

Response: D2

Prompt: To point:

Response: D3

Prompt: To point:

Response: D4

Prompt: To point:

Response: D5 ↵ {or type "C" and press Enter to close the box}

Figure 3-3
Locate Text

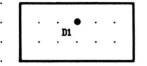

Figure 3-4
Lettering for the
First Block

Figure 3-5
Window the Block
to Copy

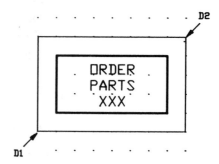

Now depress the middle button on the mouse to end the sequence, or press Enter on the keyboard. You should have a white box.}

Prompt: Command:

Response: {Digitize} LAYER {from the Root Menu and} SET {from the LAYER Menu}

Prompt: New current layer <THICK>:

Response: LETTER ↵ {then press Enter again after the next prompt}

Prompt: Command:

Response: DTEXT {from second page of the DRAW Menu, push *next* to get to the next page of the DRAW Menu}

Prompt: DTEXT start point or Align/Center/Fit/Middle/Right/Style:

Response: {Digitize} CENTER {on the menu}

Prompt: Center point:

Response: {Digitize center of box ¼″ from top as in Figure 3-3}

Prompt: HEIGHT <0.2000>: {or whatever the default height is set on}

Response: .1 ↵

Prompt: Rotation angle <0>:

Response: ↵ {or 0 if the number shown in the brackets is not 0}

Prompt: TEXT:

Response: ORDER ↵

Prompt: TEXT:

Response: PARTS ↵ {then press Enter again}

Prompt: TEXT:

Response: XXX

Figure 3-6
Multiple Copy

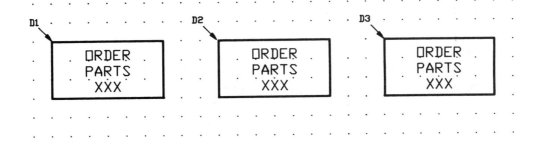

You now have three lines of text that should look like Figure 3-4. The XXX will be used later.

Prompt: Command:

Response: {Select} COPY

You will find this in the EDIT Menu. Release 9 has EDIT Menus on both the right side and the top of the display.

Prompt: Select objects:

Response: {Digitize} WINDOW {on the COPY Menu or type W from the keyboard}

Prompt: First corner:

Response: {Digitize as D1 in Figure 3-5}

Prompt: Other corner:

Response: D2 {as in Figure 3-5}

Prompt: Select objects:

Response: ↵ {or middle button on the mouse}

Prompt: <Basepoint or displacement>/Multiple:

Response: {Digitize} MULTIPLE {or type M from the keyboard}

Prompt: Base point:

Response: D1—Figure 3-6

Prompt: Second point of displacement:

Response: D2

Prompt: Second point of displacement:

Response: D3

Figure 3-7
Change Lettering

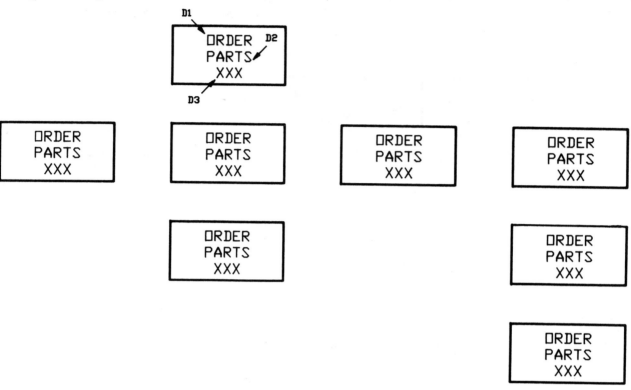

Prompt: Second point of displacement:

Response: D4,D5,D6,D7,D8 {place all boxes as shown in Figure 3-7}

Place boxes where you want them (about ¾″ apart horizontally and ½″ apart vertically). If you make a mistake and wish to move a box, select MOVE from the EDIT Menu, WINDOW from the MOVE Menu, window the box you want to move, and digitize the corner of the box in its original location and where you want to move it to. Press Enter.

Step 6. Change lettering in all boxes.

Prompt: Command:

Response: {Digitize} CHANGE {on the EDIT Menu}

Release 9 does not contain CHANGE on the menu at the top of the display.

Prompt: Select objects:

Response: {Digitize the lines} ORDER,PARTS,XXX {in the second box (Figure 3-7 D1, D2, D3) then press Enter}

You may digitize anywhere on the word. You may have to press F9 to place SNAP in the OFF position to do this easily. Be sure to put SNAP On again before you draw or move any lines, arrows or boxes.

Prompt: Properties/<CHANGE POINT>:

Response: ↵

Prompt: Enter text insertion point:

Response: ↵ {do not change the insertion point}

Prompt: Text style: STANDARD—new style or Enter for no change:

Response: ↵ {standard is the style desired}

Prompt: New height <0.1000>:

Response: ↵ {this is the correct height}

Prompt: New rotation angle <0>:

Response: ↵ {0 is the correct angle}

Prompt: New text <ORDER>:

Response: ORDER TO ↵

Prompt: Enter text insertion point:

Response: ↵ {this is so you can change the second line PARTS to ELECTRONIC}

Prompts will be the same until you get to: new text <PARTS>. Just press Enter quickly five times to get to this prompt <PARTS>, then type ELECTRONIC. Continue the same procedure for all lines of lettering. Use Erase on the EDIT Menu to get rid of any line of lettering that is not needed. After the lettering has been completed, proceed to the next step.

Step 7. Draw the lines connecting the boxes.

Prompt: Command:
Response: LAYER

Prompt: ?/Make/Set/New/- - -/Thaw:
Response: SET

Prompt: New current layer <LETTER>:
Response: THIN ↵

Prompt: Command:
Response: {Digitize} LINE {on the DRAW Menu}

Figure 3-8
Drawing Connecting Lines

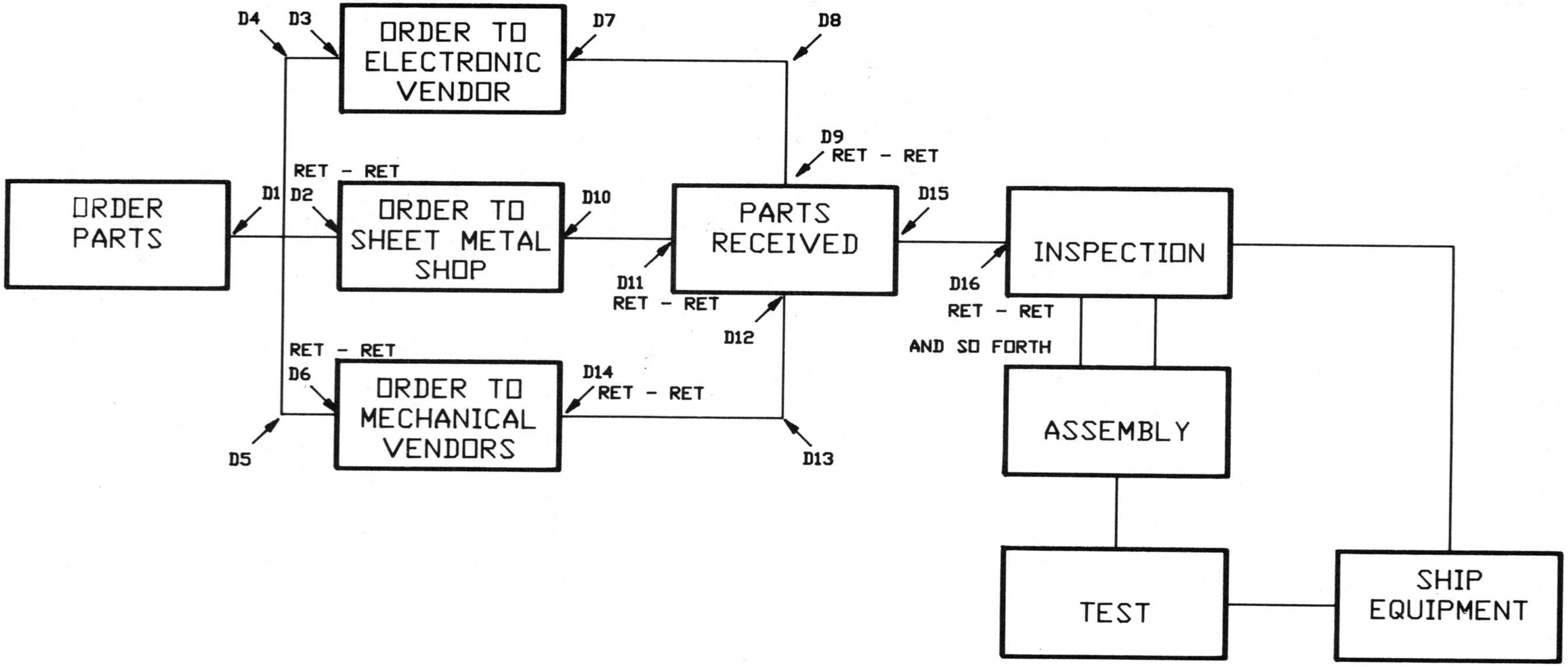

Prompt: LINE from point:

Response: {Digitize D1 from Figure 3-8—be sure SNAP and ORTHO (keys F8 and F9) are ON}

Prompt: To point:

Response: {Digitize D2}

Prompt: To point:

Response: ↵ {or the middle button on the mouse}

The command is now completed.

Prompt: Command:

Response: ↵ {or the middle button on the mouse—the previous command is activated}

Prompt: Line from point:

Response: {Digitize D3, D4, D5}

Note: *If you make a line in the wrong place, digitize "undo" on the LINE Menu (or press U on the keyboard) and the incorrect line you make will disappear. If you continue to hit "undo," all lines back to the start of the command will disappear. If you accidentally UNDO too much, type REDO from the keyboard or select REDO from the screen menu to replace an undone line.*

Prompt: Command:

Response: LINE

Prompt: From point:

Response: {Now draw the rest of the lines; be sure to press Enter after you have completed each line}

Step 8. Now the arrows must be drawn.

Draw one in an open area beneath the drawing and copy it several times. Another way to do this will be covered later with a BLOCK command.

A good arrowhead for this size drawing is ⅛". Change the grid to ⅛" (.125"); draw the arrowhead ¼" and shrink it to fit. Follow this sequence:

Prompt: Command:

Response: ZOOM {from DISPLAY Menu}

Figure 3-9
Digitize a Window
for the Arrowheads

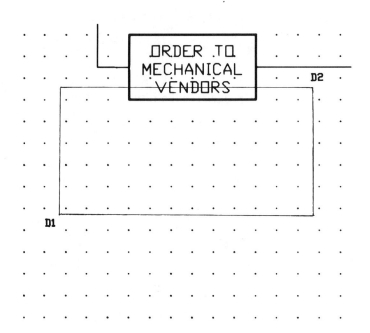

Release 9 has DISPLAY Menus at both the top and side menus—the first three selections from the top pull-down menu are ZOOM commands.

Prompt: All/Center/Dynamic/Extents/Left/Previous/Window/Scale (X):

Response: {Digitize} WINDOW {or type W ↵}

Prompt: First Corner:

Response: D1 {Figure 3-9}

Prompt: Second Corner:

Response: D2

Figure 3-10
Make Arrowheads

You should now have a large ⅛″ grid on your screen. Experiment with the PAN command at this point. PAN allows you to move the display area from one point to another at the same scale.

Prompt: Command:

Response: SOLID {from the DRAW Menu, second page; also digitize FILL ON under the SOLID command so your arrowhead will be solid}

Prompt: First Point:

Response: {Digitize D1; see Figure 3-10}

Prompt: Second point:

Response: {Digitize D2}

Prompt: Third point:

Response: {Digitize D3}

Prompt: Fourth point:

Response: ↵ {do not go to fourth point}

You should have a solid ¼″ arrowhead. Now, reduce it to ⅛″:

Prompt: Command:

Response: SCALE: {from second page of EDIT Menu}

Prompt: Select objects:

Response: {Digitize} WINDOW {or type W to digitize a window around the arrowhead}

Response: D1 {not shown}

Prompt: Second corner:

Response: D2 {not shown—after D2, "1 found" should appear on the prompt line}

Prompt: Select objects:

Response: ↵

Prompt: Base Point:

Response: D1 {the tip of the arrowhead as shown in Figure 3-11}

Prompt: <Scale Factor>/Reference:

Response: .5 {meaning 50% of the original size}

You should now have a ⅛″ arrowhead. Three versions of it will be needed: pointing up, down, and to the right. Use ROTATE on the EDIT Menu to do that. First, copy the arrow twice.

Prompt: Command:

Response: COPY {from EDIT Menu}

Prompt: Select objects:

Response: {Digitize the arrowhead D1, Figure 3-12}

You may need to take SNAP-F9-OFF to digitize it. Put SNAP back ON after digitizing.

Prompt: Select objects:

Response: ↵

Figure 3-11
Reduce the
Arrowhead to ⅛″

D1

Figure 3-12
Copy the Arrowheads
and Rotate the Copies

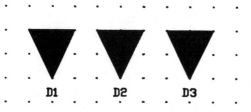

D1   D2   D3

Prompt: <Base point or displacement>/Multiple:
Response: {Digitize} MULTIPLE {or type M ↵}

Prompt: Base point:
Response: {Digitize tip of the arrowhead, D1, Figure 3-12}

Prompt: Second point of displacement:
Response: {Digitize D2 and D3, Figure 3-12, then press ↵}

Prompt: Command:
Response: ROTATE {from the EDIT Menu, second page}

Prompt: Select objects:
Response: D2 {digitize second arrowhead, Figure 3-12}

Prompt: Select objects:
Response: ↵

Prompt: Base point:
Response: D2 {digitize tip of the second arrowhead}

Prompt: <Rotation angle>/Reference:
Response: 180 ↵

Prompt: Command:
Response: ROTATE {you may activate the command you have used
              previously by pressing ↵}

Prompt: Select objects:
Response: {Select third arrowhead}

Prompt: Base point:
Response: {Digitize tip of third arrowhead}

Prompt: <Rotation Angle>/Reference:
Response: 90 ↵

Figure 3-13
Complete Block Diagram

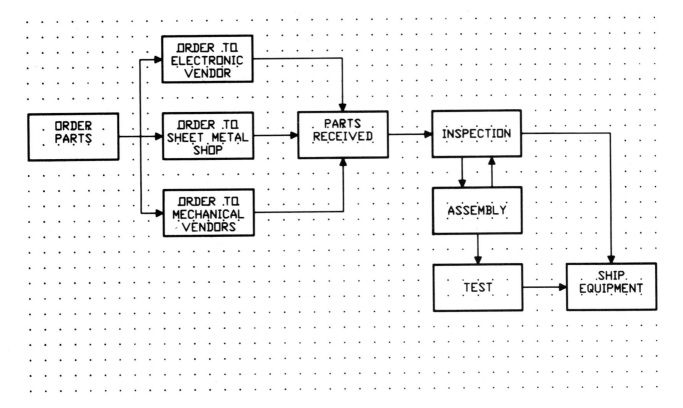

Return to the complete drawing by using the ZOOM then ALL command. You should now have three arrowheads that may be copied onto the connecting lines as shown in Figure 3-13. Use the COPY command and the MULTIPLE subcommand when appropriate for speed. Be sure SNAP is ON when you place arrowheads.

Step 9. Clean up the drawing.

After you place the arrowheads, clean up the drawing using ERASE, ERASE-WINDOW from the EDIT Menu, and REDRAW from the DISPLAY Menu.

When you use ERASE from the Release 9 pull-down menu, remember that the entity vanishes immediately when you select it.

Note: *Release 9 Users—The EDIT commands, ERASE, MOVE and COPY have the immediate selection feature. They also have a feature allowing a selection window to be created when no entity is digitized. Moving upward to the right creates a selection window. Moving downward to the left creates a crossing window. A selection window requires that any drawing entity be contained entirely within the window. A crossing window selects any entity contained entirely within or crossed by the window.*

Place your name ½″ over and ½″ up from the lower right corner using TEXT from the second page of the DRAW Menu and RIGHT from the TEXT Menu. You have now drawn a block diagram.

Step 10. Save your drawing.

SAVE your drawing onto both the hard disk (if the computer has one) and your own floppy disk. Having copies in two different places is an absolute necessity as insurance in case one of them is damaged. To save a drawing, follow this procedure:

Place a formatted floppy disk in the A drive. Consult the appendix for information on formatting a floppy disk.

Prompt: Command:

Response: {Select} SAVE {from the ACAD (AutoCAD) Menu, also on the upper FILE Menu on Release 9}

Prompt: SAVE File name <current drawing name>:

Response: A: DRAWING NAME {of 8 characters or less, Example: A:MK1}

This saves the drawing on the floppy disk, which is in the A drive.

Prompt: Command:

Response: QUIT

Prompt: Really want to discard all changes to drawing?

Response: {Digitize} YES {or type Y ↵}

Using QUIT after your SAVE will discard all changes since the last SAVE. Since you did not make any changes, YES is the correct response. END may also be used to SAVE a drawing on the drive from which it was activated. Using END eliminates the need to use the QUIT command, but it does not prompt you with the drawing name which is sometimes useful.

Step 11. EXIT from AutoCAD.

Use 0 on the Main Menu before turning off your computer to avoid creating "lost clusters"—scattered bits of information on the hard disk. These lost clusters can take up a great deal of space over a period of time. They may be removed by using a DOS command called CHKDSK C:/F (if C is the hard drive). This creates a file of the lost clusters, which may be deleted. See the Appendix for more information on DOS.

Exercise 1

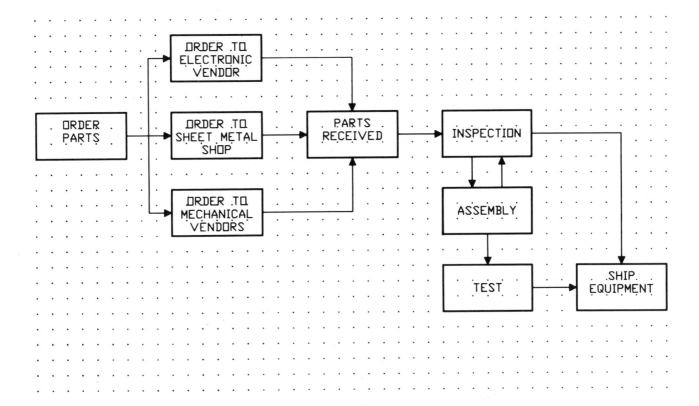

EXERCISE 1

If you have not already done so, draw the Block Diagram shown as Figure 3-1. Do it exactly as described in this chapter.

NAME this drawing BLK1-(your initials)

Example: BLK1-MK

The drawing shown as Exercise 1 shows grid spacing.

Exercise 2

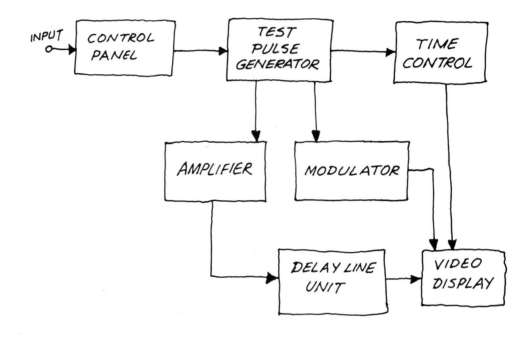

EXERCISE 2

Make a block diagram from the sketch shown above. Put it on an A-size sheet (8½ × 11″). Use the same colors, sizes, lines, and lettering as you used on your first block diagram.

> NAME this drawing BLK2-(your initials)
>
> Example: BLK2-MK
>
> SUGGESTION: Copy BLK1-MK and name it BLK2-MK

From the Main Menu do this:

Prompt: Enter selection:

Response: 6 {File utilities}

Prompt: Enter selection (0 to 5) <0>:

Response: 5 {Copy file}

Prompt: Enter name of source file:

Response: A:BLK1-MK.DWG

Be sure to type the correct name of the drive that BLK1 is on—drive A in this example—and to add the .DWG extension to identify it as a drawing file.

Prompt: Enter name of destination file:

Response: A:BLK2-MK.DWG

If you did it correctly, the computer will respond with "COPIED 4320bytes (approximately) press Enter to continue:"

Response: ↵

Prompt: Enter selection (0 to 5)<0>:

Response: ↵ {exit file utilities}

Prompt: Enter selection:

Response: 2 {edit an existing drawing}

Prompt: Name of drawing:

Response: A:BLK2-MK

Now you have a copy of BLK1 that may be erased, copied, moved or changed in any manner to make BLK2.

Another method that may be used to do the same thing is to start a new drawing and make it equal to the previous one. To do this, follow these steps from the Main Menu:

Prompt: Enter selection:

Response: 1 {begin a new drawing}

Prompt: Name of drawing:

Response: A:BLK2-MK=A:BLK1-MK

The new drawing (BLK2-MK) appears looking the same as BLK1-MK. This new drawing may now be modified. The original BLK1-MK remains on the A drive in its original form.

EXERCISE 3

Make an AutoCAD drawing of the block diagram in the illustration on the next page. Spaces and sizes of blocks should be approximately the same as shown. Lettering should be .08″ high. Place your name in the lower right corner. Limits should be 8.5″ × 11″.

The limits command is used to control the size of your drawing. This command is found on the SETTINGS Menu. To set limits for this drawing do the following:

Prompt: Command:

Response: LIMITS

Prompt: Lower left corner <0,0>:

Response: ↵

Prompt: Upper right corner <12,9>: {or another default value}

Response: 8.5,11 ↵ {this gives you a vertical page}

EXERCISE 4

Make an AutoCAD drawing of the block diagram shown on the next page. Spaces and sizes of blocks should be approximately the same as shown. Lettering should be approximately .05″ high. Limits should be 17 × 11″. Place your name in the lower right corner.

Exercise 3

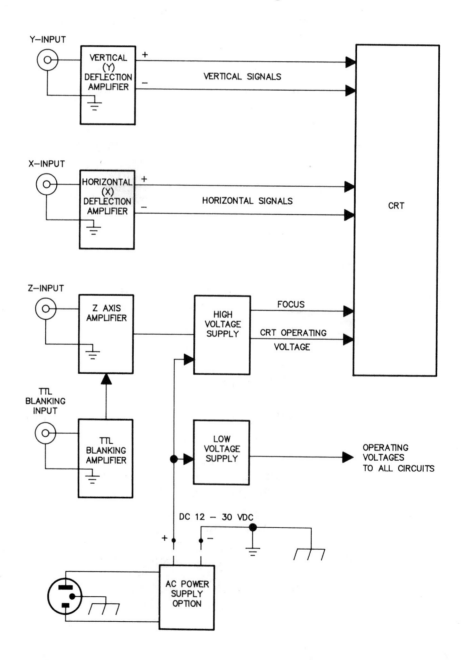

Exercise 4

49

Test on Objectives—Chapter 3

(It is suggested that the student complete this test at the computer with Figure 3-13 displayed.)

Circle the correct answer.

1. From which command is the paper size selected?
   a. GRID
   b. PAPER
   c. SETUP
   d. SETTINGS
   e. UTILITY

2. If you want a SNAP setting of ½″, what is the correct response to the prompt "SNAP spacing or ON/OFF/aspect/rotate/style < > :"?
   a. .5
   b. ½
   c. 2
   d. one half
   e. .05 in

3. If you have a grid setting of ¼″ (.25) and you wish to change it to ⅛″, on which of these menus would you find the GRID command?
   a. UTILITY
   b. SETUP
   c. SETTINGS
   d. EDIT
   e. INQUIRY

4. Which of the following series of responses can be used to make a new layer named "GLINE" on which green lines will be drawn?
   a. LAYER - NEW - GLINE - GREEN - SET - GLINE
   b. LAYER - NEW - GLINE - COLOR - GREEN
   c. LAYER - NEW - GLINE - COLOR - GREEN - GLINE
   d. LAYER - NEW - GLINE - GREEN - COLOR
   e. LAYER - NEW - COLOR - GLINE - GREEN

5. Two layers can have the same color.
   a. true
   b false

6. When you respond to the LAYER prompt, "?/Make/Set/New/ON/ OFF/Color/Ltype/Freeze/Thaw:" with a "?" and ↵, what appears on the screen?

   a. a listing of all layers, their colors, linetypes, names, and on or off status
   b. a listing of the current layer and its status
   c. a listing of all layers but the current layer and their status
   d. a listing of the unused layer colors
   e. a help display, which tells you how to use the layer command

7. The function key, F1, described in this chapter, does which of the following?

   a. sets SNAP ON or OFF
   b. flips the screen from the text display to the graphics display
   c. sets the GRID ON or OFF
   d. sets ORTHO ON or OFF
   e. sets coordinates ON or OFF

8. The function key, F7, described in this chapter, does which of the following?

   a. sets SNAP ON or OFF
   b. flips the screen from the text display to the graphics display
   c. sets the GRID ON or OFF
   d. sets ORTHO ON or OFF
   e. sets coordinates ON or OFF

9. The function key, F9, described in this chapter, does which of the following?

   a. sets SNAP ON or OFF
   b. flips the screen from the text display to the graphics display
   c. sets the GRID ON or OFF
   d. sets ORTHO ON or OFF
   e. sets coordinates ON or OFF

10. The function key, F8, described in this chapter, does which of the following?

   a. sets SNAP ON or OFF
   b. flips the screen from the text display to the graphics display
   c. sets the GRID ON or OFF
   d. sets ORTHO ON or OFF
   e. sets coordinates ON or OFF

11. If the Enter key is pressed immediately after a centered line of text has been entered on the drawing, another centered line of text may be entered after the prompt "TEXT."

    a. true
    b. false

12. When the COPY command is used with a window (not a crossing window),

    a. everything the window touches is copied.
    b. everything entirely within the window is copied.
    c. only the symbols or blocks within the window are copied.
    d. everything within the screen is copied.
    e. everything within the window except text is copied.

Figure 3-13

13. A response of 90 to the ROTATE prompt, "(Rotation angle)/ Reference" will move the arrow in Figure 3-13 to which of the following positions?

    a.   **b.**   **c.**   **d.**   **e.**

14. The COPY "multiple" command will allow how many copies to be made?

    a. one
    b. up to five
    c. up to 10
    d. up to 20
    e. unlimited

15. Circle the most complete response. The CHANGE command can be used to change which of the following text features?

    a. the words itself, height, style, insertion point, rotation
    b. the words itself, height, style, insertion
    c. the words itself, height, style
    d. the words itself, height
    e. the words itself

16. A solid triangle may be created using the SOLID command and which of the following?

    a. FILL ON, DIGITIZE THREE POINTS, ENTER
    b. FILL ON, DIGITIZE THREE POINTS, DIGITIZE BACK TO FORTH POINT
    c. FILL OFF, DIGITIZE FOUR POINTS, ENTER
    d. FILL OFF, DIGITIZE SIX POINTS, DIGITIZE BACK TO ORIGIN
    e. FILL OFF, DIGITIZE THREE POINTS, STOP

17. The three different positions of the arrowhead were created using COPY, MULTIPLE and ROTATE commands. Which of the following would have been faster?
    a. draw the arrowhead, copy it in rotation mode
    b. draw the arrowhead, copy it 2 times, use CHANGE command
    c. draw the arrowhead in three different positions
    d. draw the arrowhead, copy it everywhere you need it, then rotate to another position
    e. the original method was faster than any other method

18. The SCALE command can be used to do which of the following?
    a. to enlarge only
    b. to reduce only
    c. to enlarge and reduce
    d. to set the drawing units
    e. none of these ways

19. When a 2 is entered after the SCALE prompt "(scale factor)/reference" what happens?
    a. the selected object is reduced to ½
    b. the selected object is enlarged 2 times
    c. another object may be selected
    d. a second scale is described for the entire drawing
    e. two images of the selected object appear

20. Using SAVE instead of END has which of the following advantages?
    a. makes a backup file
    b. discards all changes since the last SAVE
    c. allows the drawing to be saved in two places
    d. allows an erased object to be regained
    e. saves space on the disk

21. List the two types of A-size sheets that are available on AutoCAD.
    a. _____
    b. _____

22. Describe the difference between the SNAP and the GRID settings.
    _____
    _____

23. Which of the LAYER commands changes the active layer on the screen?
    _____

24. How many layers may be turned off at the same time?

_____

25. Which function key is used to turn the GRID ON and OFF?

_____

26. Which function key is used to turn the coordinates line ON and OFF?

_____

27. List three choices the D-TEXT command allows.

    a. _____

    b. _____

    c. _____

28. Describe how WINDOW is used in the COPY command.

_____

_____

29. Describe how ROTATE may be used with the COPY command to make four of the same size arrows: one pointing up, one down, one left and one right.

_____

_____

_____

30. Which command can be used to enlarge a part to two times its original size?

_____

_____

4

Geometric Constructions

Objectives

From given instructions the student will:

■ draw points, lines, circles, arcs, and ellipses and use them in common geometric constructions

■ answer review questions regarding the following commands:

LINE	OFFSET
CIRCLE	ROTATE
ARC	DIVIDE
COPY	ELLIPSE
ARRAY	POLYLINE
SETUP	BEGIN A NEW DRAWING
UNDO	SAVE
REDO	

Before beginning to make production drawings that can be used to build or assemble products, a chapter containing many of the drawing constructions is needed. Familiarity with geometric constructions shown in this chapter will allow later drawings to be done much faster. At least one method is shown for each of the constructions presented. You will discover other methods; you may even find faster methods.

Geometric Constructions

The geometric constructions of this chapter are:

- lines and points
- parallel lines
- perpendicular lines
- breaking lines
- dividing lines into equal parts
- fillets
- chamfers
- circles
- tangents
- arcs
- curves through points
- breaking a polyline
- similar shapes
- arrays of circles and lines
- polygons
- solid shapes
- ellipses and tangents to them

Construction Methods

Setting Up

Begin by setting up the drawing area and deciding on a page size and scale. From the Main Menu:

Response: {Select} 1: Begin a NEW drawing

Prompt: Enter NAME of drawing:

Response: {Type the name of your NEW drawing in eight characters or less, Example: CONST-MK}

You may leave off the extension .DWG, which is automatically added. The full name of the file is CONST-MK.DWG. (An extension is the set of up to three letters following the period after the drawing name.)

Prompt: Command:

Response: SETUP {from the Root Menu}

Prompt: Select the units from the screen menu:

Response: 2 ⏎ {decimal}

Prompt: Select the scale from the screen menu:

Response: FULL

Prompt: Select the paper size from the screen menu:

Response: A-8.5 × 11 {a vertical page}

Prompt: Command:

Response: {Pick SETTINGS from the Root Menu, then select GRID}

Prompt: GRID spacing (X) or ON/OFF/SNAP/Aspect <0.000>:

Response: .25 ⏎

Prompt: Vertical spacing (X) <0.0000>:

Response: .25 ⏎

Prompt: Command:

Response: {Select} GRID = SNAP {from the menu}

Prompt: SNAP spacing or ON/OFF/Aspect/Rotate/Style:

Response: Aspect ⏎

Prompt: Horizontal spacing:

Response: .25 ⏎

You should now have an 8½ × 11″ drawing area with lower left corner coordinates at 0,0 and upper right corner coordinates at 8.5000, 11.0000 (horizontal direction is first (X) and vertical direction is second (Y). You should have a ¼″(.25″) GRID and the SNAP should be on every dot on the GRID. To check this, press function key F6 (the coordinates key) to turn coordinates ON, and F7 to display the GRID. The coordinates will appear in the upper right of your screen. Move the cursor to the lower left corner of your page (0,0) then to the upper right corner (8.5000, 11.0000). Now, draw some points and lines on a magenta layer called LINE.

Note: *Do not be afraid to try any command. You can always return to where you were before the command was issued by using UNDO (type U on the keyboard). You can also REDO an UNDO by typing REDO or selecting it from the screen menu. Also, if you get into the middle of a command sequence and you do not want to finish it, press Ctrl-C to cancel.*

Begin drawing points and lines on a magenta layer called LINE.

Prompt: Command:

Response: {Select} LAYER {from the Root Menu or MODIFY LAYER from the Release 9 MODES pull-down menu}

Prompt: ?/Make/Set/New/ON/OFF/Color/L Type/Freeze/Thaw:

Response: NEW

Prompt: New layer name(s):

Response: LINE {you may also use L for LINE or M for the color magenta—a single letter or number reduces the typing ·needed to change layers}

Prompt: ?/Make/. . . . . /Color/. . . . . /Thaw:

Response: COLOR

Prompt: COLOR:

Response: Magenta {or M}

Prompt: Layer name(s) for color 6 (magenta) <0>:

Response: LINE ↵

Prompt: ?/Make/Set/. . . . . /Thaw:

Response: SET

Prompt: New current layer <0>:

Response: LINE ↵ ↵ {press Enter twice}

You should now have displayed at the upper left of your drawing the following:

Layer LINE ORTHO SNAP (If this is not what you find, you may
    need to use the function keys to turn on SNAP, GRID, and
    ORTHO.)

F7 GRID FUNCTION

F8 ORTHO FUNCTION

F9 SNAP FUNCTION

With the GRID, ORTHO, and SNAP ON, it is very easy to draw points or lines in increments of 1/4", or whatever your SNAP setting is. To do this, select the DRAW Menu from the Root Menu and follow this sequence:

Figure 4-1
Points

× × × ×

POINTS

Lines and Points

To draw points on a grid (Figure 4-1):

Prompt: Command:
Response: POINT {from the DRAW Menu}

Prompt: POINT Point:
Response: DIGITIZE ONE POINT

Prompt: Command:
Response: {Use the Enter key or the middle button on the mouse to repeat the command—repeat this sequence three times}

Figure 4-2
Line 2″ long

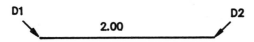

To draw a horizontal line 2″ in length half an inch from the upper left corner (Figure 4-2):

Prompt: Command:
Response: LINE

Prompt: Line from point:
Response: D1 {Figure 4-2}

Prompt: To point:
Response: D2 {move eight ¼″ grid spaces to the right, Figure 4-2}

Figure 4-3
Horizontal Line
2.615″ Long

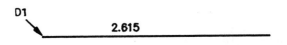

To draw a horizontal line 2.615″ long (Figure 4-3):

Prompt: Command:
Response: LINE

Prompt: Line from point:

Response: D3 {Figure 4-3}

Prompt: To point:

Response: @2.615 < 0 ↵ {hold down the shift key to type @ and < (on the commonly used keyboards they are above the two and the comma)}

Figure 4-4
AutoCAD Directions

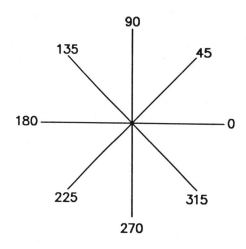

You have told AutoCAD to draw a line 2.615″ long in the 0 direction. Figure 4-4 shows the direction for all lines.

Figure 4-5
Line 2.100″ Long,
10° Angle

To draw a line 2.100″ long at a 10° angle to the upper right (Figure 4-5):

Prompt: Command:

Response: LINE

Prompt: Line from point:

Response: D1 {Figure 4-5}

Prompt: To point:

Response: @2.1 < 10 ↵

**Figure 4-6
Line, Start One Location,
End Another Location**

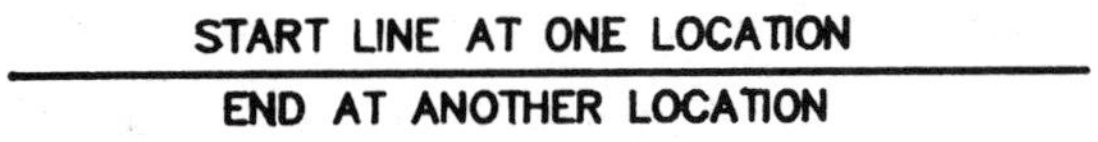

<u>START LINE AT ONE LOCATION</u>
END AT ANOTHER LOCATION

**To draw a line from one location to another location
(Figure 4-6):**

GIVEN: Start the line ¾″ from the left side of the page and 2″
from the top of the page. End it 3.832″ from the left side and 2″
from the top.

Prompt: Command:
Response: LINE

Prompt: Line from point:
Response: .75, 9 ↵ {11″ − 2″ = 9″}

Prompt: To point:
Response: 3.834, 9 ↵

**Figure 4-7
Parallel Lines .517″ Apart**

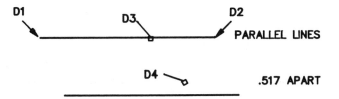

Parallel Lines

To draw 2″ lines parallel to each other, .517″ apart (Figure 4-7):

Prompt: Command:
Response: LINE

Prompt: Line from point:
Response: D1

Prompt: To point:
Response: D2 ↵ {2″ to the right of D1, use the grid spaces for
reference}

Prompt: Command:
Response: OFFSET {from the EDIT Menu}

Prompt: Offset distance or through:

Response: .517 ↵ {the distance that the lines are apart}

Prompt: Select object to offset:

Response: D3 {select the line anywhere on it}

Prompt: Side to offset?

Response: D4 {anywhere on the side you want the other line to appear}

Figure 4-8
Line, Perpendicular
Through a Point

GIVEN

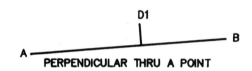

D1

A ———————————————— B

PERPENDICULAR THRU A POINT

Perpendicular Lines

To draw a line perpendicular to another line through a point (Figure 4-8):

GIVEN: Assume the point and line exist:

Prompt: Command:

Response: LINE

Prompt: Line from point:

Response: {Select NODE from the OSNAP Menu (press the third button on the mouse for the OSNAP Menu or **** on the Main Menu) then digitize the point (D1)}

Prompt: To point:

Response: {Select PERPEND from the OSNAP Menu}

Prompt: PERPEND to:

Response: {Digitize any point on the line AB}

Figure 4-9
Simple Line Break

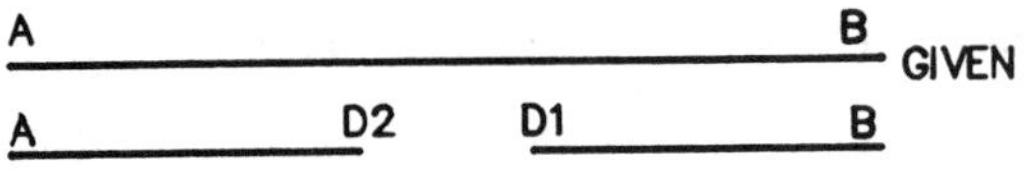

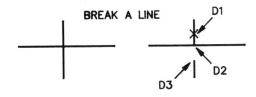

Breaking Lines

To break a line AB with no interference from other lines (Figure 4-9):

Prompt: Command: *from Edit*
Response: BREAK

Prompt: Select object:
Response: {Select the line by digitizing at one end of where the break will be made} D1 ↵

Prompt: Enter second point (or F for first point):
Response: {Digitize the second point—the other end of the break} D2 ↵

Figure 4-10
Coupled Break

BREAK A LINE

To break a line at an intersection with another line (Figure 4-10):

Prompt: Command:
Response: BREAK

Prompt: Select object:
Response: {Select line to be broken} D1 ↵

Prompt: Enter second point (or F for first point):
Response: F {from keyboard}

Prompt: Enter first point:
Response: {Select} INTersec {from the OSNAP Menu and digitize the intersection of the two lines} D2 ↵

Prompt: Enter second point:
Response: {Digitize the end of the break} D3 ↵

Figure 4-11
Divide a Line into
Equal Parts

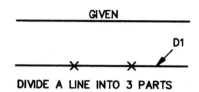

GIVEN

D1

DIVIDE A LINE INTO 3 PARTS

Dividing Lines into Equal Parts

To divide a given line into 3 equal parts (Figures 4-11):

First set PDMODE and PDSIZE. Set PDMODE to "3" so a point will appear as an X. To do this, select the SETVAR command from the SETTINGS Menu, enter PDMODE at the SETVAR variable name prompt, then set PDSIZE to .1 for a tenth-inch-high X. You may also use the POINT Menu to set PDMODE and PDSIZE. PDMODE examples are also found on this menu. For example: a PDMODE selection of 64 gives you a point with a square around it.

Prompt: Command:
Response: DIVIDE

Prompt: Select objects to divide:
Response: {Digitize anywhere on the line} D1 ↵

Prompt: <Number of segments>/Block:
Response: 3 ↵

Note: *The line has not been broken into three parts; a node, or point, has been placed at the proper interval so further construction may be made at those points.*

Figure 4-12
Divide a Line into
Certain Size Parts

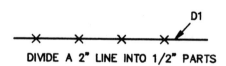

D1

DIVIDE A 2" LINE INTO 1/2" PARTS

To divide a line into certain size parts (Figure 4-12):

GIVEN: Divide a 2¼" line into ½" parts.

Prompt: Command:
Response: MEASURE {select from the EDIT Menu}

Prompt: Select object to measure:
Response: D1 {Figure 4-12}

Prompt: <Segment length>/block:

Response: .5 ↵

Note: *The divisions start from the end of the line closest to the digitized point. The ¼" left over appears on the left because the ½" parts were measured beginning from the right end of the line.*

Figure 4-13
Fillet and Chamfer

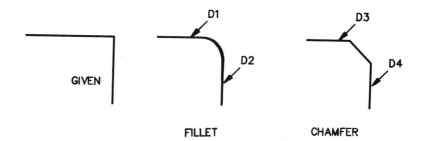

Fillets

To make a fillet (a radius of a specific size) at the junction of two lines (Figure 4-13):

Prompt: Command:

Response: FILLET {from the EDIT Menu}

Prompt: Fillet Polyline/Radius/<Select two objects>:

Response: {Select} RADIUS {or type R}

Prompt: Enter fillet radius (0.0000):

Response: .25 {or the size radius desired} ↵

Prompt: <Select two objects>:

Response: D1, D2 {Figure 4-13}

Chamfers

To make a chamfer (an angle of a specific size) at the junction of two lines (Figure 4-13):

Prompt: Command:

Response: CHAMFER

Prompt: Chamfer Polyline/Distance/<Select first line>:

Response: DISTANCE

Prompt: Enter first chamfer distance:

Response: .25 ↵

Prompt: Enter second chamfer distance <0.2500>:

Response: ↵ {to make a 45° chamfer}

Prompt: Select first line:

Response: D3 ↵

Prompt: Select second line:

Response: D4 ↵

SUGGESTION: Try another chamfer giving different measurements for each leg of the chamfer.

**Figure 4-14
Methods of Drawing
Circles**

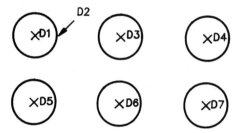

Circles

To draw circles of a specific size at a specific location (Figure 4-14):

GIVEN: Draw six ½″-diameter circles, 1″ between centers, in 2 rows of 3 each.

Prompt: Command:

Response: CIRCLE – CEN RAD {from the DRAW Menu}

Prompt: Circle 3P/2P/TTR/<Center Point>:

Response: D1 ↵ {with SNAP ON, GRID at .25}

Prompt: Diameter/<Radius>: DRAG

Response: .25 ↵ {because radius is in the default brackets, .25 is the radius for this circle}

       or

   D2 {the digitized point will specify the radius—notice DRAG shows you how big the circle will be}

       or

   D {type the letter D to tell AutoCAD you want to specify a diameter}

Prompt: Diameter:

Response: .5 ↵

GIVEN: Draw 5 more circles of the same size on 1″ centers.

Prompt: Command:

Response: COPY

Prompt: Select object:

Response: {Digitize anywhere on the circle circumference}

Prompt: Select objects:

Response: ↵

Prompt: <Base point or displacement>/Multiple:

Response: {Select} MULTIPLE {from the screen menu}

Prompt: Multiple base point:

Response: D1 {the center of the first circle}

Prompt: Second point of displacement:

Response: D3, D4, D5, D6, D7 ↵

**Figure 4-15
Tangents to Circles
and Arcs**

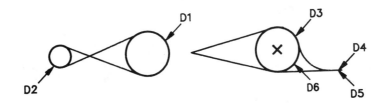

Tangents

To draw a line tangent to a circle (Figure 4-15):

Prompt: Command:

Response: LINE

Prompt: LINE from point:

Response: TANGENT {from OSNAP Menu}

Prompt: Tangent to:

Response: D1

Prompt: To point:

Response: TANGENT

Prompt: Tangent to:

Response: D2

Note: *The half of the circle that is digitized is the half where the tangent occurs. The other line tangents were drawn in the same manner.*

Arcs

To draw an arc of a given radius tangent to a circle and a line (Figure 4-15):

    GIVEN: R = .375

Prompt: Command:

Response: FILLET

Prompt: Fillet Polyline/Radius/<Select two objects>:

Response: R ↵ {from the keyboard or RADIUS from the screen menu}

Prompt: Enter fillet radius <0.0000>:

Response: .375 ↵

Prompt: Command:

Response: ↵

Prompt: Fillet Polyline/Radius/<Select two objects>:

Response: D3, D4 ↵

Prompt: Command:

Response: CHANGE

Prompt: Select objects:

Response: D5 ↵

Prompt: Properties/<change point>:

Response: TANGENT

Prompt: Tangent to:

Response: D6

Figure 4-16
Methods of
Drawing Arcs

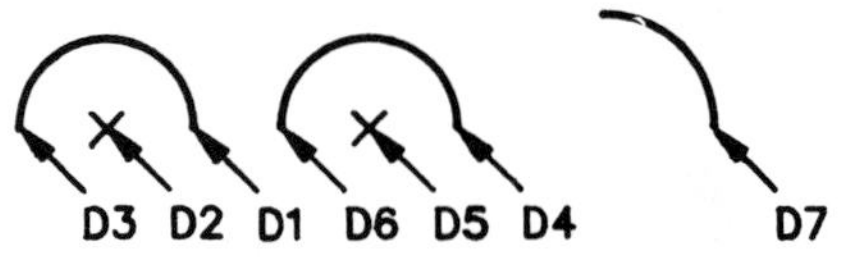

D3 D2 D1   D6 D5 D4   D7

To draw arcs of a specific size or angle (Figure 4-16):

Note: *These are two different methods for the same arc.*

Method using 3-point selection on ARC Menu:

Prompt: Command:
Response: ARC 3 {point}

Prompt: ARC center/<start point>:
Response: D1 {since default is the start point}

Prompt: Center/End/<Second Point>:
Response: C

Prompt: Center:
Response: D2

Prompt: Angle/Length of Chord/<End Point>:
Response: D3

Method using S, C, E on the ARC Menu:

Prompt: Command:
Response: ARC S, C, E:

Prompt: ARC Center/<Start Point>:
Response: D4

Prompt: C Center:
Response: D5

Prompt: Angle/Length of Chord/<End Point>: DRAG
Response: D6

Figure 4-17
Elements of an Arc

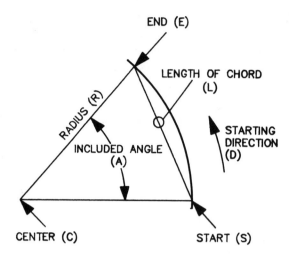

Now that you have drawn two arcs of the same size and shape, consider the choices you have in making an arc. First, look at the definitions given for the elements of an arc, Figure 4-17.

S   Start—the beginning point of the arc (does not always have to be the first point digitized).

C   Center—the center of the arc radius.

E   End—the ending point of the arc.

L   The length of the chord—a straight line connecting the ends of the arc.

D   Starting direction—used only in the S, E, D sequence; all other sequences draw the arc in a counterclockwise direction.

R   Radius—the radius of the arc.

There are several methods of drawing arcs for specific situations or preferences. We will cover one other method in this chapter and others later where drawing problems will require the use of them.

To draw an arc of a specific radius to include a specific angle (Figure 4-16):

GIVEN: R = .315, included angle = 90°.

Prompt: Command:
Response: ARC S, C, A

Prompt: ARC Center/<Start point>:
Response: D7

Prompt: C Center:

Response: @.315 < 180 ↵

Prompt: A included angle:

Response: 90 ↵

**Figure 4-18
Curve Through Points**

Curves through Points

To draw a curve through given points (Figure 4-18):

GIVEN: points marked as X's were given

Prompt: Command:

Response: PLINE (from the DRAW Menu)

Prompt: From point:

Response: D1

Prompt: Arc/Close/Halfwidth/Length/Undo/Width
/<Endpoint of line>:

Response: {Digitize each point from D2 to D14 one-by-one}

Prompt: Command:

Response: PEDIT {from the EDIT Menu}

Prompt: PEDIT select polyline:

Response: D15

Prompt: Close/Join/Width/Edit vertex/Fit curve/Decurve/Undo
/Exit<X>:

Response: FIT CURVE {select from the screen menu}

The Release 9 version of AutoCAD has a SPLINE feature that draws the curve to fit the average distance assumed by the points. It is used in the same manner as "fit curve." Try it if you have Release 9.

Figure 4-19
Break a Polyline

To break a polyline (Figure 4-19):

Prompt: Command:
Response: BREAK

Prompt: Select object:
Response: D1

Prompt: Enter second point (or F for first point):
Response: D2

Figure 4-20
Parallel Shapes

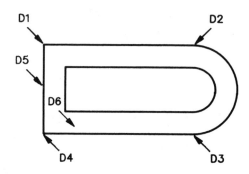

Similar Shapes

To draw a shape inside of a similar shape (Figure 4-20):

GIVEN: all points of the inner shape are the same distance from the outer shape; the inner shape is .25″ smaller than the outer shape.

Prompt: Command:
Response: PLINE (from the DRAW Menu)

Prompt: From point:
Response: D1

Prompt: <Endpoint of line>:
Response: D2

Prompt: Arc/Close/Halfwidth/Length/Undo/Width/<Endpoint of line>:
Response: ARC {or A from the keyboard}

Prompt: <Endpoint of arc>:

Response: D3

Prompt: <Endpoint of arc>:

Response: LINE {or L from the keyboard}

Prompt: <Endpoint of line>:

Response: D4

Prompt: <Endpoint of line>:

Response: CLOSE {or C from the keyboard}

Prompt: Command:

Response: OFFSET

Prompt: Offset distance or Through <Through>:

Response: .25

Prompt: Select object to offset:

Response: D5 {anywhere on the PLINE}

Prompt: Side to offset?

Response: D6 {anywhere inside the shape}

Figure 4-21
Rectangular Arrays

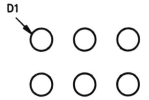

Arrays of Circles and Lines

To draw arrays of circles and lines or any other shape (Figure 4-21):

GIVEN: draw two rows of three .25 DIA circles each; all circles
½″ (.5) from center to center:

Prompt: Command:

Response: CIRCLE CEN – DIA

Prompt: <Center point>:

Response: {Digitize the center of the circle}

Prompt: Diameter:

Response: .25 ↵

Prompt: Command:

Response: ARRAY {from the EDIT Menu}

Prompt: Select objects:

Response: D1 {or window an object completely}

Prompt: Rectangular or Polar array (R/P):

Response: R ↵ {from the keyboard or RECTANG from the screen menu}

Prompt: Number of rows (- - - - - -) <1>:

Response: 2 ↵

Prompt: Number of columns (III) <1>:

Response: 3 ↵

Prompt: Unit cell or distance between rows (- - - -):

Response: .5↵ {rows form upward—a response of −.5 forms rows downward}

Prompt: Distance between columns (III):

Response: .5 ↵ {columns form to the right—a response of −.5 forms columns to the left}

**Figure 4-22
Row of Equally
Spaced Lines**

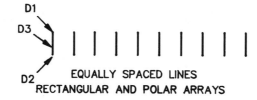

EQUALLY SPACED LINES
RECTANGULAR AND POLAR ARRAYS

To draw a row of ten ¹/₄″ (.25) lines spaced ¹/₄″ (.25) apart (Figure 4-22):

Prompt: Command:

Response: LINE

Prompt: From point:

Response: D1

Prompt: To point:

Response: D2

Prompt: Command:

Response: ARRAY

Prompt: Select objects:

Response: D3 ↵

Prompt: Rectangular or Polar array (R/P):

Response: R ↵

Prompt: Number of rows (- - - - -) <1>:

Response: ↵

Prompt: Number of columns (111) <1>:

Response: 10 ↵

Prompt: Distance between columns (111):

Response: .25 ↵ {the columns will form to the right—a response of −.25 forms columns to the left—you may also digitize two points to specify the spacing between columns or rows}

**Figure 4-23
Polar Array**

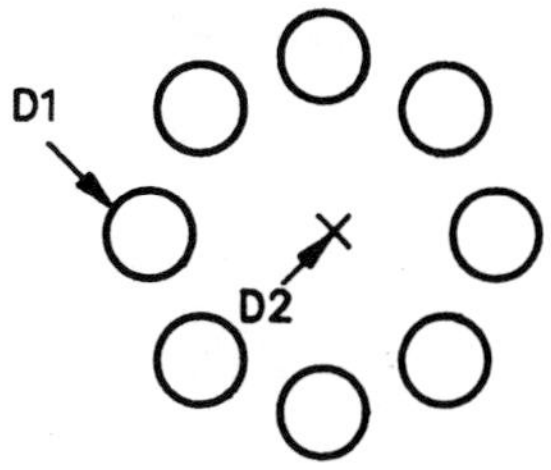

To draw a circular (polar) pattern of eight $^1/_4''$ (.25) circles on a 1″ diameter bolt circle (circular center line) (Figure 4-23):

Prompt: Command:

Response: CIRCLE CEN – DIA

Prompt: Center:

Response: {Digitize the center}

Prompt: Diameter:

Response: .25 ↵

Prompt: Command:

Response: ARRAY

Prompt: Select objects:

Response: D1 ↵

Prompt: Rectangular or Polar array (R/P):

Response: P ↵

Prompt: Center point of array:

Response: D2 ↵ {D2 is .5″ from the center of the digitized circle}

Prompt: Number of items:

Response: 8 ↵

Prompt: Angle to fill (t = CCW, − = CW) <360>:

Response: ↵ {CCW means counterclockwise, CW is clockwise, 360 is the number of degrees in a circle—you may specify fewer than 360}

Prompt: Rotate objects as they are copied? (Y)

Response: ↵ {in this case yes or no will give the same pattern; rotation of the objects keeps them perpendicular to a radius drawn from the center of a circle}

Figure 4-24
Polygons

Polygons

To draw polygons (Figure 4-24):

GIVEN: polygons are to be drawn inside an imaginary ½″ (.5) diameter circle.

Prompt: Command:

Response: POLYGON {from the DRAW Menu}

Prompt: Number of sides:

Response: 5 ↵ {or 3, 6, or 8}

Prompt: Edge/<Center of polygon>:

Response: D1 {digitize the center of the polygon}

Prompt: Inscribed in circle/circumscribed about circle (I/C):

Response: I ↵

Prompt: Radius of circle:

Response: .25 ↵

Figure 4-25
A Solid Triangle

Solid Shapes

To draw a solid triangle (Figure 4-25):

Prompt: Command:

Response: SOLID

Prompt:	First point:
Response:	FILL ON {from the screen menu}

Prompt:	First point:
Response:	D1

Prompt:	Second point:
Response:	D2

Prompt:	Third point:
Response:	D3 ↵ {be sure to strike ↵}

Prompt:	Third point:
Response:	↵

Figure 4-26
A Solid Square

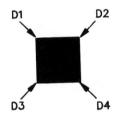

To draw a solid ¹/₂″ square (Figure 4-26):

GIVEN: draw a 4-sided polygon circumscribed around a .5″ diameter circle.

Prompt:	Command:
Response:	SOLID

Prompt:	First point:
Response:	D1

Note: *Digitizing must be done in the order in which it appears in Figure 4-26.*

Prompt:	Second point:
Response:	D2

Prompt:	Third point:
Response:	D3

Prompt:	Fourth point:
Response:	D4

Prompt:	Third point:
Response:	↵

Figure 4-27
Isometric Cylinder

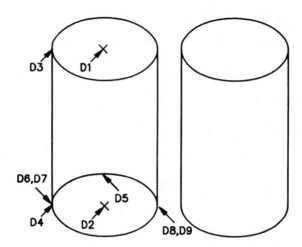

Ellipses and Tangents to Them

To draw a 1″ diameter isometric cylinder (Figure 4-27):

Note: *Other ellipses will be covered later.*

Prompt: Command:

Response: SNAP {from the SETTINGS Menu}
STYLE {from the screen menu}
ISO {from the screen menu}
GRID ON {press F7}

Prompt: Iso Vertical spacing <0.1250>:

Response: .125 ↵ {or just ↵ if spacing is already .125}

Prompt: Command:

Response: {Press the Ctrl key and the letter E at the same time until
the last bracket reads <Isoplane Top>}

Response: ELLIPSE

Prompt: <Axis endpoint 1>/Center/Isocircle:

Response: Iso {from screen menu}

Prompt: Center of circle:

Response: D1

Prompt: <Circle radius>/Diameter:

Response: .5 ↵ {the radius for the ellipse}

Prompt: Command:

Response: ELLIPSE

Prompt: <Axis endpoint 1>/Center/Isocircle:

Response: Iso {from screen menu}

Prompt: Center of circle:

Response: D2 {below the first ellipse on the same center line}

Prompt: <Circle radius>/Diameter:

Response: .5 ↵

Prompt: Command:

Response: LINE

Prompt: From point:

Response: NEArest {from OSNAP Menu}

Prompt: Nearest to:

Response: D3 {the outermost left point on the ellipse}

Prompt: To point:

Response: TANGENT {from OSNAP Menu}

Prompt: Tangent to:

Response: D4

Draw another line to form the right side of the cylinder in a similar manner.

Removing the back half of the bottom ellipse requires a little cleverness. One method is to break the ellipse in a counterclockwise direction. For some reason, however, this does not work consistently. The most consistent method requires breaking the ellipse at the same point on both ends of the ellipse and then erasing. The TRIM command may also be used and is probably the fastest method.

The BREAK command method is as follows:

Prompt: Command:

Response: BREAK

Prompt: Select object:

Response: D5 {Figure 4-27}

Prompt: Enter second point (or F for first point):

Response: F ↵

Prompt: Enter first point:

Response: D6

Prompt: Enter second point:

Response: D7 {or @}

Prompt: Command:

Response: ↵

Prompt: BREAK Select object:

Response: D5

Prompt: Enter second point (or F for first point):

Response: F ↵

Prompt: Enter first point:

Response: D8

Prompt: Enter second point:

Response: D9 {or @}

Prompt: Command:

Response: ERASE

Prompt: Select objects:

Response: D5 ↵ {you may need to select two segments}

Prompt: Command:

TRIM may also be used by selecting the vertical lines as the boundaries, pressing Enter, then selecting the back half of the ellipse as the object to be trimmed.

Response: SAVE ↵ {or END, save your drawing on a floppy disk and on the hard drive—you will have to initiate the SAVE command twice, specifying the floppy drive once and the hard drive the second time}

The preceding paragraphs cover many of the constructions you will encounter in this book and in the drafting industry. Other constructions are presented in later chapters, but understanding how to use these will provide a basis for your later work.

EXERCISE 1

Set up an 8½ × 11″ sheet and draw a ½″ border inside of it. Place your name ¼″ up and ¼″ over from the lower right corner in .1″ high letters. Set SNAP, ORTHO, and GRID at a setting you think is convenient. Arrange the following in order on your sheet inside the border leaving approximately ½″ between each problem.

1. Draw a line 2.0″ long.

2. Draw a line 3.125″ long at a 30° angle upward to the right.

3. Draw lines 3.5″ long, parallel to each other, .375″ apart.

4. Draw a 2″ line with a .5″ line perpendicular to it, .625″ from the left end.

5. Draw a line 3″ long and divide it into 7 equal parts; an X must appear where each division occurs.

6. Draw a 3″ line and divide it into .625″ segments; an X must appear where each segment ends.

7. Draw two lines 1″ long to form a 90° angle. Make a .25 chamfer at the corner.

8. Draw two 1″ lines to form a 90° angle. Make a .250 fillet at the corner.

9. Draw a polar array of eight .25″-diameter circles on a 2″-diameter circular center line.

10. Draw three 1″-diameter semicircles using three different ARC commands. Label each arc with the command used, for example: S,C,E.

11. Draw an arc with a radius of .45″ and include an angle of 60°.

12. Draw a 1½″ square using the POLYLINE command. Draw a 1¼″ and a 1″ square using the OFFSET command; all squares must be concentric.

13. Draw a hexagon inscribed inside a 1″-diameter circle.

14. Draw a solid triangle inscribed inside a ½″-diameter circle. Make an array of these triangles 3 rows by 3 columns, 1″ from center to center both vertically and horizontally.

15. Draw a ¾″-diameter isometric cylinder, 1″ tall. Be sure to erase the hidden portion of the bottom ellipse.

Exercise 2

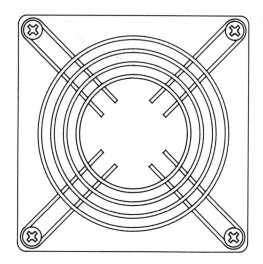

Exercise 3

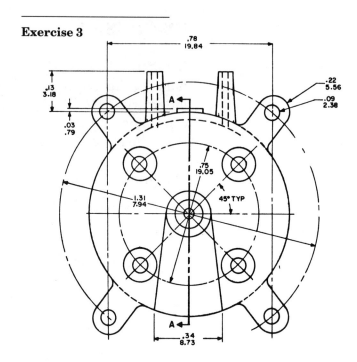

EXERCISE 2

Make an AutoCAD drawing of the fan shown in the illustration. Measure the picture and duplicate it on a vertical 8.5 × 11″ sheet. Place your name in the lower right corner.

EXERCISE 3

Make an AutoCAD drawing of the model airplane motor part shown in this illustration. Make the drawing four-times-size on a vertical 8.5 × 11″ sheet. The upper dimensions are in inches. The lower dimensions are in millimeters. Approximate any dimensions not given. Place your name in the lower right corner. Do not put any dimensions on your drawing.

EXERCISE 4

Follow the same instructions as given for Exercise 3.

EXERCISE 5

Follow the same instructions given for Exercise 3 except make the drawing the same dimensions as shown and place it on a horizontal 11 × 8.5″ sheet. Do not put any dimensions on your drawing.

Exercise 4

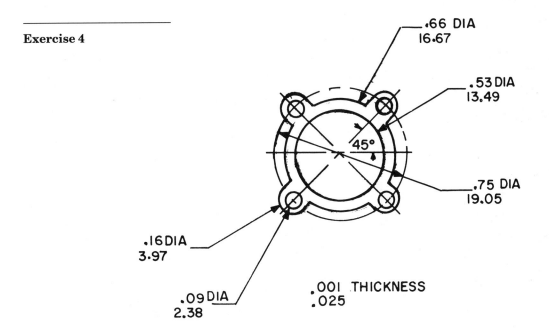

.66 DIA
16.67

.53 DIA
13.49

.75 DIA
19.05

45°

.16 DIA
3.97

.09 DIA
2.38

.001 THICKNESS
.025

Exercise 5

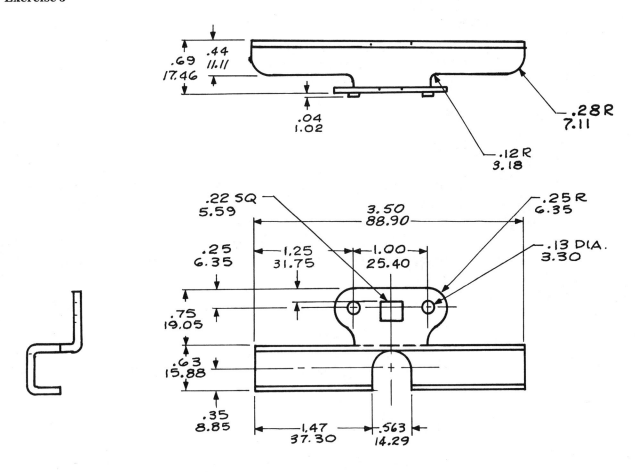

.44
11.11

.69
17.46

.04
1.02

.28 R
7.11

.12 R
3.18

.22 SQ
5.59

.25 R
6.35

3.50
88.90

.13 DIA.
3.30

.25
6.35

1.25
31.75

1.00
25.40

.75
19.05

.63
15.88

.35
8.85

1.47
37.30

.563
14.29

Exercise 6

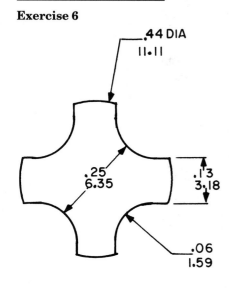

Exercise 7

EXERCISE 6

Follow the same instructions given for Exercise 3.

EXERCISE 7

Make an AutoCAD drawing of the door shown in this illustration. Measure the drawing and reproduce it as accurately as possible. Place it on a vertical 8.5 × 11″ sheet. Place your name in the lower right corner.

EXERCISE 8

Follow the same instructions as given in Exercise 7.

Exercise 8

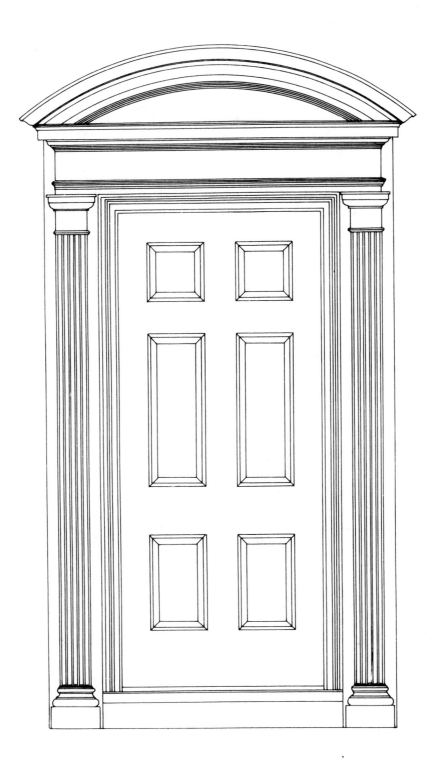

Exercise 9

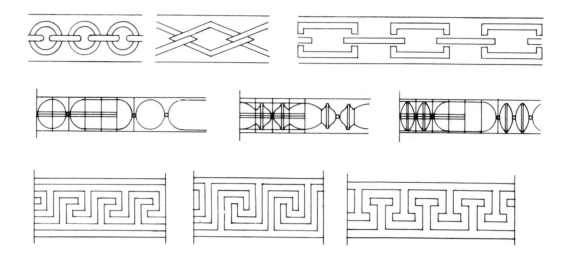

EXERCISE 9

Draw the patterns for molding twice the size shown in this illustration. Place it on a horizontal 11 × 8.5″ sheet. Place your name in the lower right corner.

Test on Objectives—Chapter 4

Circle the correct answer.

1. The maximum number of characters that may be used for a drawing name is?
   a. 2
   b. 4
   c. 6
   d. 8
   e. any number

2. If the GRID spacing is .25″ and the SNAP must touch every line of the GRID, the SNAP should be set at?
   a. .06
   b. .125
   c. .1
   d. .2
   e. .3

3. The layer name that will allow layers to be changed fastest is?

   a. GREEN

   b. LINE

   c. THIN

   d. SET

   e. G

4. From the LINE prompt "to point," which is the correct response to draw a horizontal line 4.501 long to the right of the starting point?

   a. 4.501 <180 ↵

   b. 4.501 ↵

   c. <180° <4.501 ↵

   d. @4.501 <0 ↵

   e. <0° 4.501 ↵

5. To draw a line 5.000″ long that proceeds downward at a 45° angle to the right, which is the correct response to the prompt "to point"?

   a. @5 <135

   b. @5.00 <45

   c. @5.00, <−45

   d. 5.000, 135

   e. 5.000 <45°

6. To draw a line parallel to another line, which of the following commands should be used?

   a. LINE PARALLEL

   b. PARALLEL

   c. OFFSET

   d. OFFSET PARALLEL

   e. LP

7. To draw a line perpendicular to another line from a point, the following modifier should be used?

   a. SQUARE

   b. RT ANGLE

   c. PERPENDICULAR (from the OSNAP Menu)

   d. 90° ANGLE

   e. @90°

8. If you have just drawn a line at the wrong angle and you want to return to the starting point of the line, enter:

   a. REDO

   b. R

   c. U

   d. CONTROL-C

   e. ERASE

9. If you need to break a line at the intersection of another line, select the line to be broken and enter:

   a. the second point—not the intersection
   b. F
   c. the first point
   d. BREAK
   e. CHANGE

10. The variable setting used to make a point appear as an X is?

    a. NODE
    b. POINT SET
    c. PDSIZE
    d. PDMODE
    e. NODE SET

11. To divide a given line into five equal parts, which of the following commands should be used?

    a. MEASURE
    b. DIVIDE
    c. BREAK
    d. CHANGE
    e. POLYLINE

12. To divide a given line into ½″ increments, which of the following commands should be used?

    a. MEASURE
    b. DIVIDE
    c. BREAK
    d. CHANGE
    e. POLYLINE

13. To make a 45° angle at the corner of two intersecting lines, which of the following commands should be used?

    a. MEASURE
    b. FILLET
    c. BREAK
    d. CHANGE
    e. CHAMFER

14. To make a ¼″ radius at the intersection of two lines, which of the following commands should be used?

    a. MEASURE
    b. FILLET
    c. BREAK
    d. CHANGE
    e. CHAMFER

15. A response of .5 to the prompt "diameter/<radius>" will produce a circle of?

    a. .5000 radius
    b. .5000 diameter
    c. .5 chord
    d. .5000 circumference
    e. .5000 chord

16. To produce a circle with a diameter of .5000, the correct response to the prompt "diameter/<radius>" is?

    a. D—then .5
    b. R—then .500
    c. .50
    d. circle-diameter
    e. .5000—then ⏎

17. Multiple copy is often faster than ARRAY if a small number of parts is to be copied.

    a. true
    b. false

18. A pattern of 16 holes on a circular centerline may be drawn fastest using?

    a. RECTANGULAR ARRAY
    b. MULTIPLE COPY
    c. COPY CIRCULAR
    d. REPEAT
    e. POLAR ARRAY

19. The command _____ was used to draw the arc shown below.

    a. ARC C,E,S
    b. ARC E,C,S
    c. ARC C,S,E
    d. ARC S,C,E
    e. ARC S,C,A

D3 D2 D1

20. A polyline is used when a series of lines must all be treated as a single entity as in OFFSET.

    a. true
    b. false

21. An array of 5 rows and 1 column with a .5 distance between rows will produce which of the following patterns?

22. Which of the following commands should be used to draw a hexagon?

    a. POLYGON
    b. HEXAGON
    c. POLYLINE
    d. FILLET
    e. CHAMFER

23. Which of the following sequences will produce a solid square using a solid command?

24. The isoplane top condition will produce which of the following isometric ellipses?

25. Which of the following menus contains the command to establish an isometric grid?

    a. GRID
    b. EDIT
    c. UTILITY
    d. SNAP
    e. DRAW

5

Drawing Orthographic Views

Objectives

The student will:

- make two-dimensional drawings to scale from two-dimensional and three-dimensional sketches using the following commands:

ARC	LINE
CHAMFER	OSNAP
CIRCLE	PAN
DISK	REDRAW
FILLET	TRIM
HELP	UNDO
LIMITS	VIEW

- correctly answer questions regrading the above commands

Two-Dimensional Drawings

Two-dimensional drawings are those showing only two of the three dimensions of an object in any one view. Figure 5-1 illustrates the three most commonly used two-dimensional views. The top view shows width and depth. The front view shows width and height. The right side view shows height and depth.

AutoCAD has excellent capabilities for drawing in two dimensions. The drawings can be extremely accurate and can be dimensioned in a manner ensuring correct results. Although a checking procedure is introduced in this chapter, dimensioning accurately is covered in a later chapter. In this chapter the mechanics of drawing in two dimensions and the procedures needed to move quickly from one view to another

Figure 5-1
The Most Commonly
Used Views

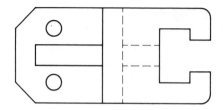

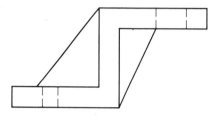

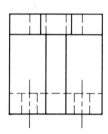

are covered. Orthographic projection (two-dimensional drawing) is a major part of any good basic drafting textbook. This is a good time to review if you have questions regarding view placement or line identification. Let us begin two-dimensional drawing with a reasonably simple flat object (Figure 5-2).

Drawing Two-Dimensional Views

To draw a single two-dimensional view:

Step 1. Load AutoCAD. Begin a new drawing and name it 5-1-(your initials).

Step 2. Select a scale and a paper size.

Prompt: Command:
Response: SETUP

Prompt: Select the units from the screen menu:
Response: 2 ↵ {decimal}

Prompt: Select scale from the screen menu:
Response: FULL

Prompt: Select the paper size from the screen menu:
Response: A-11 × 8.5

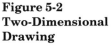

Figure 5-2
Two-Dimensional
Drawing

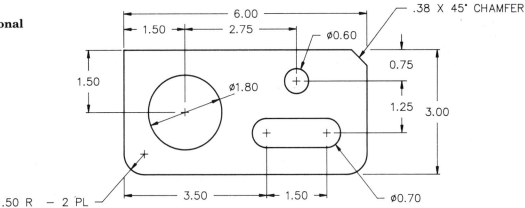

Step 3. Select GRID and SNAP settings.

Prompt: Command:
Response: SETTING – GRID

Prompt: GRID spacing (X) or ON/OFF/Snap/Aspect < >:
Response: .25 ↵

Prompt: Command:
Response: GRID = SNAP {from GRID Menu}

Prompt: SNAP spacing or ON/OFF/Aspect/Rotate/Style< >:
Response: .25 ↵

Prompt: Command:

Step 4. Create the drawing layers. You will need separate layers for LINES and CIRCLES.

Prompt: Command:
Response: {Digitize} LAYER {from the screen menu or use the Release 9 procedure described in Chapter 3}

Prompt: Layer/Make/Set/New/ON/OFF/ColorLtype/Freeze/Thaw:
Response: NEW {from LAYER Menu}

Prompt: New layers name(s):
Response: 1,2 ↵ {type from the keyboard}

Prompt: ?/Make/Set/New/ON/OFF/Color/Ltype/Freeze/Thaw:
Response: C ↵ {or digitize color}

Prompt: Color:
Response: R ↵ {or digitize RED}

Prompt: Layer name(s) for color 1 (red) < >:
Response: 1 ↵ {type from the keyboard}

Prompt: ?/Make/Set/New/ON/OFF/Color/Ltype/Freeze/Thaw:
Response: C ↵ {or digitize color}

Prompt: Color:
Response: Y ↵ {or digitize yellow}

Prompt: Layer names(s) for color 2 (yellow) < >:
Response: 2 ↵ {type from the keyboard}

Prompt: ?/Make/Set/New/ON/OFF/Color/Ltype/Freeze/Thaw:
Response: ? {from the keyboard or screen}

Note: *Make sure all layers are ON.*

If all layers are not on, do the following:

Prompt: ?/Make/Set/New/ON/OFF/Color/Ltype/Freeze/Thaw:
Response: ON ↵

Prompt: Layer Name(s) to turn ON:
Response: * ↵ {* is a symbol meaning ALL, and applies to layers and filenames}

Prompt: ?/Make/Set/New/ON/OFF/Color/Ltype/Freeze/Thaw:
Response: SET {type or select from menu}

Prompt: New current layer < >:
Response: 1 ↵

Prompt: ?/Make/Set/New/ON/OFF/Color/Ltype/Freeze/Thaw:
Response: ↵ {or press space bar}

Prompt: Command:
Response: F1 {for Flip Screen}

You are now ready to draw on Layer 1. Your status line in the upper left corner should read Layer 1 ORTHO SNAP. If ORTHO and SNAP are not ON, activate them from function keys F8 and F9 (IBM AT/XT).

Figure 5-3
Draw Object

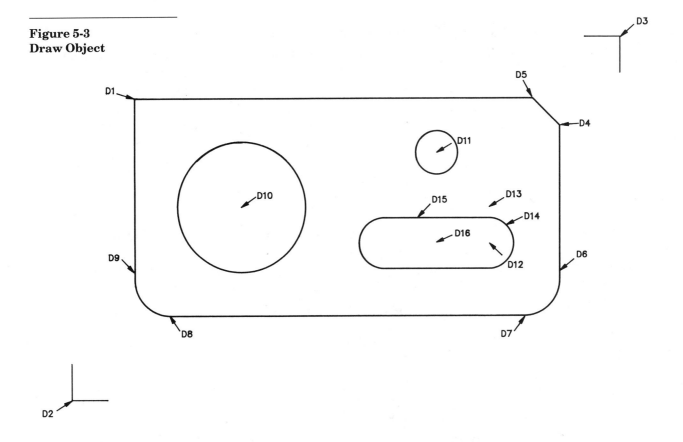

Step 5. Draw the outline of Figure 5-2.

Prompt: Command:

Response: {Digitize} LINE {from DRAW Menu or type LINE from the keyboard}

Prompt: Line from point:

To digitize a point (Figure 5-3):

Response: D1

Prompt: To point:

Response: @6 < 0 ↵

Prompt: To point:

Response: @3 < 270 ↵

Prompt: To point:

Response: @6 < 180 ↵

Prompt: To point:

Response: C ↵ {or digitize CLOSE—the close option will cause the last point entered to connect back to the first point entered}

You should now have a closed red box on the screen. If a mistake is made while entering line coordinates, type UNDO and press Enter. This returns the cursor to the last line entered. Now add the chamfer and the fillets to the outline.

Prompt: Command:

Response: {type or digitize} ZOOM {from DISPLAY Menu}

Prompt: All/Center/Dynamics/Extents/Left/Previous/Window /Scale(x):

Response: W ↵ {or select Window}

Prompt: First corner:

Response: D2 {Figure 5-3}

Prompt: Other corner:

Response: D3 {Figure 5-3}

Prompt: Command:

Response: CHAMFER {or select from EDIT Menu}

Prompt: Polyline/Distances/<Select first>:

First select the chamfer distances.

Response: D ↵ {or select DISTANCE from screen menu}

Prompt: Enter first chamfer distance <0.0000>:

Response: .38 ↵ {type from the keyboard}

Prompt: Enter second chamfer distance <0.3800>:

Response: .38 ↵

At this point you may have to press the space bar or Enter to get back to the CHAMFER command.

Prompt: Chamfer Polyline/Distances/Select first/Line:

Response: D4 {Figure 5-3}

Prompt: Select second line:

Response: D5 {Figure 5-3}

Prompt: Command:

Response: FILLET {or select FILLET from the EDIT Menu}

Prompt: Fillet Polyline/Radius/<Select two objects>:

First enter the fillet radius.

Response: R ↵ {or select RADIUS from FILLET Menu}

Prompt: Enter fillet radius <0.0000>:

Response: .5 ↵   16.5

Prompt: Command:

Response: ↵ {or press the space bar to get back to the FILLET command}

Prompt: Fillet Polyline/Radius/<Select two objects?:

Response: D6 D7 ↵ ↵ D8 D9

Prompt: Command:

Step 6. Add the circles and the slot to the drawing.

Prompt: Command:

Response: LAYER {or select LAYER from Root Menu; Release 9: digitize "current for layer 2" on the Modify Layer chart under the MODES Menu}

Prompt: Layer?/Make/Set/New/ON/OFF/Color/Ltype/Freeze/Thaw:

Response: SET {or select SET from LAYER Menu}

Prompt: New current layer <1>:

Response: 2 ↵ {type from the keyboard}

Prompt: Layer?/Make/New/ON/OFF/Color/Ltype/Freeze/Thaw:

Response: ↵ {or press space bar}

Prompt: Command:

Response: CIRCLE {or select CIRCLE from DRAW Menu}

When you select the menu, digitize CEN,RAD: to change the prompt.

Prompt: 3P/2P/TTR/ Center point:

Response: D10 {Figure 5-3}

Pick a point 1.5 inches from the top edge and 1.5 inches from the left edge. Press the appropriate function key to turn the GRID ON.

Prompt: Diameter/<Radius>:

Response: .9 ↵ {radius is the default}

Prompt: Command:

Response: CIRCLE {or select CIRCLE from DRAW Menu and select CEN,RAD:}

Prompt: 3P/2P/TTR/<Center Point>:

Response: D11 {Figure 5-2}

Pick a point .75 inches from the top edge and 1.75 inches from the right edge. Remember the SNAP and the GRID are set to .25 inches.

Prompt: Diameter/<Radius>: DRAG

Response: D

Prompt: Diameter:

Response: .6 ↵

Prompt: Command:

Now, draw the slot.

Response: ARC {or select ARC from the DRAW Menu}

Prompt: Center/ Start point:

Response: C {or select C,S,E, from ARC Menu}

Prompt: Center:

Response: D12 {Figure 5-3}

Pick a point 1.00 inch from the right edge and 1.00 inch from bottom edge.

Prompt: Start point:

Response: @.35 < 270 ↵

Prompt: Angle/Length of chord/<Endpoint>:

Response: D13

Digitize on GRID dot 90° opposite of start point.

Prompt: Command:

Response: LINE {or select from DRAW Menu}

Prompt: From point:

Response: END ↵ {or press space bar}

Prompt: From point: END of

Move the cursor and notice the target box. Position the box near the top part of the arc. If you have difficulty because the SNAP command is ON, then toggle F9 OFF, digitize the point, and toggle F9 back ON.

Response: D14

Prompt: To point:
Response: @1.5 < 180 ↵

Prompt: To point:
Response: ↵ {or press space bar}

Prompt: Command:
Response: OFFSET {or select from DRAW Menu}

Prompt: Offset distance or Through <Through>:
Response: .70 ↵ {this sets the distance to the end of the arc}

Prompt: Select object to offset:
Response: {Turn off} SNAP {then} D15 {Figure 5-3}

Prompt: Side to offset:
Response: D16 {notice how the offset line connects exactly on the end of the ARC}

Prompt: Select object to offset:
Response: ↵

Prompt: Command:
Response: {Turn} SNAP {function key back} ON {select} ARC {from the DRAW Menu, then select CONTIN: from ARC Menu}

Prompt: End point: DRAG

Now move the cursor around. Notice how the ARC drags.

Response: @.7 <270 ↵

Prompt: Command:
Response: REDRAW {from the DISPLAY Menu—the REDRAW command will remove the digitized points from the screen}

Step 7. Plot the drawing on an A-size (11 × 8.5″) sheet. Respond to the plot prompts as follows:

Prompt: Command:

Response: PLOT {from the screen menu or 3 from the Main Menu}

Prompt: Specify the part of the drawing to be plotted by entering: Display, Extents, Limits, View or Window <L>:

Response: ↵ {or L if the default is other than L}

Prompt: Do you want to change anything: <N>

Response: Y

Prompt: Do you want to change any of the above parameters? <N>:

Response: Y

Prompt: Layer color 1 (Red) – Pen No. 1 – Line Type 0 – Pen Speed 36 – Pen Number <1>:

Response: 2

This will allow you to place a thicker pen in the No. 2 slot in the open carrousel if your plotter is so equipped. To change other pens or other features on other layers, type "C" and the layer color number, for example: C5 ↵. This will change the prompt to "Layer Color No. 5." Type "X ↵" to proceed.

Prompt: Write the plot to a file? <N>:

Response: ↵

Prompt: Size Units (Inches or Millimeters) <I>:

Response: ↵

Prompt: Plot origin in Inches <0.00,0.00>:

You may need to move the origin depending on how your plotter is set up. The first dimension is the long side of the paper.

Response: ↵

Prompt: Standard Values for plotting size: Enter the size or Width, Height (in inches) <USER>:

Response: 11, 8.5 {or ↵ if the USER shows this size}

Prompt: Rotate 2D Plots 90 degrees clockwise? <N>:

Response: ↵ {respond with Y for a vertical page}

Prompt: Pen width <0.010>:

Note: *This is used only for very accurate artwork such as printed circuit artwork.*

Response: ↵

Prompt: Adjust area fill boundaries for pen width? <N>: {used only for very accurate artwork}

Response: ↵

Prompt: Remove hidden lines? <N>:

Response: ↵

Prompt: Plotted Inches = Drawing Units or Fit or ? <F>:

Response: 1 = 1

Prompt: Position paper in plotter:
                Press Return to continue, or S to stop for hardware setup.

Check the plotter pens to make sure they are working, and load the paper in your plotter. Press the appropriate controls on the plotter to make sure it will respond, then press ↵ on the computer keyboard. The plot should begin.

Now draw an object using the three most common views so you can see the relationship between views and see how easy it is to move from one view to another.

To draw three, two-dimensional views of an object (Figure 5-4):

Step 1. Load AutoCAD 1. Begin a new drawing and name it 5-2-(your initials).

Step 2. Select UNITS, LIMITS, GRID and SNAP.

Prompt: Command:

Response: {Type} UNITS {or select from SETTINGS screen menu}

Prompt: System of Units:

                  1. Scientific
                  2. Decimal
                  3. Engineering
                  4. Architectural
                  5. Fractional

                Enter choice, 1 to 4 <2>:

Response: ↵ {this defaults to decimal}

Figure 5-4
Three Views of an Object

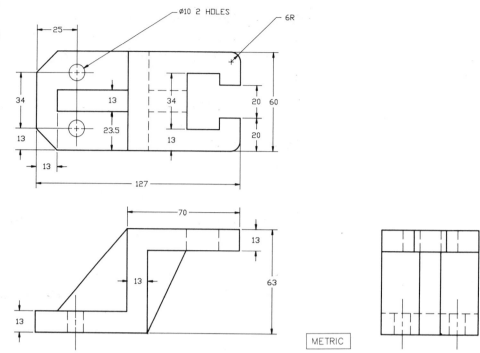

METRIC

Prompt: Number of digits to the right of decimal point (0 to 8) <4>:

Response: ↵ {this defaults to 4}

Prompt: Systems of angle measure:

    1. Decimal degrees
    2. Degrees/Minutes/Seconds
    3. Grads
    4. Radians
    5. Surveyor's units

Enter choice, 1 to 5 <1>:

Response: ↵ {this defaults to 1}

Prompt: Number of fractional places for display of angles (0 to 8) <0>:

Response: ↵ {this defaults to 0}

Prompt: Direction for angle 0:

East   3 o'clock = 0
North   12 o'clock = 90
West   9 o'clock = 180
South   6 o'clock = ²70

Enter direction for angle 0 <0>:

Response: ↵ {this will default to current settings on screen}

Prompt: Do you want angles measured clockwise: <N>

Response: ↵ {this defaults to No}

Prompt: Command:

At this point you may have to return to the drawing (use F1 flip screen key).

Response: LIMITS {or select from SETTINGS screen menu}

Prompt: ON/OFF/ Lower left corner <0.0000,0.0000>:
Response: ↵ {this will default the lower left corner to 0.0000,0.0000}

Prompt: Upper right corner <12.0000,9.0000>:
Response: 420,297 {this sets up a METRIC drawing on a 11 × 17″ sheet, respond with 297,210 for an A-size sheet}

Prompt: Command:
Response: GRID {or select from SETTINGS screen menu}

Prompt: Grid spacing (x) or ON/OFF/Snap/Aspect <0.0000>:
Response: 10 ↵

Prompt: Command:
Response: SNAP {or select GRD = SNAP from screen menu}

Prompt: SNAP spacing or ON/OFF/Aspect/Rotate/Style <0.0000>:
Response: {Type} 10 ↵

Prompt: Command:
Response: ZOOM {or select from DISPLAY on screen menu}

Prompt: All/Center/Dynamics/Extents/Left/Previous/Window/ <Scale (x)>:
Response: A ↵ {or select ALL from screen menu}

Prompt: Layer?/Make/Set/New/ON/OFF/Color/Ltype/Freeze/Thaw:
Response: NEW {or select NEW from LAYER Menu}

Prompt: New layer name(s):
Response: 1,3 ↵ {type from keyboard}

Prompt: Layer?/Make/Set/New/ON/OFF/Color/Ltype/Freeze/Thaw:
Response: C ↵ {type from keyboard}

Prompt: Color:
Response: R ↵ {for red}

Prompt: Layer name(s) for color 1 (red) <0>:
Response: 1 ↵

Prompt: Layer?/Make/Set/New/ON/OFF/Color/Ltype/Freeze/Thaw:
Response: C ↵

Prompt: Color:
Response: G ↵ {for green}

Prompt: Layer name(s) for color 3 (green) <1>:
Response: 3 ↵

Now select a linetype for LAYER 3. LAYER 3 is the layer to be used for HIDDEN lines.

Prompt: Layer?/Make/Set/New/ON/OFF/Color/Ltype/Freeze/Thaw:
Response: LTYPE {or select from LAYER Menu}

Prompt: Line type (or ?) <CONTINUOUS>:
Response: HIDDEN ↵

Prompt: Layer name(s) for Ltype hidden <1>:
Response: 3 ↵ {the name of the layer to be hidden}

If it is not changed, AutoCAD will default to the current drawing layer.

Prompt: Layer?/Make/Set/New/ON/OFF/Color/Ltype/Freeze/Thaw:
Response: ?

Prompt: Layer name(s) for listing <*>:
Response: {Press the ↵ key for a complete listing of all layers created; notice LAYER 3—the linetype has now been changed to HIDDEN}

Prompt: Layer?/Make/Set/New/ON/OFF/Color/Ltype/Freeze/Thaw:
Response: SET {or select SET from LAYER Menu}

Prompt: New current layer <0>:
Response: 1 ↵ {layer 1 is the red layer}

Prompt: Layer?/Make/Set/New/ON/OFF/Color/Ltype/Freeze/Thaw:
Response: ↵ {or press space bar}

Prompt: Command:
Response: F6 {function key, or the coordinate function key if it is not F6 on your computer keyboard}

You are now ready to draw on Layer 1. The status line in the upper left corner should read: Layer 1 ORTHO SNAP. If ORTHO and

Figure 5-5
Create View Areas

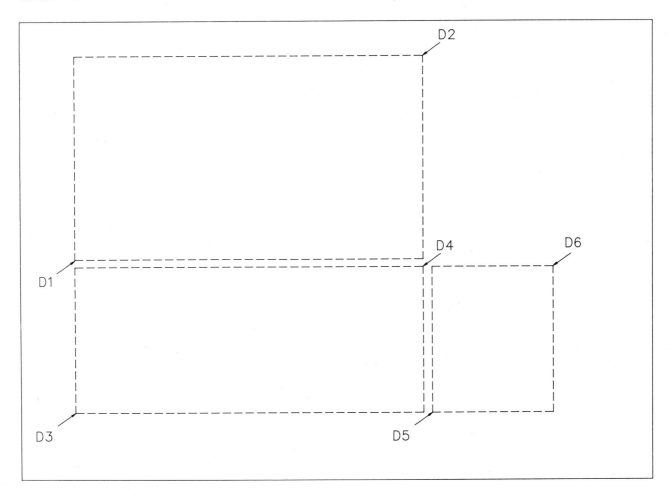

SNAP are not ON, activate them from the appropriate function keys (F8 and F9—IBM AT/XT).

Begin drawing by creating areas for the front, top, and right side views. Window an area for the front view (name it F or Front), an area for the top view (name it T or Top), and an area for the right side view (name it S or SIDE). As you draw these views you will find it helpful to project surfaces from one view to another. Using the VIEW-RESTORE command allows you to move from one view to another quickly without going through ZOOM dynamic to get there. Naming the views with a single letter reduces the amount of typing needed to change views. Follow this sequence to create views (Figure 5-5).

Prompt: Command:

Response: VIEW {type or select from DISPLAY Menu}

Prompt: View?/Delete/Restore/Save/Window:

Response: W ↵ {or WINDOW from the menu}

Prompt: View name to save:
Response: T ↵ {or TOP from the keyboard}

Prompt: First corner:
Response: D1 {Figure 5-5}

Prompt: Other corner:
Response: D2

Prompt: Command:
Response: ↵

Prompt: VIEW ?/Delete/Restore/Save/Window:
Response: W ↵

Prompt: View name to save:
Response: F ↵ {front}

Prompt: First corner:
Response: D3

Prompt: Other corner:
Response: D4

Prompt: Command:
Response: ↵

Prompt: VIEW ?/Delete/Restore/Save/Window:
Response: W ↵

Prompt: View name to save:
Response: R ↵ {right side}

Prompt: First corner:
Response: D5

Prompt: Other corner:
Response: D6

Now move from one view to another to observe the VIEW command in action.

Prompt: Command:
Response: VIEW

Prompt: VIEW ?/Delete/Restore/Save/Window:
Response: R ↵ {from the keyboard or RESTORE from the menu}

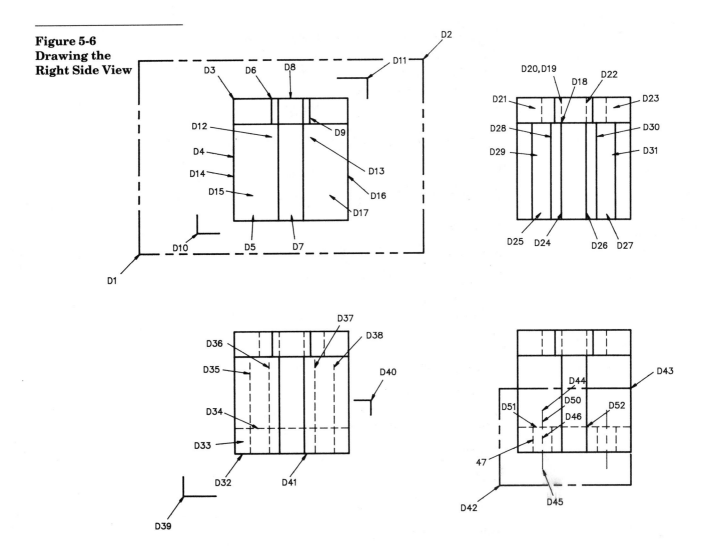

**Figure 5-6
Drawing the
Right Side View**

Prompt: View name to restore:

Response: T ↵ {top}

You should have the area reserved for the top view on your screen now. Draw the object lines of the top view in this area using the commands you used to draw Figure 5-2. Take your measurements from Figure 5-4. Then use ZOOM dynamic to display an area that shows both the front and top views. Use the top view to line up the surfaces in the front as you draw that view. Once the views are placed, you will be able to move quickly from one view to another by using the VIEW-RESTORE command. After you have completed the top and front views, RESTORE the area for the right side view and use the following sequence of steps to draw that view. (After you have completed the right side view you may need to return to the front and top views to add center lines and hidden lines to those views.)

Step 4. Draw object lines for the right side view.

Prompt: Command: <ORTHO ON> <Coords ON>

ZOOM in closer for a better VIEW of the drawing.

Response: ZOOM {or select from DISPLAY Menu}

Prompt: All/Center/Dynamics:
Response: W ↵ {or select WINDOW from screen menu}

Prompt: First corner:
Response: D1 (70.,70) {Figure 5-6}

Prompt: Other corner:
Response: D2 (220,170)

Prompt: Command:
Response: LINE {or select LINE from screen DRAW Menu}

Prompt: LINE from point:
Response: D3 (120,150)

Prompt: To point:
Response: @60 <0 ↵

Prompt: To point:
Response: @63 <270 ↵

Prompt: To point:
Response: @60 <180 ↵

Prompt: To point:
Response: C ↵ {this response closes the figure back to the beginning point}

Prompt: Command:

Now, use the OFFSET command for drawing the other vertical lines in the side view.

Response: OFFSET {or select from DRAW Menu}

Prompt: OFFSET distance or Through <Through>:
Response: 20 ↵

Prompt: Select object to offset:

Response: D4 {notice the change in the line}

Prompt: Side to offset:

Response: D5 {notice how the line has been copied and moved 20mm to the right}

Prompt: Select object to offset:

Digitize the new line just created.

Response: D6

Prompt: Side to offset:

Response: D7

Prompt: Select object to offset:

Response: ↵ {or press space bar}

Now use the OFFSET command to create a horizontal line.

Prompt: Command:

Response: ↵ {or press space bar; this returns the prompt to the last command entered: OFFSET}

Prompt: Offset distance or Through <20.0000>:

Response: 13 ↵

Prompt: Select object to offset:

Response: D8

Prompt: Side to offset:

Response: D9

Prompt: Select object to offset:

Response: ↵ {or press space bar}

Prompt: Command:

Now the two vertical lines may be trimmed to meet the horizontal line.

Response: TRIM {or select from EDIT Menu}

Prompt: Select cutting edge(s). . .
Select objects:

At this point the target cursor should appear on the screen. This cursor may be used to Select objects. A window can also be used to Select objects.

Response: W {and press space bar}

Prompt: First corner:
Response: D10

Prompt: Other corner:
Response: D11

Prompt: Select object:
Response: ↵ {or press space bar}

Prompt: Select object to trim:
Response: D12 {the bottom part of this line is now gone in Figure 5-5}

Prompt: Select object to trim:
Response: D13

Prompt: Select object to trim:
Response: ↵ {or press space bar}

At this point, the screen may be cluttered with digitized marks. Use the REDRAW command to clean up the screen.

Prompt: Command:
Response: REDRAW {or select from DISPLAY Menu}

Prompt: Command:
Response: OFFSET {or select from EDIT Menu}

Prompt: Offset distance or Through <Through>:
Response: 23.5 ↵

Prompt: Select object to offset:
Response: D14

Prompt: Side to offset:
Response: D15

Prompt: Select object to offset:
Response: D16

Prompt: Side to offset:
Response: D17

Prompt: Select object to offset:

Response: ↵ {or press space bar}

Step 5. Use the BREAK command to divide the lines describing the web lines into lines partially hidden and partially solid. (The CHANGE command can be used to put part of the line on the hidden layer.)

Prompt: Command:

Response: BREAK {or select from the EDIT Menu}

Prompt: Select object:

You will need to turn off SNAP (F9) in order to digitize the line.

Response: D18

Prompt: Enter second point (or F for first point):

Response: F ↵

Prompt: Enter first point:

Response: INT {or select from **** (OSNAP Menu) on screen menu (INTersec)}

Notice target box; try to align it on the intersection of two lines.

Prompt: Intersec of:

Response: D18

Prompt: Enter second point:

Response: @.↵ {or select the symbol "@" from the screen menu to break the line at the same point as the first break point}

Prompt: Command:

Response: CHANGE {or select from EDIT Menu}

Prompt: Select objects:

Response: D19

Prompt: 1 selected, 1 found.
Select objects:

Response: ↵ {or space bar}

Prompt: Properties/<change point>:

Response: LA ↵ {LAyer or select from CHANGE command on screen menu}

Prompt: New layer <1>:

Now you can enter Layer 3, which is the HIDDEN Layer.

Response: 3 ↵ ↵

Notice that the Layer has changed color but still looks like continuous linetype. This is because the line scale is too small. It can be changed by using the LTSCALE command.

Prompt: Command:

Response: LTSCALE {or select from SETTINGS on screen menu}

Prompt: Ltscale new scale factor <1.0000>:

Entering a decimal value of less than one will result in a smaller line segment.

Note: *Those who are using mm as the measured value must remember that the length of the line segments must increase when using metric values.*

Response: 25.4 ↵

The line is now hidden and on the proper layer. Repeat Step 5 for other hidden lines on the web. Remember to leave the SNAP function OFF until you are ready to go to the next step. Add the other hidden lines by offsetting the hidden lines just drawn.

Prompt: Command:

Response: OFFSET {or select from the EDIT Menu}

Prompt: Offset distance or Through <Through>:

Response: 10.5 ↵

Prompt: Select object to offset:

Response: D20 {same as D19}

Prompt: Side to offset:

Response: D21

Prompt: Select object to offset:

Response: D22

Prompt: Side to offset:

Response: D23

Prompt: Select object to offset:

Response: ↵ ↵

The OFFSET command may be used again for creating the bottom hidden lines, a procedure similar to Step 5.

Prompt: Offset distance or Through <10.5000>:

Response: 5.5 ↵

This is one edge of the holes in the bottom portion.

Prompt: Select object to offset:

Response: D24

Prompt: Side to offset:

Response: D25

Prompt: Select object to offset:

Response: D26

Prompt: Side to offset:

Response: D27

Prompt: Select object to offset:

Response: ↵ ↵

Prompt: Offset distance or Through <5.500>:

Change the offset distance for the other edge of the hole.

Response: 10 ↵

Prompt: Select object to offset:

Response: D28

Prompt: Side to offset:

Response: D29

Prompt: Select object to offset:

Response: D30

Prompt: Side to offset:

Response: D31

Prompt: Select object to offset:

Response: {Press space bar twice}

Now OFFSET the horizontal hidden line in the view. (It will not be hidden at this time.)

Prompt: Offset distance or Through <10.0000>:
Response: 13 ↵

Prompt: Select object to offset:
Response: D32

Prompt: Side to offset:
Response: D33

Prompt: Select object to offset:
Response: ↵

Prompt: Command:

These lines can now be trimmed and changed to the hidden layer.

Response: TRIM {or select from the EDIT Menu}

Prompt: Select cutting edge(s) . . . .
            Select objects:
Response: D34

Prompt: Select objects:
Response: ↵

Prompt: Select objects to trim:
Response: D35

Prompt: Select objects to trim:
Response: D36

Prompt: Select object to trim:
Response: D37

Prompt: Select object to trim:
Response: D38

Prompt: Select object to trim:
Response: ↵

Prompt: Command:
Response: CHANGE {or select from the EDIT Menu}

Use CHANGE command to make the solid lines hidden. Change the lines to the hidden layer.

Prompt: Select objects:

Response: W ↵ {or select WINDOW from the screen menu}

Prompt: First corner:

Response: D39

Prompt: Other corner:

Response: D40

Prompt: Select objects:

Response: R ↵ {or select REMOVE from the screen menu}

Prompt: Remove Objects:

Response: D41 {this removes the bottom line from the lines selected to be changed}

Prompt: Remove Objects:

Response: ↵

Prompt: Properties/<Change point>:

Response: LA ↵ {or select LAyer from CHANGE command screen menu}

Prompt: New layer <1>:

Response: 3 ↵ ↵

Prompt: Command:

The drawing is complete except for the center lines. Create a new layer for the center lines called 5.

Step 6. Create center lines and move them to their correct position.

Response: LAYER {or select from AutoCAD Menu—Release 9: select the modify layer icon}

Note: *linetypes must be loaded from the LAYER screen menu as described in the procedure below before they can be used in the Release 9 layer chart.*

Prompt: Layer?/Make/Set/New/ON/OFF/Color/Ltype/Freeze/Thaw:

Response: N ↵ {or select New from Layer Menu}

Prompt: New layer name(s):

Response: 5 ↵

Prompt: Layer?/Make/Set/New/ON/OFF/Color/Ltype/Freeze/Thaw:
Response: C ↵ {or select Color from LAYER Menu}

Prompt: Color:
Response: B ↵ {or select BLUE from Color screen menu}

Prompt: Layer Name(s) for color 5 (blue) <1>:
Response: 5 ↵

Prompt: Layer?/Make/Set/New/ON/OFF/Color/Ltype/Freeze/Thaw:
Response: L ↵ {or select Ltype from LAYER Menu}

Prompt: Linetype (or ?) <CONTINUOUS>:
Response: CENTER {or select from LINETYPE on LAYER Menu}

Prompt: Layer name(s) for linetype CENTER <1>:
Response: 5 ↵

Prompt: Layer?/Make/Set/New/ON/OFF/Color/Ltype/Freeze/Thaw:
Response: ? {make sure new layer is created}

Prompt: Layer name(s) for listing <*>:
Response: ↵

Prompt: Layer?/Make/Set/New/ON/OFF/Color/Ltype/Freeze/Thaw:
Response: S ↵ {or select SET from LAYER menu}

Prompt: New current layer <1>:
Response: 5 ↵ ↵ {check status for Layer 5}

Note: *If you use MAKE instead of NEW to create a new layer, AutoCAD sets the newly created layer as the current active layer automatically.*

Prompt: Command:
Response: ZOOM {or select from DISPLAY Menu}

Prompt: All/Center/Dynamic/Extents/Left/Previous/Window/ <Scale(x)>:
Response: W ↵ {or select Window on ZOOM Menu}

Prompt: First corner:
Response: D42

Prompt: Other corner:
Response: D43

Prompt: Command:

Response: LINE {or select from DRAW Menu}

Prompt: LINE from point:

Toggle the SNAP key ON.

Response: D44

Estimate the point at which the center line should start. Be sure SNAP is OFF and ORTHO is ON.

Prompt: To point:
Response: D45

Prompt: To point:
Response: ↵

Notice that the line is probably not centered on the hole. The DIST command will give a distance between lines and points. Use the DIST command to determine the position of the centered line.

Prompt: Command:
Response: DIST {or select from INQUIRY Menu}

Prompt: Dist first point:
Response: MIDPOINT {select from the OSNAP Menu}

Prompt: Midpoint of:
Response: D46

Prompt: Second point:
Response: PERPENDICULAR {select from the OSNAP Menu}

Prompt: Perpend to:
Response: D47

Prompt: 5.2928
Response: ↵

Prompt: Command:
Response: MOVE

Once MOVE has been selected as the command, move the center line to its correct location. In the case described above, the procedure would then continue as follows:

Prompt: Select objects:

Response: D48

Prompt: Select objects:

Response: ↵ {or space bar}

Prompt: Base point or displacement:

Response: D49 {digitize anywhere}

Prompt: Second point of displacement:

Response: @.2928 < 180 ↵

   Now use the DIST command, in the same manner as you did
before, to check the position of the center line. If the center line is not
5mm from the left vertical dotted line, move it to that location.
   If you make a mistake and wish to return to the drawing condition
before the mistake, do the following:

Response: U ↵ {or select UNDO from EDIT Menu}

Prompt: Auto/Back/Control/End/Group/Mark/<number>:

   To undo the last command:

Response: ↵

Prompt: Command:

   If you now decide that the mistake was not a mistake:

Response: REDO {or select from the screen menu}

   Notice what happens to the drawing.

Prompt: Command:

   Now the center line can be copied to the other hole.

Response: COPY {or select from the EDIT Menu, toggle SNAP OFF}

Prompt: Select objects:

Response: D50

Prompt: Select objects:

Response: ↵

Prompt: <Base point or displacement> / Multiple:

Response: INT {or select INTersec from **** (OSNAP) screen menu}

Prompt: Intersec of:

Response: D51

Prompt: Second point of displacement:

Response: INT {from the OSNAP Menu then} D52 ↵

Prompt: Command:

Response: VIEW {or select from DISPLAY Menu}

Prompt: ?/Delete/Restore/Save/Window:

Response: R ↵ {or select RESTORE from screen menu}

Prompt: View name to restore:

Response: F ↵

You have now completed the right side view. At this point you should return to the front and top views to create hidden lines and center lines in those views. After you have completed all three views, plot the drawing on a 17 × 11″ sheet of paper. Respond to all plot prompts as you did for Figure 5-2 except for the following:

Prompt: Size units (inches or millimeters) <I>:

Response: M ↵

Prompt: Standard values for plotting size

SIZE	WIDTH	HEIGHT
A4	285.00	198.00
MAX	399.24	254.23

Enter the size or Width, Height (in Millimeters)<MAX>:

Response: 420,297

Prompt: Plotted Millimeters = Drawing Units or Fit or ? 1 = 1:

Response: ↵

This should produce a metric drawing in millimeters on a B-size (17 × 11″) sheet of paper.

EXERCISE 1

Draw Figure 5-2 on an 11 × 8.5″ sheet of paper using the sequence of steps shown for that figure. Place your name in the lower right corner .50″ to the left and .50″ up from the bottom edge of the sheet. Center the drawing on the paper.

EXERCISE 2

Draw Figure 5-4 on an 11 × 17″ sheet of paper using the sequence of the steps shown for that figure. Place your name in the lower right corner ½″ from the left edge and ½″ from the bottom of the sheet. Center the drawing on the paper.

Exercise 3

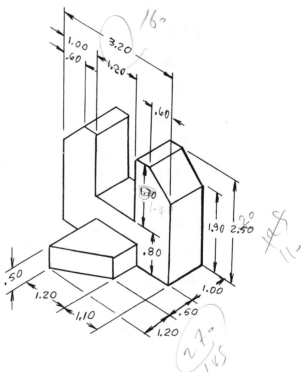

EXERCISE 3

Draw three orthographic views of the object shown above using the following specifications :

    full-scale

    17 × 11″ sheet of paper

    name in lower right corner

    object lines—thick

    all other lines and text—thin

    no dimensions

Test on Objectives—Chapter 5

Circle the correct answer.

1. In drawing an object full-scale using decimal dimensions, which of the following menus must be used first to begin the drawing?

   a. DRAW
   b. EDIT
   c. BLOCKS
   d. SETUP
   e. DISPLAY

2. If the grid is set at .25 and the operator wishes SNAP to fall on every GRID and also half way between each GRID, on what value should SNAP be set?

   a. .10
   b. .12
   c. .125
   d. .25
   e. .50

3. What is the advantage in naming layers with either a single letter or a single number?

   a. saves ZOOM time
   b. saves typing time
   c. saves drawing time
   d. saves plotting time
   e. saves all of the above

4. How many standard layer colors are there? (Find them in the SETTINGS Menu under COLOR.)

   a. 3
   b. 5
   c. 7
   d. 9
   e. Unlimited

5. How many standard linetypes are there? (Find them in the SETTINGS Menu under LINETYPE.)

   a. 3
   b. 5
   c. 7
   d. 9
   e. Unlimited

6. If three lines of a rectangle have been drawn, which letter may be pressed to complete the rectangle?

   a. L
   b. C
   c. D
   d. R
   e. Z

7. Which of the following will produce a vertical line 3½″ long downward from a point?

   a. 3.50×90
   b. @3.50 < 0
   c. @0 < 3.50
   d. @3.50 < −90
   e. 90 < 3.50

8. When a new layer is created with the name R, it automatically assumes the color RED unless otherwise assigned.

   a. true
   b. false

9. Which of the following is used to change the current screen layer?

   a. NEW
   b. ON
   c. THAW
   d. SET
   e. MAKE

10. Which of the following will turn on all unfrozen layers?

    a. ALL
    b. *
    c. U
    d. C
    e. CONTROL A

11. 45° angle at a corner may be obtained most easily with the use of which of the following commands?

    a. CHAMFER
    b. FILLET
    c. DRAW
    e. OFFSET
    e. BREAK

12. A rounded corner may be obtained most easily with the use of which of the following commands?

   a. CHAMFER

   b. FILLET

   c. DRAW

   d. OFFSET

   e. BREAK

13. Which of the following circles is produced if ".50" is entered in response to the circle prompt "Diameter/<Radius>:"?

   a. .50 DIAMETER

   b. .25 RADIUS

   c. 1.00 RADIUS

   d. 1.00 DIAMETER

   e. .25 DIAMETER

14. The letters C,S,E on the ARC Menu are labels for

   a. Center,start,end

   b. Center,start,clockwise

   c. Clockwise,start,end

   d. Clockwise,start,edit

   e. Counterclockwise,start,end

15. The three digitized points below will produce which of the following C,S,E arc?

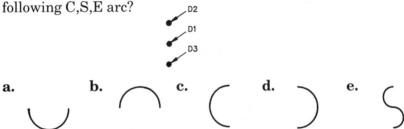

   a.   **b.**   **c.**   **d.**   **e.**

16. Which of the following commands can most easily be used to produce parallel PLINES?

   a. PARALLEL

   b. DRAW

   c. OFFSET

   d. CHANGE

   e. OSNAP

17. Which of the following commands can be used most quickly to remove digitized points from the screen?

   a. ZOOM

   b. PAN

   c. CHANGE

   d. REMOVE

   e. REDRAW

18. Which of the following is the correct response to the plot prompt for an 8½ × 11″ horizontal page size?

   a. 11 × 8½

   b. 11,8.5

   c. 8.5,11

   d. 8.5 × 11

   e. 8-½, 11

19. If the drawing is to be plotted at half the size it was drawn, what is the correct response to the plot prompt: "Plotted Inches = Drawing Units or Fit or ? <F>:"?

   a. .05

   b. 2 = 1

   c. 1 = 2

   d. ↵

   e. ½

20. Which of the following VIEW prompts allows views to be changed quickly?

   a. DYNAMIC

   b. WINDOW

   c. SAVE

   d. RESTORE

   e. VIEW

21. List three prompts that the SETUP command displays.

_____

22. Name the menu that is used to establish GRID and SNAP settings.

_____

23. Write a sequence of *draw responses* to the "to point" prompt which will produce a 3 × 4½″ rectangle.

_____

_____

24. Why is the ZOOM DYNAMIC command used instead of the ZOOM ALL command?

_____

_____

25. What is the advantage of using the fewest layers possible?

_____

_____

26. How may you discover which layers exist and their status?

_____

_____

27. Write a sequence of EDIT commands that will produce a .25 fillet using the FILLET command.

_____

_____

28. Draw and label three points in sequence (D1,D2,D3) that will produce the CSE arc shown below.

_____

29. For what purpose is the VIEW command used?

_____

_____

30. List the command and the menu on which it is listed that is used to give the distance from one point to another.

_____

_____

6

Drawing a Small Office Plan and Inserting Furniture

Objectives

The student will:

- draw a small office floor plan full-scale
- draw desks, tables, and chairs full-scale as blocks
- assign attributes to all furniture
- insert furniture into the small office floor plan
- describe how to make a list of furniture part numbers from the floor plan (extract data)
- describe how to plot the floor plan on a standard-size sheet
- correctly answer questions regarding the following commands:

ATTDEF	INSERT
PLINE	BLOCK
EXPLODE	WBLOCK
DIVIDE	NODE
MEASURE	POINT
EXTEND	PERPENDICULAR
STRETCH	SCALE
OFFSET	PLOT
PEDIT	MIDPOINT
SETVAR	SETTINGS
AREA	LIMITS

Application of AutoCAD for Floor Plans

Advantages

AutoCAD has a distinct advantage over manual drafting in drawing floor plans. The plan can be drawn full-size and plotted at a size that will fit on a standard-size sheet of paper instead of drawing at a reduced scale. In this chapter you will draw a floor plan, create a library of symbols you will use to insert windows, doors, and furniture, and to label rooms correctly. The libraries you create will suffice for the drawings in this chapter, but professional use requires so many different symbols that it is often economical to buy disks containing architectural symbols for use with AutoCAD.

Drawing full-scale makes the use of standard symbols for architectural features much easier than using preprinted symbols for manual drafting. The manual symbols have to be done at a specific scale such as $\frac{1}{8}'' = 1'$, $\frac{1}{4}'' = 1'$, $1'' = 1'$, etc., and they are often done at a different scale than the one needed.

Another major advantage of many CAD programs is the ability of the program to make accurate lists of parts from the drawing. Space planning in commercial buildings is often extremely complex and tedious. After all the furniture, bookcases, shelves, partitions, lighting, and electrical outlets are drawn in place, they must be carefully counted and accurately listed. Errors in this type of work can be very costly. AutoCAD allows these lists to be made from the drawing with ease. Each part of the plan (chair, bookcase, end plate, etc.) is given a part number, a description, and any other needed information such as color and price.

These part numbers and descriptions are called *attributes*. When the item is placed into the floor plan, its attributes accompany it. After the floor plan is completed, the attributes may be used to make a complete and accurate list of all of the items placed on the floor plan. AutoCAD will write the information to a file, but the file must be created with the use of another software program. Several of the common programs such as dBASE III or a word processor can be used to create the file and print it.

To draw the office and insert furniture (Figure 6-1):

In this chapter you will make a floor plan of a small office, draw furniture as blocks, assign attributes to each block, insert the furniture into the floor plan, and examine the processes necessary to make an automatic listing of all of the furniture. Begin by drawing the office. Load AutoCAD and begin a new drawing.

Figure 6-1
Office and Furniture

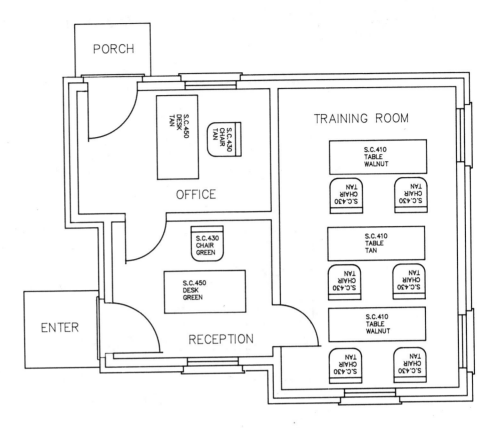

Step 1. Draw the outside walls of the office (Figure 6-2). You will not be required to place dimensions on this drawing now.

Prompt: Command:

Response: {Select} SETUP {from the AutoCAD Menu}

Prompt: Select the units from the screen menu:

Response: {Select} ARCHITECT {from the screen menu}

Prompt: Select the scale from the screen menu:

Response: {Select} FULL {from the screen menu}

Prompt: Select the paper size from the screen menu:

Response: {Select} OTHER {from the screen menu}

You are drawing full-size so the drawing will be larger than the largest page size.

Prompt: Enter the horizontal dimension of the paper:

Response: 40' ↵ {be sure to type the foot symbol}

Prompt: Enter the vertical dimension of the paper:

Response: 30' ↵ {40' × 30' will be slightly larger than the limits of the full-size drawing}

Figure 6-2
Dimensions for the Office

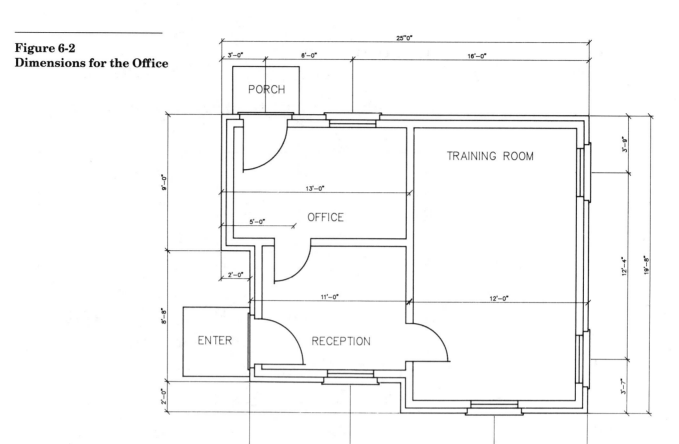

Prompt:	Command:
Response:	{Select} SETTINGS {from the AutoCAD Menu then select} GRID

Prompt:	GRID spacing (x) or ON/OFF/Snap/Aspect<0'–0'>:
Response:	1' ↵ {or 12 ↵ because the default unit is inches}

Prompt:	Command:
Response:	{Select} GRID-SNAP {from the GRID Menu}

Prompt:	SNAP spacing or ON/OFF/Aspect/Rotate/Style<0'–1">:
Response:	2" ↵

Prompt:	Command:
Response:	ZOOM-ALL

Prompt:	Command:

At this point, the layers for the walls, doors, and windows must be created.

Response:	LAYER {or select from LAYER on AutoCAD Menu}

Prompt:	Layer?/Make/Set/New/ON/OFF/Color/Ltype/Freeze/Thaw:
Response:	NEW {or select from LAYER Menu}

Prompt: New layer name(s):

Response: wall, door, window, text {or 1,2,3,4 for less typing}

Prompt: ?/Make/Set/New/ON/OFF/Color/Ltype/Freeze/Thaw:

Select the colors for the new layers.

Response: {Type color} C ↵ {or select from LAYER Menu}

Prompt: Color:

Response: R ↵ {or select RED from screen menu}

Prompt: Layer name(s) for color 1 (Red) <0>:

Response: Wall {or 1} ↵

Prompt: ?/Make/Set/New/ON/OFF/Color/Ltype/Freeze/Thaw:

Response: C ↵ {or select COLOR from LAYER Menu}

Prompt: Color:

Response: Y ↵ {or select YELLOW from COLOR Menu}

Prompt: Layer name(s) for color 2 (yellow) <0>:

Response: Door {or 2} ↵

Prompt: ?/Make/Set/New/ON/OFF/Color/Ltype/Freeze/Thaw:

Response: C ↵ {or select COLOR from LAYER Menu}

Prompt: Color:

Response: G ↵ {or select GREEN from COLOR Menu}

Prompt: Layer name(s) for color 3 (green) <0>:

Response: WINDOW {or 3} ↵

Prompt: ?/Make/Set/New/ON/OFF/Color/Ltype/Freeze/Thaw:

Response: C ↵ {or select COLOR from LAYER Menu}

Prompt: Color:

Response: C ↵ {or select CYAN from COLOR Menu}

Prompt: Layer name(s) for color 4 (cyan) <0>:

Response: TEXT {or 4} ↵

Prompt: ?/Make/Set/New/ON/OFF/Color/Ltype/Freeze/Thaw:

Response: S ↵ {or select SET from LAYER Menu}

Prompt: New current layer <0>:

Response: WALL ↵ ↵

Figure 6-3
Draw and Clean-up Walls

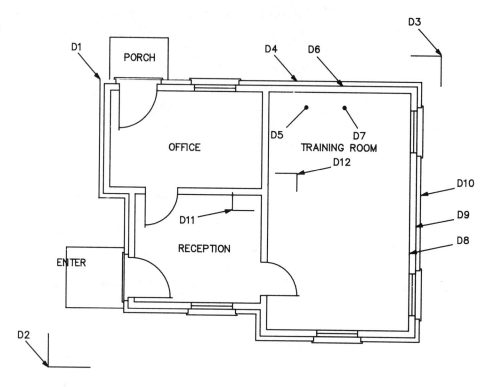

Prompt: Command:

Check the STATUS AREA of the screen. It should read "Layer Wall Snap." If not, repeat the procedures for setting and making layers. Turn on the F6 <coords on> and F8 <ortho on> keys. The wall sections can now be drawn. Start with the outside sections first (Figure 6-3).

Response: PLINE {or select PLINE from DRAW Menu}

Prompt: From point:
Response: D1

Prompt: Current line width is 0′ -0″
Arc/Close/Halfwidth/Length/Undo/Width
/<Endpoint of line>:
Response: @25′ <0 ↵

Prompt: Arc/Close/Halfwidth/Length/Undo/Width
/<Endpoint of line>:
Response: @19′8″<270 ↵

Prompt: Arc/Close/Halfwidth/Length/Undo/Width
/<Endpoint of line>:
Response: @12′7″<180 ↵

Prompt: Arc/Close/Halfwidth/Length/Undo/Width
/<Endpoint of line>:

Response: @2'<90 ↵

Prompt: Arc/Close/Halfwidth/Length/Undo/Width
/<Endpoint of line>:

Response: @10'5"<180 ↵
@8'8" <90 ↵
@2'<180 ↵

Prompt: Arc/Close/Halfwidth/Length/Undo/Width
/<Endpoint of line>:

Response: C ↵ {or select CLOSE from PLINE on the screen menu}

Prompt: Command:

Response: ZOOM {or select from the screen menu}

Prompt: All/Center/Dynamic/Extents/Left/Previous/Window
/Scale (X):

Response: W ↵ {or select WINDOW from ZOOM Menu}

Prompt: First corner:

Response: D2 ↵

Prompt: Other corner:

Response: D3 ↵

Prompt: Command:

The brick veneer of the wall can be added by using the OFFSET command.

Response: OFFSET {or select from the DRAW Menu}

Prompt: Offset distance or Through <Through>:

Response: 4 ↵

Prompt: Select object to offset:

Response: D4 ↵

Prompt: Side to offset:

Response: D5

The exterior line is a closed polyline; thus, all the lines are OFFSET.

Prompt: Select object to offset:

Response: ↵ ↵

Prompt: Offset distance or through <0'–4">:

Response: 6 ↵

Prompt: Select object to offset:

Response: D6

Prompt: Side to offset:

Response: D7 {same as D5}

Prompt: Command:

The EXPLODE command is used to break the POLYLINES into separate entities. Then the interior walls are created using the DRAW-LINE command with ORTHO ON.

Response: {Select} EXPLODE {from the EDIT Menu}

Prompt: Select block reference, polyline, or dimension:

Response: D8,D9,D10

Prompt: Command:

Response: {Draw the interior lines using the exterior shape as a reference. Use the LINE command with SNAP and ORTHO ON or use the EXTEND, OFFSET and CHANGE commands.}

Prompt: Command:

The TRIM command is used to edit the interior walls. First ZOOM closer to the sections to be trimmed.

Response: ZOOM {or select from DISPLAY on screen menu}

Prompt: All/Center/Dynamic/Extents/Left/Previous/Window /<Scale(X)>:

Response: W ↵ {or select Window from screen menu}

Prompt: First corner:

Response: D11

Prompt: Other corner:

Response: D12

Prompt: Command:

Response: TRIM {or select from EDIT Menu}

Prompt: Select cutting edge(s) . . . Select objects:

You may also select CROSSING from the screen and select all lines at once.

Response: D13 {D13 through D19 are not illustrated because they may vary depending on how you drew your interior walls}

Prompt: Select objects:

Response: D14

Prompt: Select objects:

Response: D15

Prompt: Select objects:

Response: D16

Prompt: Select object to trim:

Response: D17,D18,D19

Remove all other unwanted lengths using the TRIM or CHANGE commands. The walls are now drawn. The next steps are to draw the windows and doors, save them as blocks, and insert them into the walls.

Step 2. Create windows and doors (Figure 6-4).

Use the dimensions shown in Figure 6-4 to draw the doors and windows. After the doors and windows have been drawn successfully, create blocks of them using the following procedure:

Prompt: Command:

Response: BLOCK {select the BLOCK Menu from the Root Menu and then select the BLOCK command}

Prompt: Block name (or ?):

Response: W ↵ {or WINDOW}

Prompt: Insertion base point:

Response: D1 {select MIDPOINT on the OSNAP Menu to select the exact center of the window}

Prompt: Select objects:

Response: W ↵ {or select WINDOW from the screen menu}

Prompt: First corner:

Response: D2

Figure 6-4
Create Windows
and Doors

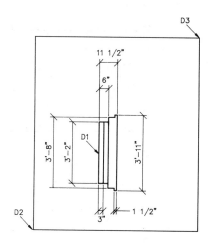

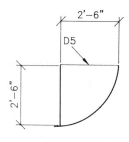

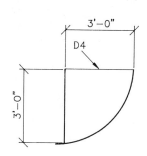

Prompt: Other corner:

Response: D3

Prompt: Select objects:

Response: ↵

The drawing should vanish. You now have a block named "W" that you may call up anytime this drawing is active. If you want to use this same block on later drawings place a copy of it on your hard disk so it may be inserted on any drawing you choose. This is called "writing it out to the hard disk."

To write it out to the hard disk, follow these instructions:

Prompt: Command:

Response: WBLOCK {from the BLOCKS Menu}

Prompt: Wblock filename:

Response: W ↵ {this is the name of the block; you may call it something else for the permanent block, but many people prefer to keep the WBLOCK name and the BLOCK name the same}

Figure 6-5

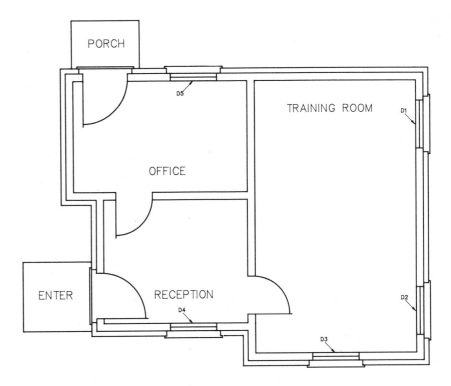

Prompt: Block name:

Response: W ↵ {or ↵ because the BLOCK name and the WBLOCK name are the same}

The window named W now exists on the hard disk as well as on the drawing currently active.

Repeat the procedure just described for both doors. Name one of them DI (inside door) and the other DO (outside door). Be sure to place D4 and D5 in the exact center of the opening; these are insertion points. You should now have three blocks on this drawing: DI, DO, and W. Remember where their insertion points are and proceed to the next step.

Step 3. Insert doors and windows (Figure 6-5).

Use the dimensions from Figure 6-2 to locate the center of windows and doors. You may want to draw a construction line perpendicular to the location. This line may be erased later.

Another means is to identify the location of corners of the house and place the block using the @_<– command as if you were drawing a line. To identify a location, select ID from the INQUIRY Menu and digitize the point in question. However you choose to locate the centers, use this procedure to insert the doors and windows:

Prompt: Command:

Response: INSERT {from the DRAW Menu}

Figure 6-6
Insert Windows and Doors

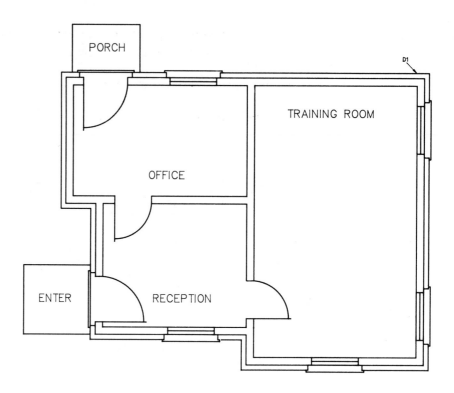

Prompt: Block name (or?):

If you enter a ?, a listing of the blocks for this drawing will appear.

Response: W ↵

Prompt: Insertion point:
Response: DI {Figure 6-5}

Prompt: X-scale factor <1> 1 corner/XYZ:
Response: ↵

The door should be the same size as it was drawn. You may enlarge or reduce a block using numbers larger than one to enlarge, or smaller than one to reduce. A response of 2 will make the block twice the size; .5 will make the block half the size.

Prompt: Y-scale factor (default = X):

The vertical size may be changed at this time. This is valuable for some blocks; not for this one.

Response: ↵

Prompt: Rotation angle <0>:

Any rotation angle may be entered at this time. D3 and D4 will require 90 (or 270) rotation. D5 will require 90 rotation.

Response: ↵ {for 0-degree rotation}

The first window will appear.

To insert a block without first locating the centers (Figure 6-6):

Prompt: Command:
Response: ID: {from the INQUIRY Menu}

Prompt: ID Point:
Response: D1 {select NEAREST on the OSNAP Menu to digitize the exact location of the outside wall. Notice that the digitized point is on the inside wall vertically because the insertion point for the window is on the inside wall}

Prompt: Command:
Response: INSERT {from the DRAW Menu}

Prompt: Block name (or?):
Response: W ↵

Prompt: Insertion point:
Response: @3'9"<–90

Prompt: X-scale factor <1>/corner/XYZ:
Response: ↵

Prompt: Y-scale factor (default = X):
Response: ↵

Prompt: Rotation angle <0>:
Response: –90 ↵ {select the correct rotation angle}

The window should appear in the correct location.
Use a procedure similar to these to insert the other windows. Notice that the BLOCK prompt gives you the name of the last block used as a default. To insert the same block again, use ↵ to avoid typing the name again. Insert doors in a similar manner.
After all doors and windows are in place, use the BREAK or TRIM command to remove unwanted lines. Draw the ends of the partitions next to the doors using the LINE command. Use the ZOOM command if necessary to make the drawing larger on the screen.

Figure 6-7

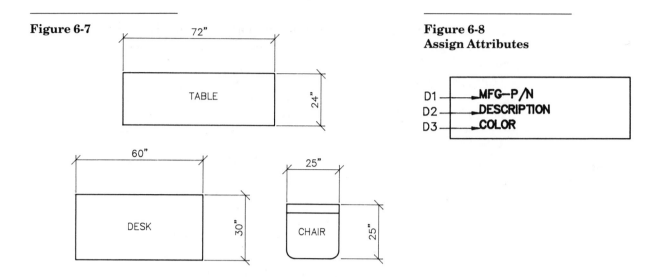

Figure 6-8
Assign Attributes

Step 4. Draw furniture (Figure 6-7).

Draw the furniture using the dimensions shown in Figure 6-7. You may draw these objects in any open area. Use the LINE command for drawing the rectangles and the FILLET command for rounding the corners on the chair.

Step 5. Assign attributes to the table (Figure 6-8).

An attribute is a label that contains text. These labels are placed on drawings of parts. They contain important information, such as the part number and description of the part. These part numbers and descriptions may later be extracted from the drawing to form a list of all of the parts (in this case the furniture) used in the drawing. This becomes a very important function of the system.

To assign attributes to the table follow this procedure:

Note: *If you make typing mistakes, correct them by using the backspace key. If the mistake cannot be corrected in that manner, use Ctrl-C to cancel the command and start over. Also, set SNAP at 2".*

Prompt: Command:

Response: ATTDEF {attribute definition from the DRAW Menu}

Prompt: Attribute modes-Invisible: N constant:N Verify:N Enter (ICV) to change, RETURN when done:

The "N" following the attribute mode indicates that the mode is not being used; "Y" would indicate that it was being used. These attribute modes are explained in detail in the *AutoCAD Reference Manual*, but briefly they are:

Invisible   The attribute will not appear on the drawing when the block is inserted. We want these to be visible. (The "price" might be something that should be invisible.)

Constant   The attribute is the same for every insertion of the block and cannot be changed.

Verify   The value of the attribute may be verified during insertion.

If none of these modes is selected then the attribute is a variable one.

Response: ↵

None of the three modes described above is useful for this attribute.

Prompt: Attribute tag:

Response: MFG-P/N ↵

This is the label's identifying text, which may be used later to extract this information from the drawing.

Note: *IMPORTANT: DO NOT USE SPACES IN THE ATTRIBUTE TAG; use of the space bar moves you to the next prompt. If you make a mistake and press the space bar, use Ctrl-C to cancel the command and start over.*

Prompt: Attribute prompt:

This is the prompt that will appear on the screen when you insert the block. Make the prompt whatever is necessary to make sure the correct information is inserted.

Response: INSERT ABBREVIATED MANUFACTURER'S NAME AND PART NUMBER ↵ {spaces may be used in the prompt}

Prompt: Default attribute value:

This is the label that will be inserted if one is not typed in response to the prompt.

Response: NONE

Prompt: Start point or Align/Center/Fit/Middle/Right/Style:

Response: D1

Prompt: Height <0′–3″>:

Response: ↵ 3″ {if the default is not 3″ this will produce letters ¹⁄₁₆″ high on the finished drawing}

Prompt: Rotation angle <0.0>:

Response: ↵ {we want the lettering to be horizontal}

The text MFG-P/N should now appear.

Prompt: Command:

Response: ↵

Prompt: Attribute modes–Invisible:N Constant:N Verify:N Enter (ICV) to change, RETURN when done:

Response: C {let's make this attribute one that cannot be changed}

Prompt: Attribute modes–Invisible:N Constant:Y Verify:N Enter (ICV) to change, RETURN when done:

Note: *There is now a Y following the word Constant, meaning that the attribute will be constant.*

Response: ↵

Prompt: Attribute tag:

Response: DESCRIPTION {no spaces; use Ctrl-C to cancel if you make a mistake}

Prompt: Attribute value:

Response: TABLE 24 × 72″ ↵ {spaces may be used in the attribute value}

Prompt: Start point or Align/Center/Fit/Middle/Right/Style:

Response: D2

Prompt: Height <0′–3″>:

Response: ↵

Prompt: Command:

Response: ↵

Prompt: Attribute modes–Invisible:N Constant:Y Verify:N Enter (ICV) to change, RETURN when done:

Response: C ↵ {the attribute will be variable}

Prompt: Attribute tag:

Response: COLOR ↵

Figure 6-9
BLOCK the Table

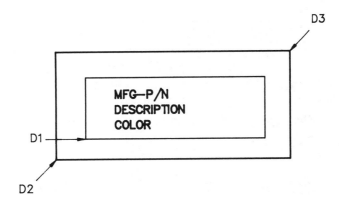

Prompt: Attribute prompt:
Response: INSERT COLOR DESIRED ↵

Prompt: Default Attribute Value:
Response: TAN ↵

Prompt: Start point or Align/Center/Fit/Middle/Right/Style:
Response: D3

Prompt: Height <0′–3″>:
Response: ↵

Prompt: Rotation angle <0.0>:
Response: ↵

The word COLOR should now appear. The three attributes required for this exercise have been created. Now, make a block of the table and insert it to test what you have done.

Step 6. Make a block of the table (Figure 6-9).

To make a block of the table follow this procedure:

Prompt: Command:
Response: BLOCK

Prompt: Block name (or?):
Response: TABLE ↵

Prompt: Insertion base point:
Response: D1

Prompt: Select objects:
Response: WINDOW {select or type W}

Prompt: First corner:
Response: D2

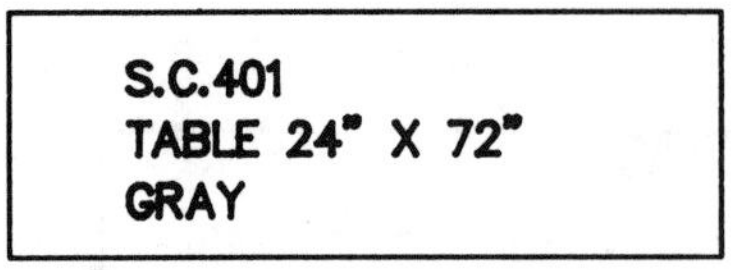

Figure 6-10
Insert Table with
Attributes

```
┌─────────────────────────┐
│  S.C.401                │
│  TABLE 24" X 72"        │
│  GRAY                   │
└─────────────────────────┘
```

Prompt: Other corner:

Response: D3

The table should disappear.

Step 7. Insert the table and answer the prompts you created (Figure 6-10).

Prompt: Command:

Response: INSERT {from the DRAW Menu}

Prompt: Block name (or?):

Response: TABLE ↵

Prompt: Insertion point:

Response: D1 {any point where you want to place a table}

Prompt: X-scale factor <1>/Corner/XYZ:

Response: ↵

Prompt: Y-scale factor (default = X):

Response: ↵

Prompt: Rotation angle <0>:

Response: ↵

Prompt: INSERT COLOR DESIRED <TAN>: {your prompt}

Response: GRAY ↵

Prompt: INSERT ABBREVIATED MANUFACTURER'S NAME AND PART NUMBER NONE: {your prompt again}

Response: S.C. 401 {or whatever the manufacturer and part number is}

The table inserted should appear as shown in Figure 6-10.

Step 8. Assign attributes to the chair and desk and insert chairs, desks, and table into the floor plan (Figure 6-11).

    a. Use the same procedures for assigning attributes to the chair and the desk. Make the second attribute for the chair and the desk a constant one.

Figure 6-11

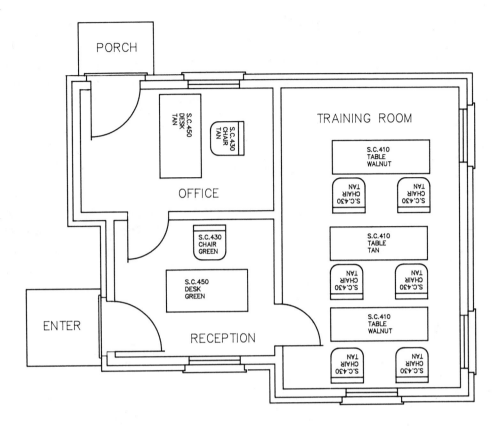

b. Insert chairs, desks, and tables in the approximate locations shown in Figure 6-10. Pay particular attention to the attributes that change.

Step 9. Label rooms using DTEXT.

Step 10. Compile a parts list of the inserted items.

See the *AutoCAD Reference Manual* for details on the ATTEXT command. Additional software programs are available that must be used in conjunction with the ATTEXT command to assemble this information.

EXERCISE 1

Draw the floor plan and furniture as shown in Figures 6-1 through 6-11. Do not show dimensions. Construct blocks and assign attributes for chair, desk, and table. You will be called upon to show blocks for these three items of furniture.

EXERCISE 2

Draw a floor plan and insert furniture as shown in the figure for Exercise 2. Construct blocks and assign attributes to all furniture. Approximate any dimensions not shown. Use the scale in the upper right corner to measure all parts.

EXERCISE 3

Draw the floor plan shown on the next page at a scale of $\frac{1}{8}'' = 1'0''$ (you may draw it full-scale and reduce it using the SCALE command). Approximate any dimensions not shown. Use the technique shown in the lower right corner for shading walls. Limits should be $11 \times 17''$ for the final sheet size.

EXERCISE 4

Draw the floor plan shown in the figure for this Exercise at a scale of $\frac{1}{8}'' = 1'0''$. (Draw full-size and reduce if you like.) Approximate any dimensions not shown or measure with an architect's scale and draw to size. Use the wall technique used for Figure 6-3. Limits should be $11 \times 17''$ for the final sheet size.

Exercise 2

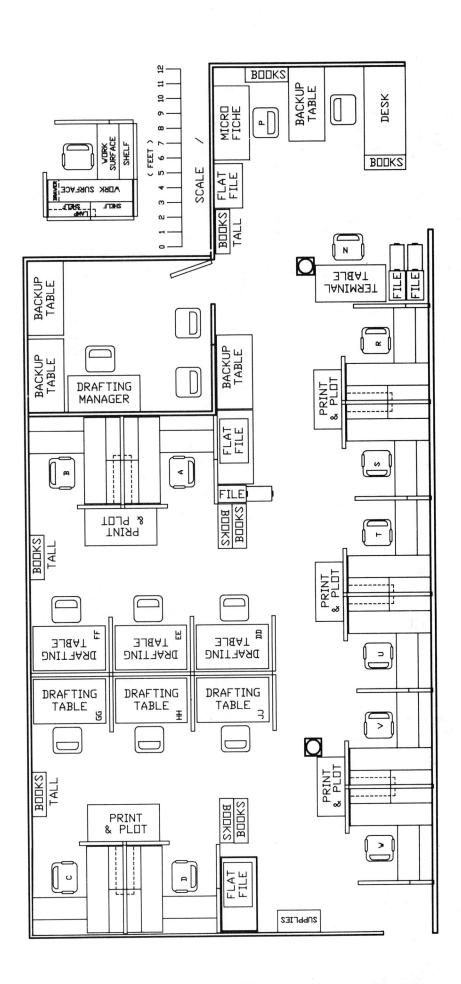

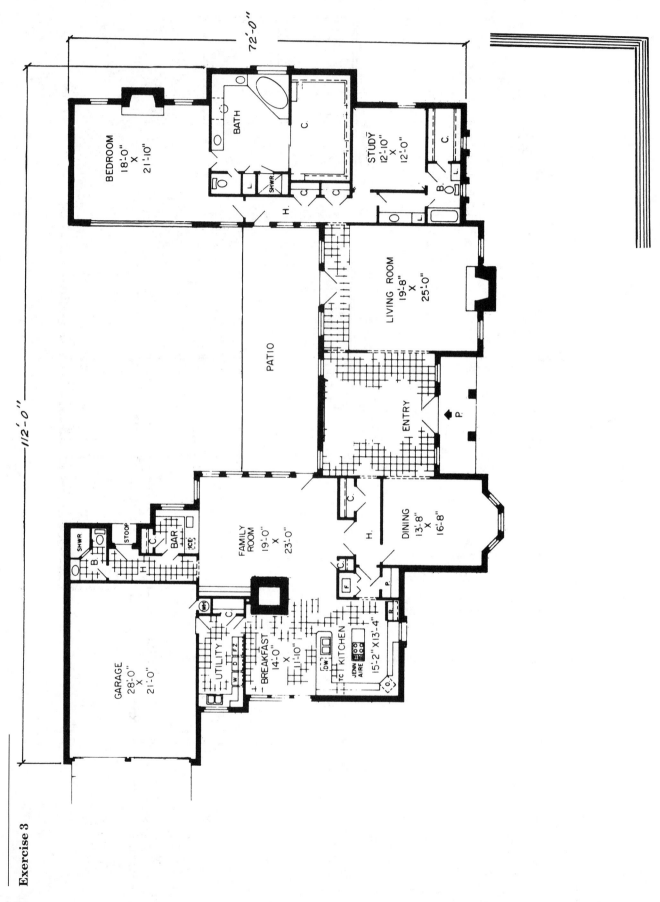

Exercise 3

152

Exercise 4

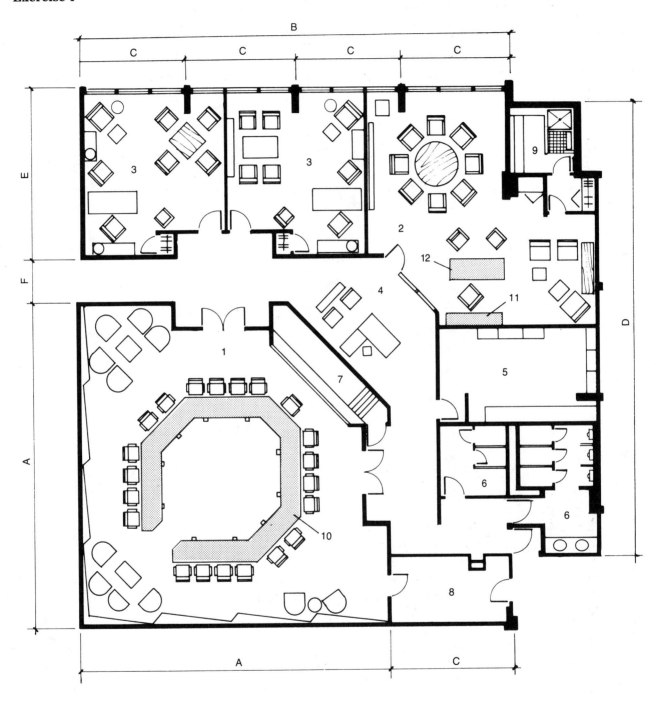

Dimensions:

	ft/in.	m
A =	46 6	14.17
B =	62	18.90
C =	15 6	4.72
D =	69±	21.03
E =	24±	7.32
F =	6±	1.83

Test on Objectives—Chapter 6

Circle the most correct answer.

1. AutoCAD contains most of the symbols needed for complete space planning.
   a. true
   b. false

2. Which of the following is an advantage of drawing a floor plan full-scale?
   a. eliminates the need for changing the scale of some objects
   b. saves time
   c. saves space
   d. is more accurate
   e. all are advantages

3. What was the GRID setting for Figures 6-1 through 6-10?
   a. 1″
   b. 1′
   c. ¼″
   d. ½″
   e. 6″

4. What was the SNAP setting for this chapter?
   a. ¼″
   b. 3″
   c. 2″
   d. ⅛″
   e. 1″

5. How many layers are needed if furniture outlines are on one layer, text is on another, walls are on another, and doors and windows occupy the same layer?
   a. 1
   b. 2
   c. 3
   d. 4
   e. 5

6. Which of the following responses may be used to establish the color of a layer from the prompt "COLOR:"?
   a. Z
   b. X
   c. D
   d. A
   e. R

7. Which of the following responses is used to change the current drawing layer?

   a. NEW

   b. LTYPE

   c. SET

   d. ON

   e. THAW

8. If lines are to be drawn on layer "G" perfectly vertical or horizontal on GRID, which of the following is the correct status line?

   a. LAYER G ORTHO SNAP

   b. LAY B VER GRID

   c. LAYER G VER/HOR GRID

   d. LAYER GREEN STR SNAP

   e. LAYER G GRID SNAP

9. Which of the following commands will most easily produce lines showing the inside edge of a wall drawn with PLINE?

   a. COPY

   b. PLINE

   c. LINE

   d. OFFSET

   e. PARALLEL

10. Which of the following commands may be used to chop off 10 lines to end on the same line?

   a. CHANGE

   b. CHOP

   c. ERASE

   d. ORTHO

   e. TRIM

11. Which of the following commands creates a block that may be used on the current drawing only?

   a. BLOCK

   b. WBLOCK

   c. ATTDEF

   d. ATTEXT

   e. ATTBLOCK

12. Which of the following commands creates a block that may be used on any drawing?

   a. BLOCK

   b. WBLOCK

   c. ATTDEF

   d. ATTEXT

   e. ATTBLOCK

13. What happens after the blocked object has been selected and ↵ (Enter) has been pressed after the prompt "Select Objects:"?
    a. the "BLOCK" prompt reappears
    b. the blocked object is displayed as before the prompt
    c. the blocked object becomes dim then reappears
    d. the blocked object disappears
    e. the blocked object flashes

14. Which of the following menus contains the INSERT command?
    a. DRAW
    b. EDIT
    c. INQUIRY
    d. DISPLAY
    e. UTILITY

15. Which of the following menus contains the ATTDEF command?
    a. DRAW
    b. EDIT
    c. INQUIRY
    d. BLOCKS
    e. UTILITY

16. Which of the following commands is used to assign attributes to a drawing?
    a. ATTEXT
    b. ATTADD
    c. ATTDEF
    d. BLOCK
    e. WBLOCK

17. Which of the following may be used to obtain a listing of all the blocks in a drawing?
    a. DIR
    b. LIST
    c. BLOCK
    d. WBLOCK
    e. ?

18. Which of the following commands may be used to identify a location from which a block may be inserted with the @2'6"< 0 response?
    a. ID
    b. ZERO
    c. OSNAP
    d. INTERSECTION
    e. NEAREST

19. If a block is to be rotated 90° in a clockwise direction, which of the following is the correct response to the prompt "rotation angle <0>"?

    a. 90

    b. 90°

    c. −90

    d. −90°

    e. 180

20. In which of the following may spaces *not* be used?

    a. attribute Value

    b. attribute Prompt

    c. attribute Tag

    d. default attribute value

    e. none may contain spaces

Write the correct answers in the spaces provided.

21. List two advantages of using PLINE over LINE in drawing the walls of a floor plan.

    a. _____

    b. _____

22. List the four attribute elements that may be changed.

    a. _____

    b. _____

    c. _____

    d. _____

23. List two commands used to BLOCK a drawing.

    a. _____

    b. _____

24. Describe how the attribute tag is used.

_____

_____

25. Describe how the attribute value is used.

_____

_____

26. Describe the difference between attribute value and default attribute value.

_____

_____

27. Describe the difference between a regular attribute and a _constant_ attribute.

_____

_____

28. Describe the characteristics of an invisible attribute.

_____

_____

29. Describe the procedure for compiling a list of furniture from a drawing containing blocks with attributes.

_____

_____

_____

30. How many attributes may a block contain?

_____

7

Dimensioning and Tolerancing

Objectives

The student will:

- use the Dimensioning Menu to dimension the following full-scale drawings of:

  architectural floor plans

  mechanical parts using decimal parts of an inch

  mechanical parts using metric measurements

- provide positive and negative tolerances for specific dimensions
- correctly answer questions regarding the following commands and settings:

DIM	DIM ALIGNED
DIM 1	DIM ROTATED
DIM HORIZONTAL	DIM BASELINE
DIM ANGULAR	DIM CENTER
DIM DIAMETER	DIM LEADER
DIM RADIUS	DIMENSIONING VARIABLES
DIM VERTICAL	

Dimensioning

Up to this point, you have made several different types of drawings. You have made block diagrams, architectural floor plans, drawings of furniture containing attributes, and two-dimensional drawings of mechanical parts.

**Figure 7-1
Drawing to be Dimensioned**

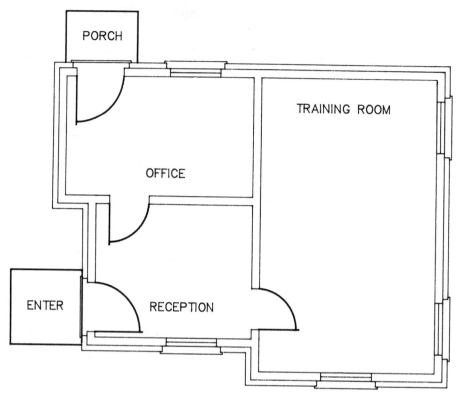

For the manufacturing and construction drawings to be used to manufacture a part or to construct a building, dimensions must be added. Adding dimensions to a drawing manually is a very time-consuming process. With AutoCAD, adding dimensions is much easier. In addition, the AutoCAD dimensioning process verifies the accuracy of the drawing. The associative dimensioning feature of the 2.62 and later versions of AutoCAD also allows a part size to be changed or corrected while the dimension changes with it automatically.

In this chapter you will dimension some of the drawings you have already made and you will make some simple drawings to demonstrate other dimensioning features. Remember that you have made these drawings full-size, so the dimensioning procedure is relatively simple. Begin with the floor plan from Chapter 6.

To dimension a floor plan (Figure 7-1):

Step 1. Display the drawing you did in Chapter 6. From the Main Menu select: "2. Edit an EXISTing drawing."

Step 2. When your drawing is displayed on the screen, make the proper settings for dimensioning the floor plan which was drawn at ¹/₄″ = 1″. If it was drawn full-scale, other settings will apply—they are also shown.

Prompt: Command:

Response: Dim {from the Root Menu}

Prompt: Dim:

Response: STATUS {from the DIM Menu}

The following listing should appear.

DIMSCALE	1.0000	Overall scale factor
DIMASZ	0.1800	Arrow size
DIMCEN	0.0900	Center mark size
DIMEXO	0.0625	Extension line origin offset
DIMDLI	0.3800	Dimension line increment for continuation
DIMEXE	0.1800	Extension above dimension line
DIMTP	0.0000	Plus tolerance
DIMTM	0.0000	Minus tolerance
DIMTXT	3.0000	Text height
DIMTSZ	0.0000	Tick size
DIMRND	0.0000	Rounding value
DIMDLE	0.0000	Dimension line extension
DIMTOL	Off	Generate dimension tolerances
DIMLIM	Off	Generate dimension limits
DIMTIH	On	Text inside extensions is horizontal
DIMTOH	On	Text outside extensions is horizontal
DIMSE1	Off	Suppress the first extension line
DIMSE2	Off	Suppress the second extension line
DIMTAD	Off	Place text above the dimension line
DIMZIN	Off	Edit zero inches
DIMALT	Off	Alternate units selected
DIMALTF	25.40	Alternate units scale factor
DIMALTD	2	Alternate units decimal places
DIMLFAC	1.0000	Linear unit scale factor
DIMBLK	DOT	Arrow block name
DIMASO	Off	Associative dimensioning
DIMSHO	Off	Update dimensions while dragging
DIMPOST		Default suffix for dimension text
DIMAPOST		Default suffix for alternate text

Figure 7-2
Tick and Arrowhead

Figure 7-3
DIMCEN

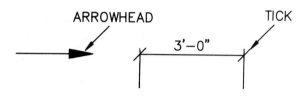

Figure 7-4
DIMEXO

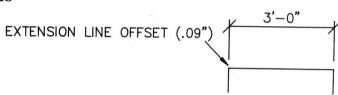

All of the dimensioning variables should be set as shown above. Notice that the text size (DIM TEXT) is 3″. On a scale of ¼″ = 1′, the dimensioning text size will be ¹⁄₁₆″ high when it is plotted. If it were changed to 6″, the text size would be ⅛″ high.

Several of the other variables require similar explanations, so each one will be examined as follows:

DIMSCALE 1.0000 (or 48 if the drawing was done full-scale)
   overall scale factor—This scale applies to all items that make up a dimensioning system.

For example, if the text size is set at 3″ when the drawing was done at ¼″ = 1′, the text will measure ¹⁄₁₆″. The same is true for arrowhead, ticks, offsets of dimension and extension lines, etc. If the scale factor DIMSCALE is set at 2.0000 the text size, all other dimensioning elements will be twice the status value displayed. In this case, text height size will increase to ⅛″.

Another approach to dimensioning is to make the drawing full-scale and use DIMSCALE to make the dimensioning elements the correct size. For example, the default size for dimensioning text height is .18. If a floor plan that will be plotted at a scale of ¼″ = 1′ is drawn full-size, the text height will be .18 of an inch at that scale (approximately .004″). That is so small that a powerful magnifier would be required to read it. Set DIMSCALE to 48 (12″ = ¼″) and the text height returns to .18″ along with all other items that make up the dimensioning package.

DIMASZ 5″ (or .10 if DIMSCALE is 48)
   Length of the arrows used at the ends of a dimension line—the dimensioning system chosen for the floor plan will use ticks such as the one shown in Figure 7-2, so the arrowhead size is set at 0. (Use tick instead of arrowhead.)

Figure 7-5
DIMDLI

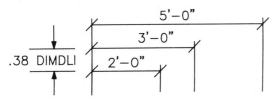

Figure 7-6
DIMEXE

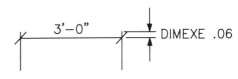

Figure 7-7
DIMTP

.250+.003

Figure 7-8
DIMTSZ

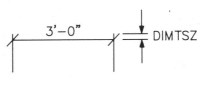

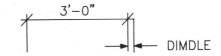

DIMCEN 1″ (or .09 if DIMSCALE is 48)
Center mark size—this is the mark at the center of a circle or arc (Figure 7-3).

DIMEXO 4.5″ (or .09 if DIMSCALE is 48)
Extension line origin offset—this is the distance from the object to the beginning of the extension line (Figure 7-4).

DIMDLI 1′-6″ (or .38 if DIMSCALE is 48)
Dimension line increment for continuation—this is the spacing of dimension lines when Baseline or Continuous modifiers are used with dimensioning as shown in Figure 7-5.

DIMEXE 3″ (or .06 if DIMSCALE is 48)
Extension above dimension line—this is the distance the extension line extends beyond the dimension lines (Figure 7-6).

DIMTP 0″
Plus tolerance—this is a positive tolerance value that will be added to the dimension text if you desire (Figure 7-7).

DIMTM 0″
Minus tolerance—this is a negative tolerance value that will be added to the dimension text if you desire.

DIMTXT 5″ (or .10 if DIMSCALE is 48)
Text size—this is the height of the text used for dimensioning.

DIMTSZ 2″ (or .04 if DIMSCALE is 48)
Tick size—this is the height of the tick used for dimensioning as shown in Figure 7-8. Where the value is set at 0 the arrowhead is used: 2″ Tick.

Figure 7-9
DIMSE1

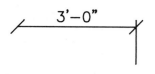

Figure 7-10
DIMSE2

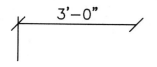

Figure 7-11
DIMTAD

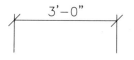

DIMRND 0″

    Rounding value—this variable is used to round all dimensions. For example, if DIMRND is set at .5, all distances will be rounded to the nearest ½ (.5) unit. With the setting at 0 units, no rounding takes place.

DIMDLE 0

    Dimension line extension—this variable extends the dimension line past the extension line when the tick is used instead of an arrowhead as shown in Figure 7-8.

DIMTOL – OFF

    Tolerance—this variable must be ON for the plus and minus tolerances to be added to dimensions.

DIMLIM – OFF

    Limits—this variable generates dimension limits as the default text. If DIMLIM is turned ON, the dimensioning tolerances are automatically turned OFF. If DIMTOL (tolerances) is turned ON, DIMLIM is automatically turned OFF.

DIMSE1 – OFF

    Suppress extension line 1—when this switch in ON, the first extension line is not drawn. This is useful in some instances to avoid drawing the same extension line twice (Figure 7-9).

DIMSE2 – ON

    Suppress extension line 2—when this switch is ON, the second extension line is not drawn (Figure 7-10).

DIMTAD – ON

    Text above dimension line—when this is ON, the dimension is placed above the dimension line (Figure 7-11).

DIMZIN – ON

    Zero feet/inch editing—this adds the 0″ when the dimension is a round number of feet: 6′-0″ (DIMZIN is ON) – 6′ (DIMZIN is OFF).

DIMALT – OFF

    Alternate units—this variable allows two systems of dimensioning to be done at the same time (usually English and metric units). The value of the basic dimension is multiplied by the DIMLFAC scale factor and that dimension is shown in brackets (Figure 7-12).

DIMALTF – 25.4

    Alternate units scale factor—this is the factor by which the basic dimension is multiplied to produce the dimension shown in brackets (Figure 7-12).

DIMALTD – 2

    Alternate units decimal places—this is the number of places to the right of the decimal point shown in the alternate dimension.

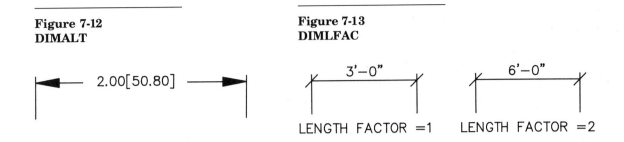

Figure 7-12
DIMALT

Figure 7-13
DIMLFAC

DIMLFAC – 48 (or 1 if the drawing was done full-scale)
Length factor—this is the factor by which all dimensions are multiplied before they are written on the drawing (Figure 7-13). This is useful when the drawing is done to a scale as in ½″ = 1.

DIMBLK – NONE
This is the name of the block that is used whenever the arrowhead or the tick is not used.

DIMASO – OFF
Create associative dimensions—the dimensions change while the part is being stretched.

DIMSHO – OFF
Update dimensions while dragging—the dimensions are displayed as the part is being lengthened or shortened.

DIMPOST
Default suffix for dimension text—this adds the unit marks to each dimension, such as inches, millimeters, feet, and so on. Example: 24″ or 24mm or 24′ or 24in.

DIMAPOST
Default suffix for alternate text—this adds the unit marks to each alternate dimension.

In a working situation these factors are usually set once for each type of dimensioning done by that company. Individual drafters seldom have to set these variables. It is very important for you to know what these variables are, however, and that they may be changed easily to do exactly the type of dimensioning you want to do. Now, proceed to dimensioning the floor plan.

Step 3. Dimension to the center of all doors, windows, and inside partitions. Dimension to the outside of the outside walls.

First, ZOOM a window to include just the north side of the office (Figure 7-14). Second, follow this procedure to dimension the north side features.

Figure 7-14
Dimension the North Side

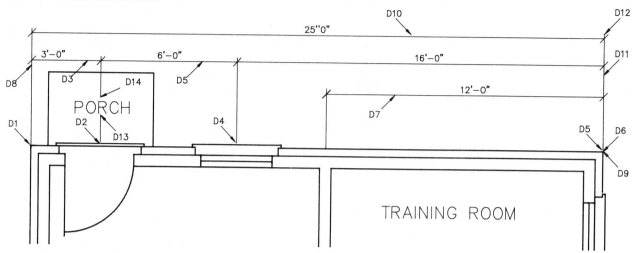

Prompt:	Command:
Response:	{Select} DIM {from the AutoCAD Root Menu}

Prompt:	Dim:
Response:	{Select} LINEAR {from the Dimensioning Menu}

Prompt:	Dim:
Response:	{Select} HORIZ {from the LINEAR Menu}

Prompt:	First extension line origin or RETURN to select:
Response:	D1 {activate OSNAP and select INTersec; then pick the exact location of the corner of the house}

Prompt:	Second extension line origin:
Response:	D2 {activate OSNAP and select MIDpoint to pick the exact center of the door}

Prompt:	Dimension line location:
Response:	D3 {use an appropriate distance from the drawing of the house, usually ½″—in this case the porch interfered with that and the available space allowed the dimension to be placed further from the outline of the office itself}

Prompt:	Dimension text <3′–0″>:

At this time the dimensions may be changed if needed. In this case, the dimension is exactly what is needed.

Response: ↵

Prompt: Dim:

Response: {Select} CONTINU {from the menu}

Prompt: Second extension line origin:

Response: D4 {activate OSNAP and select MIDpoint to pick the exact center of the window}

Prompt: Dimension text <6'–0">:

Response: ↵

Prompt: Dim:

Response: ↵

Prompt: Second extension line origin:

Response: D5 {activate OSNAP and select the exact outside wall of the house using intersection}

Prompt: Dimension text <16'–0">:

Response: ↵

Prompt: Dim:

Now, dimension to the center of the partition from the outside wall. Since the drawing was made full-scale and the partition was to have been 12' – 0" from the right corner of the building, do this:

Prompt: Dim:

Response: {Select} HORIZ {from the DIM Menu}

Prompt: First extension line origin:

Response: D6 {select the right corner of the house using OSNAP}

Prompt: Second extension line origin:

Response: @12' <180 ↵

Prompt: Dimension line location:

Response: D7

Prompt: Dimension text <12'–0">:

Response: ↵

Prompt: Dim:

Finally place the overall dimension as the outside dimension.

Prompt: Dim:

Response: {Select} HORIZ

Prompt: First extension line or RETURN to select:

Response: D8 {pick the extension line a small distance below the tick}

Prompt: Second extension line origin:

Response: D9 {OSNAP the right corner}

Prompt: Dimension line location:

Response: D10

Prompt: Dimension text <25'–0">:

Response: ↵

Prompt: Dim:

Response: {Select} EDIT {from the AutoCAD Menu and then the CHANGE command}

Prompt: Select objects:

Response: D11 ↵

Prompt: Properties/<change point>:

Note: *Be sure ORTHO is ON before D12 is digitized.*

Response: D12 {to extend the last extension line to the 25' dimension line}

Step 4. Break extension lines that interfere with lettering or dimension lines.

Prompt: Command:

Response: {Select} BREAK

Prompt: Select object:

Response: D13 ↵

Prompt: Enter second point (or F for first point):

Response: D14

Step 5. Complete dimensions for the south and east sides of the floor plan (Figure 7-15). Use methods similar to the ones used to dimension the north side of this floor plan.

Step 6. After you have completed this drawing, save it in two places. You may plot the drawing now or wait until you complete Chapter 8, which contains detailed instructions for plotting.

Figure 7-15
Complete Dimensioning

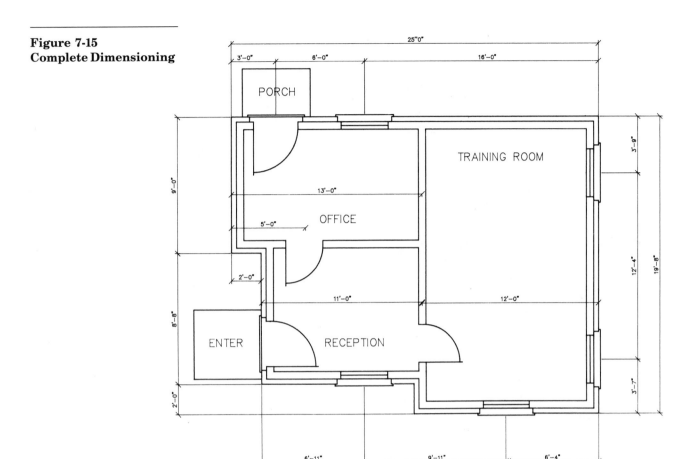

The next step is to dimension a mechanical part, such as one from Chapter 5, using decimal dimensions.

To dimension a mechanical drawing in inches using 2-place decimals (Figure 7-16):

Step 1. Call up the first drawing done in Chapter 5.

Prompt: Enter Selection:
Response: 2 {edit an EXISTING drawing}

Prompt: Enter NAME of drawing:
Response: {Use the name you gave the drawing from Chapter 5, be sure to include the drive, if it is other than the default drive, and include the directory before the name}

Step 2. Make the proper DIMVAR settings for this drawing. Most of the DIMVAR settings will be the AutoCAD default. To do this after the drawing is in place, follow this procedure:

Prompt: Command:
Response: DIM {from the Root Menu}

Figure 7-16
Drawing to be Dimensioned

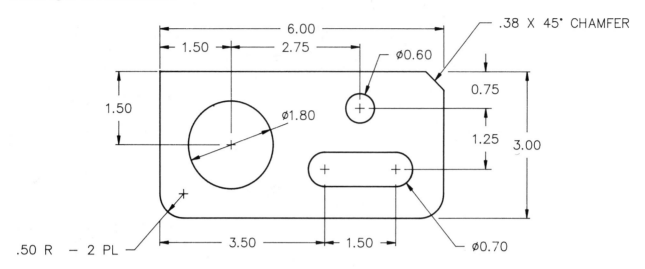

Prompt: Dim:

Response: STATUS {from the DIM Menu}

The following listing should appear:

DIMSCALE	1.000	
DIMASZ	0.18	
DIMCEN	0.09	
DIMEXO	0.06	
DIMDLI	0.38	
DIMEXE	0.06	{this is different from the AutoCAD default}
DIMTP	0.00	
DIMTM	0.00	
DIMTXT	0.125	{this is different from the default}
DIMTSZ	0.00	
DIMRND	0.00	
DIMDLE	0.00	
DIMTOL	OFF	
DIMLIM	OFF	
DIMTIH	ON	
DIMTOH	ON	
DIMSEI	ON	{prevents the first extension line being drawn}
DIMSEZ	OFF	
DIMTAD	OFF	

DIMZIN	0
DIMALT	OFF
DIMALTF	25.40000
DIMALTD	2
DIMLFAC	1.0000
DIMBLK	
DIMASO	OFF
DIMSHO	OFF
DIMPOST	
DIMAPOST	

If any of the variables on your list are different from the preceding ones change them using this procedure:

Prompt: Dim:

Response: {Select} DIM VARS {from the DIM Menu}

Prompt: Dim:

Response: {Select the variable to be changed, for Example: DIMEXE}

Prompt: DIMEXE current value <0.18> new value:

Response: .06

The variable is now changed for this drawing. If you have already started dimensioning sometimes a change in dimensioning variable will not take effect until the next command. So do not be concerned until you have used the variable twice.

Note: *PROTOTYPE DRAWING: If you want to keep the changes for later drawing, keep this as a prototype drawing (a standard drawing containing all of the settings, such as dimensioning, layers, text size, etc., just the way you want them). You may then copy the drawing file, rename it as DWG1 (or whatever you want to call your prototype) and erase anything except what you will use on later drawings. When the drawing is to be used, create a new drawing by selecting "1. Begin a NEW drawing." At the prompt, do this:*

Prompt: Name of drawing:

Response: {New drawing name—your choice} = DWG1

DWG1 will then appear with the new drawing name and the original DWG1 will remain in the file as DWG1. Now, back to the settings. Another setting that must be changed is the number of digits to the right of the decimal point. To do this:

Prompt: Command:

Response: SETTINGS {Root Menu}
UNITS {second page of SETTINGS Menu}

Prompt: System of units: (Examples)

1. Scientific
2. Decimal
3. Engineering
4. Architectural
5. Fractional

Enter choice, 1 to 5 <2>:

Response: 2 {or simply ↵ if 2 is the default}

Prompt: Number of digits to right of decimal point (0 to 8)<4>:

Response: 2 {2 places to the right of the decimal point—5.00}

When all of the settings have been made proceed with
dimensioning.

Step 3. Place center marks at the centers of all circles and arcs (Figure 7-17).

Prompt: Command:

Response: DIM {from the Root Menu} CENTER

Prompt: Dim; CENTER Select arc or circle:

Response: D1, D2, D3, D4, D5, D6 ↵

Step 4. Make the horizontal dimensions (Figure 7-17).

Prompt: Command:

Response: {Select}   DIM
LINEAR
HORIZ

Prompt: First extension line origin or RETURN to select:

Response: D7 {SNAP should be ON if the drawing was done with
SNAP ON}

Prompt: Second extension line origin:

Response: D8 {pick the end of the center mark}

Prompt: Dimension line location:

Response: D– {½″ from the object}

Figure 7-17
Dimension a Mechanical
Drawing in Inches
Using 2-Place Decimals

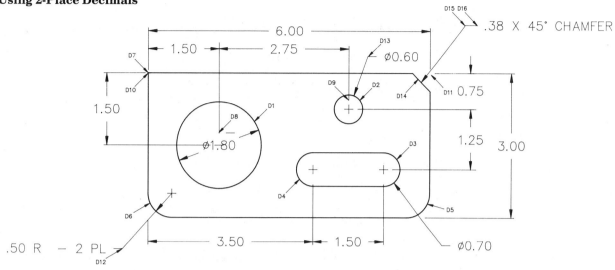

Prompt:	Dimension text <1.50>:
Response:	↵

Prompt:	Dim:
Response:	CONTINU {select from DIM Menu}

Prompt:	Second extension line origin:
Response:	D9

Prompt:	Dim:
Response:	HORIZ

Prompt:	First extension line origin or RETURN to select:
Response:	D10

Prompt:	Second extension line origin:
Response:	D11

If you have suppressed the first extension line you will have to draw it at this time using the line command or copy the last extension line to the origin. Draw the remainder of the horizontal dimensions shown at the bottom of Figure 7-17 in a similar manner.

Step 5. Make all vertical dimensions (Figure 7-17).

Use a similar procedure to the one you used to make horizontal dimensions. You may have to erase a bar on the first dimension line and move the dimension from the outside of the arrowhead to inside as shown in this figure. All other dimensions may be drawn as the horizontal dimensions were drawn.

Step 6. Dimension diameters, radii, and chamfer (Figure 7-17).

To dimension these features follow this procedure:

Prompt: Command:
Response: DIM
　　　　　　RADIUS

Prompt: RAD Select arc or circle:
Response: D6 {the same spot again}

Prompt: Dimension text (0.50):

If you don't like the default form, enter the one you like, for Example: .50R. In this case, enter .50R–2PL, which serves for both ends.

Prompt: Text does not fit. Enter leader length for text:
Response: D12

Prompt: Dim:
Response: {Select} DIAMETER

Prompt: Dim: DIAM Select arc or circle:
Response: D1 {same spot as before}

Prompt: Dimension text <1.80>:
Response: ↵

Prompt: DIAM Select arc or circle:
Response: D2 {the same as before}

Prompt: Dimension text <0.60>:
Response: ↵

Prompt: Text does not fit.
　　　　　　Enter leader length for text:
Response: D13

Prompt: Dim:
Response: {Select} LEADER

Prompt: LEADER, Leader start: (Activate OSNAP and select MIDpoint) MIDPOINT OF

Response: D14

Prompt: To point:

Response: D15

Prompt: To point:

Response: D16

Prompt: To point:

Response: ↵

Prompt: Dimension text <0.00>:

Response: .38 × .45%%D CHAMFER {%%D will display the degree symbol}

Prompt: Dim:

Response: {Select} DIAMETER

Prompt: DIAM Select arc or circle:

Response: D17

Prompt: Dimension text <0.70>:

Response: ↵

Prompt: Text does not fit
Enter leader length for text:

Response: {Be sure ORTHO is OFF} D18

Prompt: Dim:

Response: {Exit the dimensioning program by selecting or typing EXIT or Ctrl-C}

The drawing is complete except for cleaning up any lines that are too long (use the CHANGE command) or erasing features such as the center mark for the radius in the lower left corner.
  After cleanup:

Prompt: Command:

Response: SAVE {save the drawing in two places}

Hint: *Dimensioning diameters, radii, and special features before making horizontal and vertical dimensions is sometimes helpful. Planning a dimensioning approach to each drawing usually saves time.*

To dimension a drawing in millimeters using one-place decimals:

Dimensioning a metric drawing is similar to dimensioning a drawing drawn in inches, but there are a few differences. The differences are shown below. Set dimensioning variables in the same manner as you choose for dimensioning in inches, except:

DIMSCALE = 25.4

Set units (from the SETTINGS Menu) as follows:

Prompt: Systems of units:

1. Scientific
2. Decimal
3. Engineering
4. Architectural
5. Fractional

Enter choice, 1 to 5 <2>:

Response: 2 {or ↵ if 2 is the default}

Prompt: Number of digits to right of decimal point (0 to 8) <4>:

Response: 1 ↵

Press Enter in response to the other prompts. Five features you will be able to use are:

**Figure 7-18
Selected Line
for Dimension**

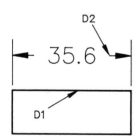

Feature 1. Respond to the DIM prompt:

Prompt: First extension line or RETURN to select:

Response: ↵ {Figure 7-18}

Prompt: Select line, arc, or circle:

Response: {Digitize the line, arc, or circle to be dimensioned} D1

This will eliminate some prompts. You will discover where it can be used most effectively, for example: overall dimensions of parts (Figure 7-18).

Prompt: Dimension line location:

Response: D2

Prompt: Dimension text <35.6>:

Response: ↵

Figure 7-19
Dimension Placement

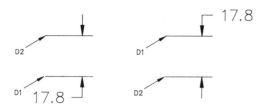

Figure 7-20
Baseline Dimensioning

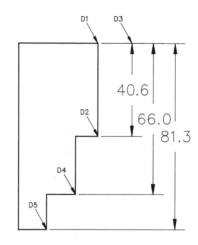

Feature 2. Notice that the sequence of extension lines selection determines where the small dimension is placed. See examples in Figure 7-19.

Feature 3. For baseline dimensioning (Figure 7-20):

Prompt:	Dim:
Response:	VERTICAL {select from LINEAR Menu}
Prompt:	First extension line origin:
Response:	D1
Prompt:	Second extension line origin:
Response:	D2
Prompt:	Dimension line location:
Response:	D3
Prompt:	Dimension text <40.6>:
Response:	↵
Prompt:	Dim:
Response:	{Select} BASELINE
Prompt:	Second extension line origin:
Response:	D4
Prompt:	Dim:
Response:	↵

**Figure 7-21
Tolerances Added**

|← ———— 3.37±.02 ————— →|

Prompt: Second extension line origin:

Response: D5

Feature 4. Associative dimensioning—use the STRETCH command to shrink or enlarge any drawing already dimensioned.

Observe that the dimension text changes with the size of the drawing (DIMASO must be ON). When DIMAZO is ON the dimension, dimension lines, arrowheads, and extension lines are inserted as a block which must be exploded if a change is needed.

Feature 5. Adding tolerances to specific dimensions—to add tolerances to a specific dimension (Figure 7-21) use the following in response to the text prompt:

Response: 3.37%%P.02

The text will appear as shown in Figure 7-21.

EXERCISE 1

Dimension the floor plan (Figure 7-1) using the procedures described in this chapter. Use the floor plan from Chapter 6 for the basic drawing. Plot the drawing or save it on a floppy disk for plotting later according to your instructor's plan.

EXERCISE 2

Dimension the mechanical part shown as Figure 7-16. Use the basic drawing from Chapter 5. Use the procedures described in this chapter. Plot the drawing or save it on a floppy disk for later use according to your instructor's plan.

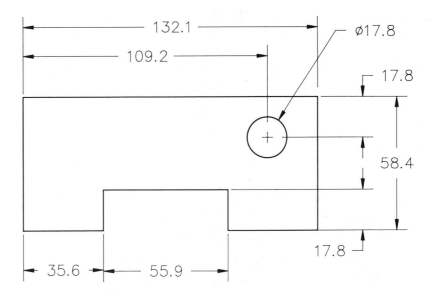

EXERCISE 3

Draw and dimension the above part using metric dimensions. Make the drawing full-scale. Set the dimensioning variables using the procedures described for Figure 7-20. Plot or save according to your instructor's directions.

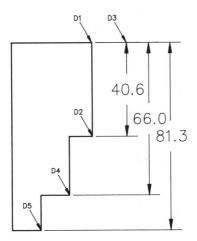

EXERCISE 4

Draw and dimension the above part using one-place decimal dimensions in millimeters. Use the baseline dimensioning system. Estimate horizontal dimensions. Plot or save as your instructor directs.

EXERCISE 5

Dimension the drawings done for Chapter 5, Exercises 5 through 10. Scale the drawings to full-size and use the AutoCAD dimensioning system. Then, enlarge them to the size you drew them originally. Set dimensioning variables so that the final drawings have the following features:

TEXT HEIGHT = .10
ARROW SIZE = .12
EXTENSION LINE OFFSET = .10
EXTENSION LINE EXTENSION = .10
show both English and metric units
use 3-place decimals for all inch dimensions = .000
use 2-place decimals for all metric units = .00

EXERCISE 6

Draw full-size and dimension the figure shown on the following page. Approximate any unknown dimensions. Show only the dimensions that appear on this figure. Use the following variables:

TEXT HEIGHT = .06
ARROW SIZE = .10
EXTENSION LINE OFFSET = .06
EXTENSION LINE EXTENSION = .06
use 2-place decimals for all inch dimensions
show only inch dimensions
place on all 11 × 17" sheet.

EXERCISE 7

Use the instructions for Exercise 6 except show only metric measurement using 1-place decimals.

Exercises 6 and 7

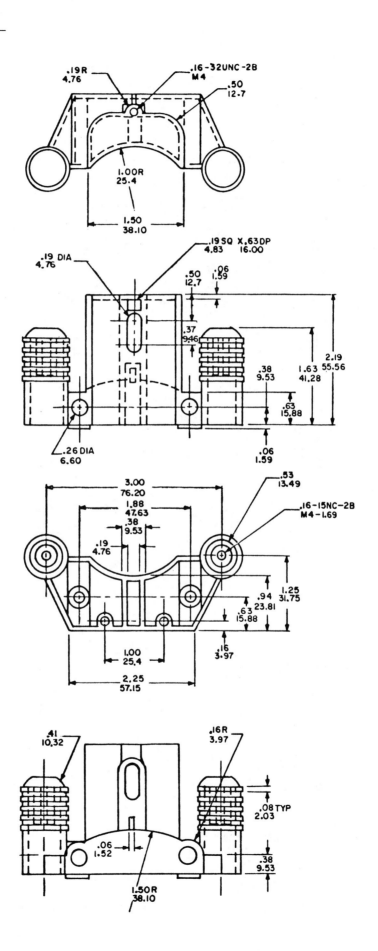

Exercise 8

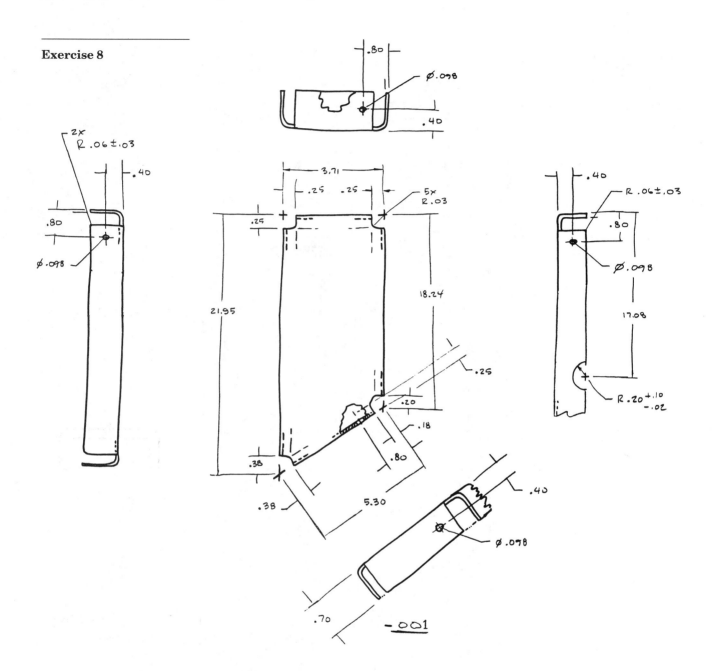

EXERCISE 8

Draw full-size and dimension the part shown in the sketch. Put it on a
22 × 34″ sheet size using the following:

DIMTXT = .18

DIMEXE = .16

DIMEXO = .16

DIMASZ = .18

DIMSCALE = 1.00

use 3-place decimals for hole sizes

use 2-place decimals for all other dimensions

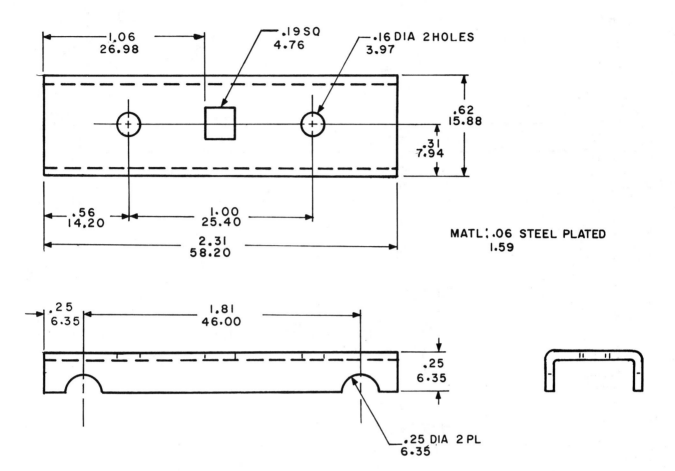

EXERCISES 9 AND 10

Draw and dimension the part shown in this figure. Make the drawing twice-size and place it on an 8.5 × 11″ horizontal sheet. Use these DIMVARS:

DIMTXT = .10

DIMEXE = .08

DIMEXO = .08

DIMASZ = .12

DIMSCALE = 2.00

use 2-place decimal inch dimensions for Exercise 9

use 2-place decimal millimeter dimensions for Exercise 10

Exercises 11 and 12

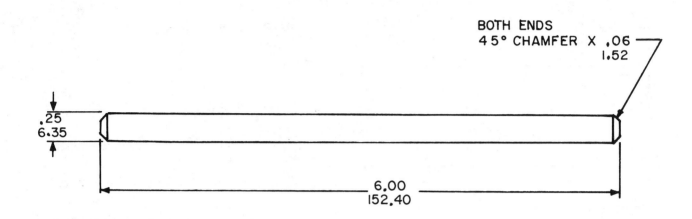

EXERCISES 11 AND 12

Draw and dimension the part shown in this figure. Make the drawing full-size and place it on an 8.5 × 11″ horizontal sheet. Use these DIMVARS:

DIMTXT = .10

DIMEXE = .08

DIMEXO = .08

DIMASZ = .12

DIMSCALE = 1.00

use 2-place decimal inch dimensions for Figure 11

use 2-place decimal millimeter dimensions for Figure 12

Test on Objectives—Chapter 7

Circle the correct answer.

1. On a scale of ¼″ = 1′ with DIMSCALE set at 1, a 3″ letter will measure:
   a. ¹⁄₁₆″
   b. ⅛″
   c. 3″
   d. ⅓″
   e. ³⁄₁₆″

2. DIMASZ determines:
   a. the height of the alternate text
   b. the height of the arrowhead
   c. the length of the arrowhead
   d. the direction of the azimuths
   e. the length of the bearing

3. DIMEXO sets:
   a. the distance from the X and Y coordinates
   b. the execute file for dimensions
   c. the distance from the object to the beginning of the extension line
   d. the distance from the end of the extension line to the dimension line
   e. the distance from the beginning of the extension line to the end of the extension line

4. DIMDLI sets:
   a. the dimension length in inches
   b. the length of the arrowhead
   c. the distance from the beginning of the dimension line to the extension line
   d. the length of dimension lines
   e. the spacing between dimension lines

5. On a scale of ¼″ = 1′ with DIMSCALE set at 1 and DIMTXT set at 6″, the text height will measure:
   a. ¹⁄₁₆″
   b. ⅛″
   c. ¼″
   d. ½″
   e. 6″

6. Which of the following places the text above the extension line?
   a. DIMSE1
   b. DIMSE2
   c. DIMTAD
   d. DIMLIM
   e. DIMTOL

7. Which of the following produces a dimension with no extension line at the beginning of the dimension?
   a. DIMSE1
   b. DIMSE2
   c. DIMTAD
   d. DIMLIM
   e. DIMTOL

8. Which of the following must be set to ON for tolerances to be added to dimensioning text?
   a. DIMSE1
   b. DIMSE2
   c. DIMTAD
   d. DIMLIM
   e. DIMTOL

9. Which of the following must be set ON for metric dimensions to be displayed with inch dimensions?
   a. DIMLIM
   b. DIMTOL
   c. DIMALT
   d. DIMALTF
   e. DIMALTD

10. Which of the following sets the number of decimal places in the alternate dimension?
   a. DIMLIM
   b. DIMTOL
   c. DIMALT
   d. DIMALTF
   e. DIMALTD

11. Which of the following menus contains a setting that fixes the number of places to the right of the decimal point in dimensioning text?
   a. EDIT
   b. DRAW
   c. TEXT
   d. SETTINGS
   e. UTILITY

12. To digitize the exact location of the upper right corner of the floor plan, which of the following OSNAP modifiers should be used?
   a. PERPENDICULAR
   b. INTERSECTION
   c. CENTER
   d. MIDPOINT
   e. LINE

13. To draw a horizontal line 12 feet long to the right on the floor plan, which of the following is the correct response?
   a. @12<0
   b. @12'–0"<0
   c. 12'–0"<180
   d. @12'–0"<180
   e. 12'R

14. Which of the following variables must be "0" for the dimension to contain an arrowhead?

    a. DIMTXT

    b. DIMTP

    c. DIMEXE

    d. DIMDLE

    e. DIMTSZ

15. If DIMSCALE is set at 1.0000, what must the setting be for an arrowhead to be ⅛" long?

    a. DIMASZ = .125

    b. DIMASZ = 1.00

    c. DIMTSZ = .125

    d. DIMTSZ = 1.00

    e. DIMASZ = 0

16. Which of the following variables must be activated if some symbol other than the tick or the arrowhead is to be used for the ends of a dimension line?

    a. DIMSHO

    b. DIMPOST

    c. DIMBLK

    d. BIMALT

    e. DIMALT 2

17. If all dimensions are to originate from the same edge, which of the following modifiers should be used?

    a. CONTINUE

    b. DATUM

    c. ORIGIN

    d. ORIGINATE

    e. BASELINE

18. If you wish to begin all dimension lines ¹⁄₁₆" from the object lines, which of the following is the correct setting?

    a. DIMZIN = 0

    b. DIMEXE = 1

    c. DIMEXO = .0625

    d. DIMLIM = .0625

    e. DIMLIM = 1

19. To place center marks at the center of all arcs and circles, which of the following DIM modifiers should be activated?

    a. CENTER

    b. INTERSECTION

    c. POINT

    d. DIAMETER

    e. RADIUS

20. Which of the following is the correct response if a 1.395-diameter dimension is needed? The prompt is XXXXX<RADIUS>?

   a. 1.395

   b. .625

   c. D

   d. R

   e. C

21. Write the dimensioning variable that sets the size of center marks at the centers of circles.

_____

22. Write the dimensioning variable that sets the overall scale of the arrowheads and text size used on a drawing.

_____

23. Write the dimensioning variable that sets the height of the text used for dimensions.

_____

24. Write the variable that sets the space between dimension lines when baseline dimensions are used.

_____

25. Write the selection from the SETTINGS Menu that may be used to set the number of places to the right of the decimal point.

_____

26. Write the correct DIMSCALE setting for a drawing done in millimeters.

_____

27. Describe the function of associative dimensioning.

_____

_____

_____

28. Describe the function of the DIMALTF variable.

_____

_____

_____

29. Describe the function of the DIMALTD variable.

_____

_____

_____

30. Write the dimensioning variable that should be used to suppress the first extension line.

_____

8
Drawing Formats for Plotting

Objectives

The student will:

- construct drawing formats for A-,B-, and C-size sheets
- place drawing within these formats and determine the scale factor
- plot A-, B-, and C-size drawings
- answer questions regarding the use of PLOT, SCALE, INSERT

Drawing Formats

Most manufacturing and construction drawings must be placed in a standard format. This format consists of the border, title blocks, revision block, and standard notes. The SCALE command allows the drawing to be drawn full-scale for convenience in measuring, and then reduced to fit within a standard size format if reduction is needed.

The format may be called up as a block with attributes and inserted around the drawing, or the drawing may be called up as a block and inserted into the format. In this chapter you will be required to make formats for the following standard size sheets:

A-11 × 8½″
B-17 × 11″
C-22 × 17″

You may wish to create larger size formats, but these are within the capability of many relatively inexpensive plotters. Using those formats, you will be asked to insert drawings you have previously made, and to plot the composite drawings.

Figure 8-1
A-size Format

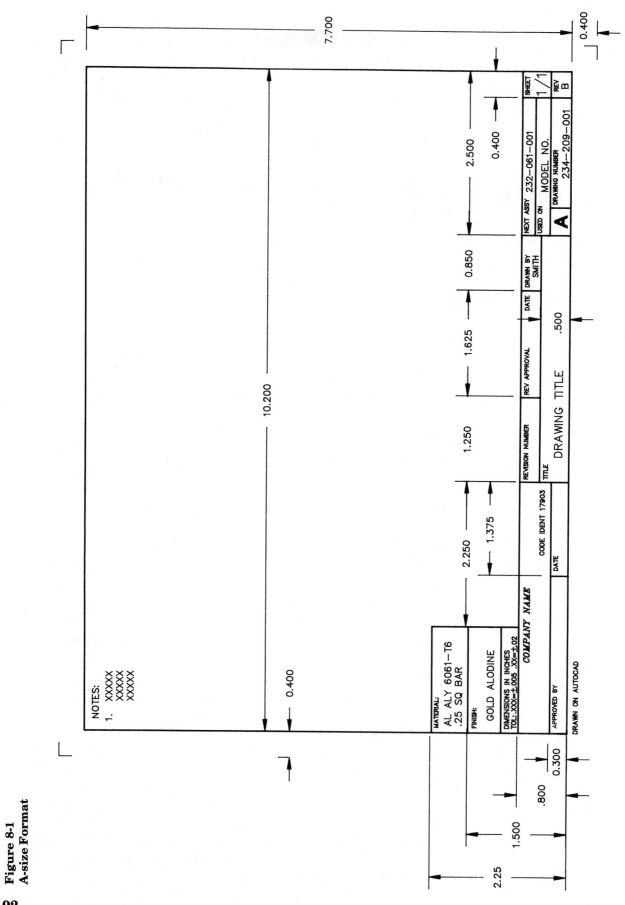

Begin with the A-size (11 × 8½″) formats. This is the only format that has both horizontal and vertical forms. The horizontal format is used more than the vertical one, so you will first learn to construct the horizontal format.

To draw the A-size horizontal format (Figure 8-1):

Load AutoCAD, begin a new drawing, and name it "A."

Prompt: Command:
Response: SETUP

If your computer will not allow SETUP to work use LIMITS and UNITS.

Prompt: Select the units from the screen menu:
Response: Decimal

Prompt: Select the Scale from the menu area:
Response: FULL

Prompt: Select the paper size from the screen menu:
Response: A-8.5 × 11 {the default is horizontal sheet}

Prompt: Command:
Response: STYLE {from the SETTINGS Menu}

Prompt: Text style name (or?)<STANDARD>:
Response: ↵

Prompt: Existing style,
Font file (txt):
Response: SIMPLEX {from the screen menu or the keyboard}

Prompt: Height (0.0000):
Response: ↵ {press Enter for default at width, obliquing, angle, backwards, upside down, and vertical prompts}

Use the LINE command to draw the lines of the format shown in Figure 8-1. Begin the drawing at .4,.4 (the lower left corner) in response to the first LINE command prompt, "From point:" then create a new layer called G (green color) and use D-TEXT to place the text in the format on the "G" layer.

Make all the labels for the spaces (such as FINISH, MATERIAL, DATE) .062 high, and all other letters. 125 high. Notice that many spaces are already filled in and the notes are located with xxx's. You may wish to change the letter style for the school or company name as was done in Figure 8-1; that style is italic. This ensures that all of these labels will be in the same place every time after the CHANGE command is used to change the label from what is in the box to what should be in the box. You may also use variable attributes for text that changes often. WBLOCK the format and type in the correct drawing number, title, etc., when the format is inserted into the drawing. Now, draw the B-size format.

To draw the B-size format (Figure 8-2):

Begin a new drawing and name it "B."

Prompt: Command:
Response: SETUP

Prompt: Select the units from the screen menu:
Response: Decimal

Prompt: Select the scale from the menu area:
Response: FULL

Prompt: Select the paper size from the screen menu:
Response: B-11 × 17

Prompt: Command:

Use the LINE command to draw the lines shown in Figure 8-2. Use the DTEXT command to place the text on a green layer similar to the A-size format. Use the same letter heights as for the A-size format. Finally, create the C-size format.

To draw the C-size format (Figure 8-3):

Create a new drawing and name it "C."

Prompt: Command:
Response: SETUP

Prompt: Select the units from the screen menu:
Response: Decimal

Prompt: Select the Scale from the menu area:
Response: FULL

Prompt: Select the paper size from the screen menu:
Response: C-17 × 22

Prompt: Command:

Draw the format and add the text as you did for the A-size format, keeping all letter heights the same as the A-size format.

Once you have completed the standard size formats for A-,B-, and C-size sheets you may use these formats for all of your drawings. Begin by selecting "2. Edit an EXISTing drawing" from the Main Menu and responding with "A" to the "Name of the Drawing" prompt. This should bring up the A-size format on your screen. Now, insert the block diagram you drew in Chapter 3 into the format. Follow this sequence:

Prompt: Command:
Response: INSERT {from the DRAW Menu}

Prompt: INSERT Block name (or?):
Response: A:BLK1 (your initials)

Use this if you have saved the BLOCK DIAGRAM on a floppy disk you have placed in the A drive and if you named the drawing in the manner suggested in Exercise 1 of Chapter 3.

Note: *This procedure is somewhat risky in that you may accidentally save the completed drawing under the name "A" and lose your A-size format. Although you may easily recover your format by copying the drawing and erasing everything but the format, an alternate procedure is described for Figure 8-6.*

Prompt: Insertion point:
Response: D1 {Figure 8-4}

Prompt: X-scale factor <1>/Corner/XYZ:
Response: ↵

Prompt: Y-scale factor (default = x):
Response: ↵

Prompt: Rotation angle <0>:
Response: ↵

The block diagram should now be positioned where you indicated you wanted it to be. Notice that complete drawings that are inserted use 0,0 as the insertion point. If it is not exactly where you think it should be, you may move it using the MOVE command. If you plan to do any editing on the block diagram, you must first EXPLODE it using the EXPLODE command on the EDIT Menu. You may now

Figure 8-2
B-size Format

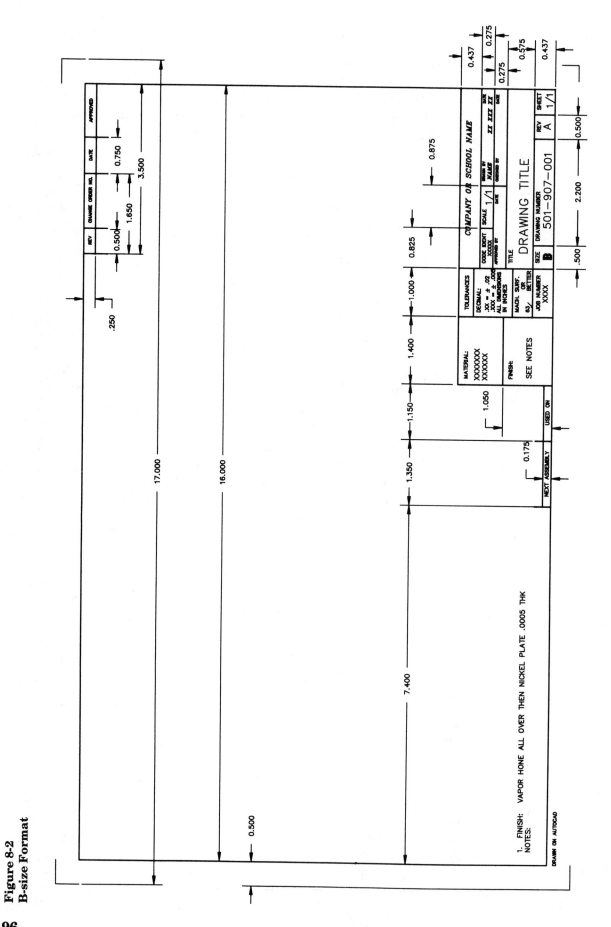

Figure 8-3
C-size Format

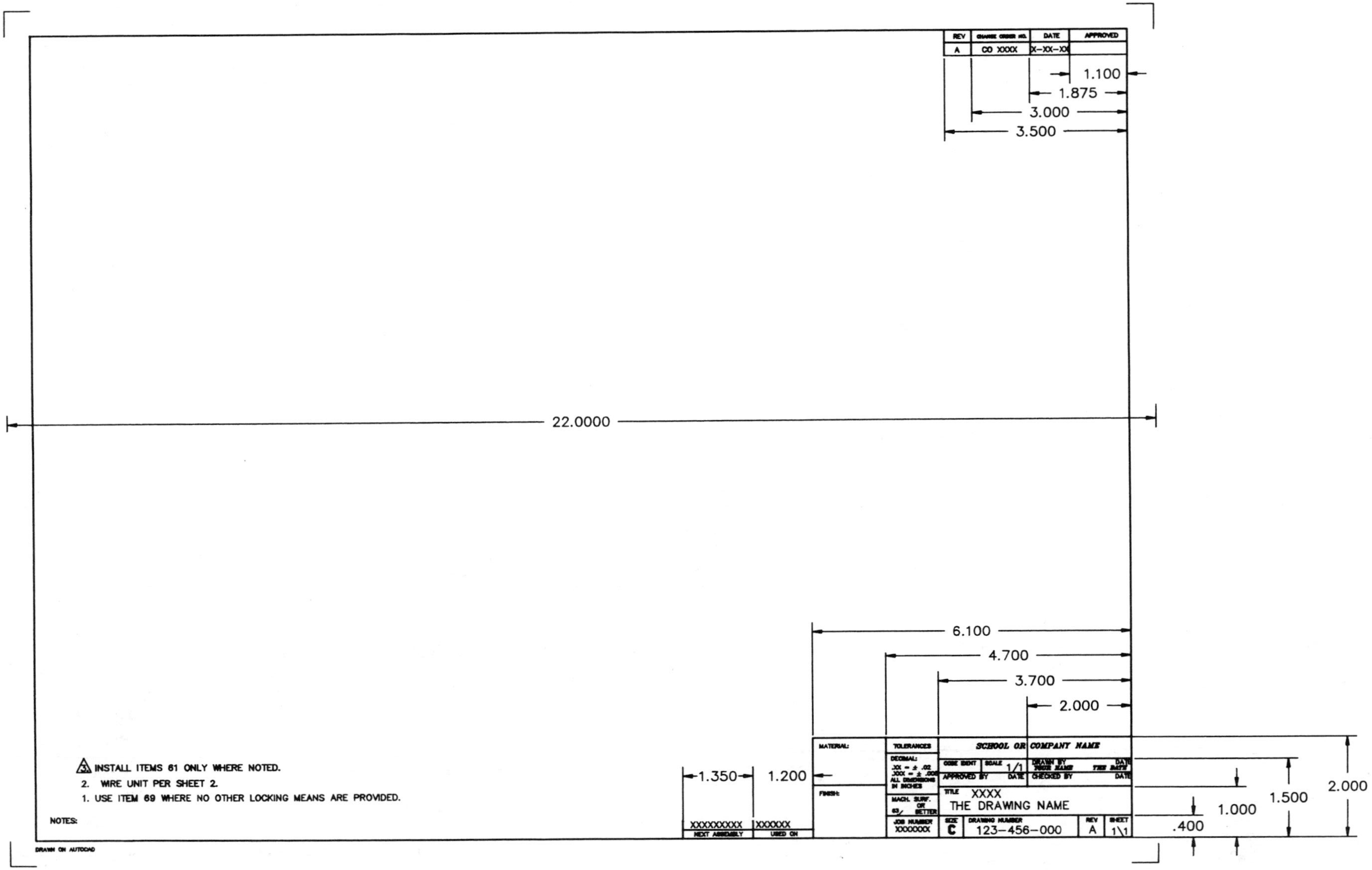

Figure 8-4
Inserting a Full-size Drawing into a Full-size Format

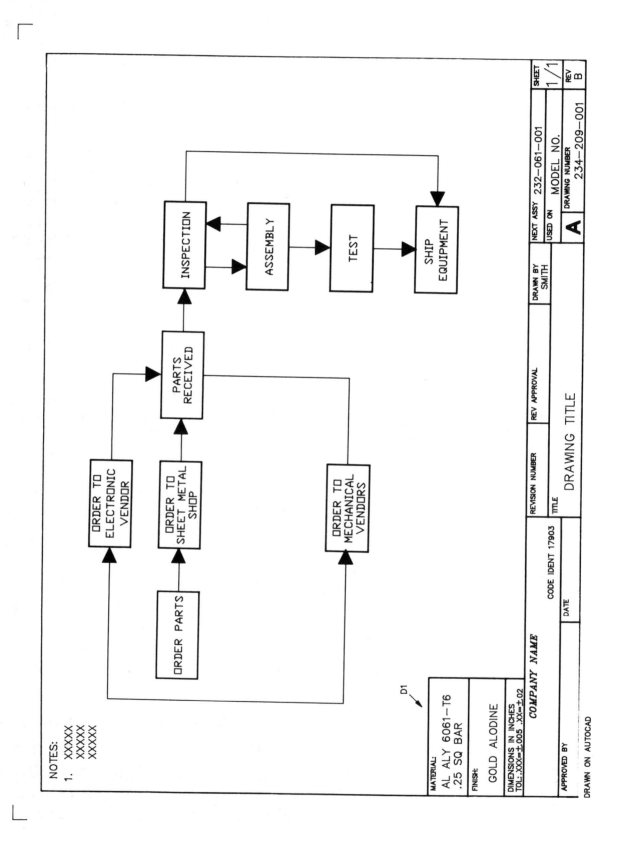

change the drawing title and any other text using the CHANGE command and then save the drawing under another name using the SAVE command as follows:

Prompt: Command:

Response: SAVE

Prompt: Filename <A: A> or the name and drive on which you saved your A-size format:

Response: A:BLKFORM ↵

Do this if you wish to save it on the floppy disk in the A drive with a name of BLKFORM. Otherwise, specify the letter of the drive you want to save the drawing on and give it a name of less than 8 characters, or do not specify a drive if you want to save the drawing on the default drive.

Prompt: Command:

Response: QUIT

Prompt: Really want to discard all changes to drawing?

Response: Y {or Yes} ↵

Other drawings may be inserted into this or other formats in a similar manner. Insertion of a large drawing into a small format is discussed later in this chapter.

You now have an A-size format intact with no block diagram on it and another drawing called BLKFORM, which contains both the format and the block diagram. SAVE gave you the BLKFORM drawing and QUIT returned the A-size format to its original state. Now, plot the drawing.

To plot the BLKFORM drawing:

Prompt: Enter NAME of drawing:

Response: BLKFORM

Remember to precede the name of the drawing with the drive and directory if different from the default drive.

Prompt: What to plot-Display, Extents, Limits, View, or Window:

Response: L ↵

The LIMITS response corresponds to the limits set when the plot was planned. The LIMITS setting is found on the SETTINGS Menu. Consult the AutoCAD manual chapters on plotting for an explanation of any of the other choices if they are not clear to you. You may find it helpful to use EXTENTS if your plot does not include everything you wanted.

Prompt: Plot will NOT be written to a selected file
Sizes are in Inches
Plot origin is at (0.00,0.00)
Plotting area is 15.75 wide by 11.20 high (MAX size)
Plot is NOT rotated 90 degrees
Pen width is 0.010
Area fill will be adjusted for pen width
Hidden lines will NOT be removed
Plot will be scaled to fit available area
Do you want to change anything?<N>:

Response: Y ↵

Prompt:

Entity Color	Pen No.	Line Type	Pen Speed	Entity Color	Pen No.	Line Type	Pen Spec
1 (red)	1	0	36	9	1	0	36
2 (yellow)	1	0	36	10	1	0	36
3 (green)	1	0	36	11	1	0	36
4 (cyan)	1	0	36	12	1	0	36
5 (blue)	1	0	36	13	1	0	36
6 (magenta)	1	0	36	14	1	0	36
7 (white)	1	0	36	15	1	0	36
8	1	0	36				

Line types   0 = continuous line
1 = ...
2 = ...
3 = ----------
4 = - - - - -

Do you want to change any of these parameters? <N>:

{Do you want to change any of the above pens?}

Response: Y ↵

Prompt:

Layer Color	Pen No.	Line Type	Pen Speed	
1 (red)	1	0	36	Pen number <1>:

Response: C7 ↵

Prompt:

Layer Color	Pen No.	Line Type	Pen Speed	
7 (white)	1	0	36	Pen Number<1>:

Response: 2 ↵

Now all lines on all layers will be drawn with pen No. 1 except the lines on layer 7, which will be drawn with pen No. 2.

Prompt:

Layer Color	Pen No.	Line Type	Pen Speed	
7 (white)	2	0	36	Line type <0>:

Response: X ↵ {this allows you to exit from that sequence}

Prompt: Write the plot to a file <N>:

Response: ↵ {no need to write it to a file}

Prompt: Size units (Inches or Millimeters) <I>:

Response: ↵ {the drawing was made in inches}

Prompt: Plot origin in Inches <0.00,0.00>:

Response: ↵

The first 0.00 is the long side of the paper, the second is the short side. You may have to play around with these numbers to make the plot fit your application. Usually −.5 to +.5 in both directions is the range for the plot origin. On some plotters it is necessary to plot a drawing on the next larger paper size (Example: A-size on a B-size) because the rollers that grip the paper roll through the plotted area.

Prompt: Standard values for plotting size

SIZE	WIDTH	HEIGHT
A	10.50	8.00
B	16.00	10.00
C	21.00	16.00
D	33.00	21.00
E	43.00	33.00
MAX	44.72	35.31
USER	8.50	11.00

These values may be abbreviated for your plotter.
Enter the Size or Width, Height (in units) <default>:

Response: 11,8.5 ↵

This produces a plot of a horizontal A-size sheet.

Prompt: Rotate 2-D plots 90 degrees clockwise? <N>:

Response: ↵ {a response of Y would turn the plot 90°—a vertical A-size page}

Prompt: Pen width <0.010>:

Response: ↵ {this is useful on drawings which must be plotted extremely accurately—within .005 inches or less}

Prompt: Adjust area fill boundaries for pen width? <N>:

"No" is the correct response; "yes" adjusts for the pen size entered in the response above.

Response: ↵

Prompt: Remove hidden lines? <N>: {this is used on 3-dimensional drawings; it has nothing to do with lines you have drawn with the hidden linetype}

Response: ↵

Prompt: Plotted Inches = Drawing Units or Fit or ? <F>:

Response: 1 = 1 {this will produce a full-size plot—F fits the plot into the plotting area and often results in a drawing not to scale; sometimes Fit is the appropriate response, which you can determine as the situation arises}

Prompt: Position paper in plotter.
Press RETURN to continue or S to Stop for hardware setup:

Load the paper and check the following to be sure that:

■ the pens flow properly and are properly loaded in the carrousel (the holder for the pens),

■ the carrousel is seated properly,

■ the settings on the plotter are set for the computer from which the plot is to be made, and

■ the switch box, if you have one, is set for the correct computer.

Response: {Then press ↵ on the computer keyboard and the plot should proceed}

If the pens skip for any reason, leave the paper in the plotter and replot over the same plot after the pen problem is corrected (see Chapter 12). You may find it necessary to specify a slower pen speed, which you can do from the plotting sequence just described.

Other drawings may be inserted into the A-size format or other formats in a similar manner. If, however, you plan to insert a drawing such as a floor plan from Chapter 6, which you drew full-scale, the size of the inserted drawing must be considered. For example, consider that the floor plan FP1 (+your initials) is to be inserted into a C-size format. The building measures $42' \times 28'$. The usable area inside the format measures approximately $16'' \times 10''$. (There must be room between the drawing and the border or title block for changes and other information.) To get the approximate reduction percentage:

Change both the 42′ and the 28′ to inches: $42 \times 12 = 504''$;
$28' \times 12 = 336''$

DIVIDE 504″ into 16″ (the horizontal dimension):
$16 \div 504 = .0317$
(504″ will have to reduce to approximately 16″ or less)

DIVIDE 336″ into 10″ (the vertical dimension):
$10 \div 336 = .0296$
(336″ will have to reduce to approximately 10″ or less)

Figure 8-5
Reduction Percentages
for Commonly Used
Scales

SCALE	REDUCTION PERCENTAGE
⅛″ = 1′	.0104
¼″ = 1′	.0208
⅜″ = 1′	.0312
½″ = 1′	.0417
¾″ = 1′	.0625
1″ = 1′	.0833

Figure 8-5 shows the reduction percentages for commonly used scales. Comparing these two percentages to the percentages in Figure 8-5 shows that the standard scale that comes closest to the percentages needed is ⅜″ = 1′ or .0312. This means that the full-size drawing of the floor plan FP1 must be inserted into the C-size format at .0312 or 3.12% of its original size.

To insert the floor plan at a scale ⅜″ = 1′:

Response: 1. Begin a NEW drawing

Prompt: Name of drawing:
Response: FP1-1 = C

FP1-1 will be the floor plan inserted in the format. The drawing named C is your C-size format if that was the name assigned to it. Using this procedure prevents you from making a mistake and losing the drawing named "C" when you save or end the drawing.

Prompt: Command:
Response: INSERT {from the DRAW Menu}

Prompt: Insert block name (or?):
Response: FP1-1 {or whatever name you gave to the floor plan you drew in Chapter 6}

Figure 8-6
**Inserting a Very Large Drawing
into a Standard Format**

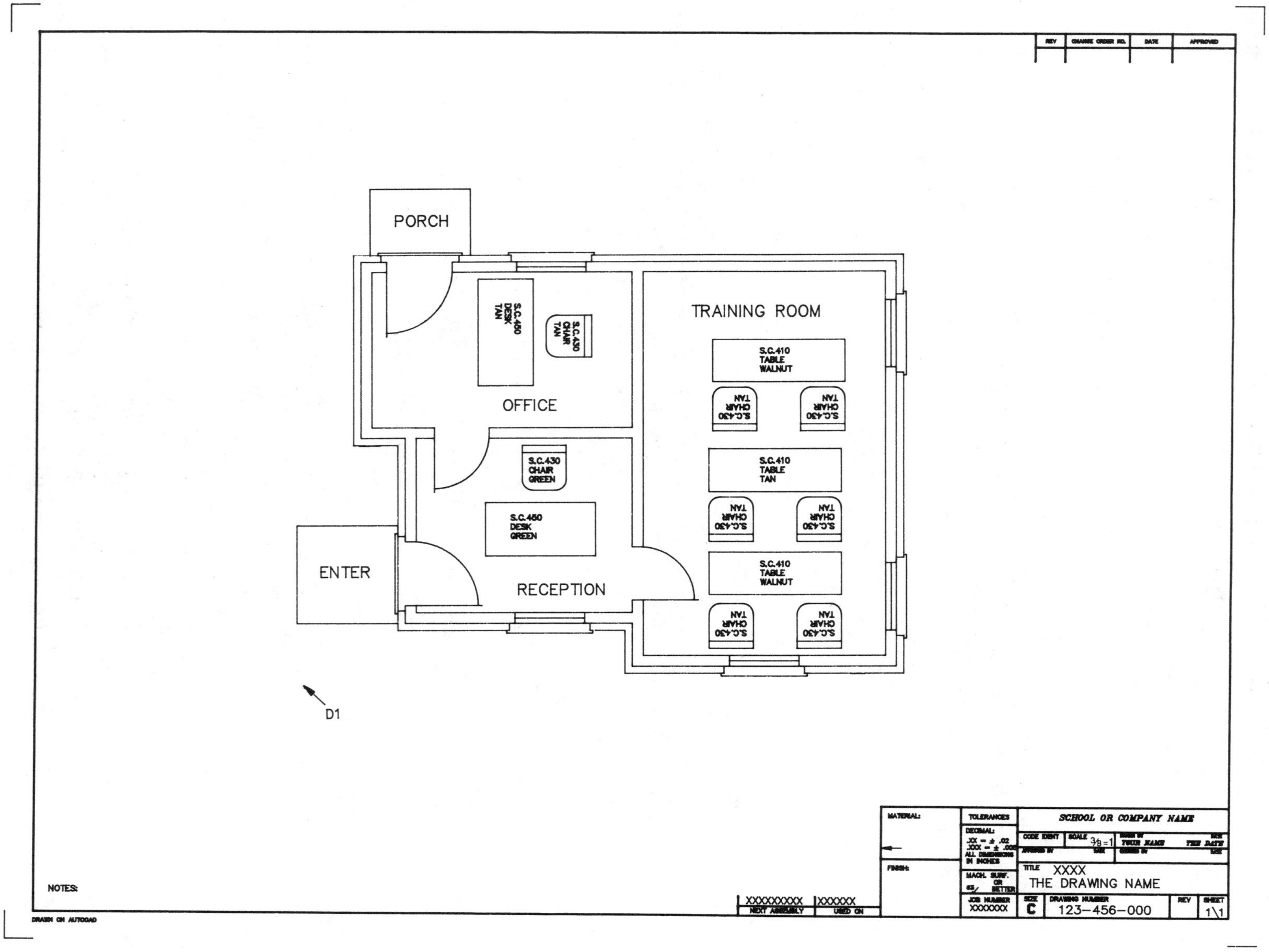

Be sure to specify the drive your floppy disk is in if the drawing is not filed on the default drive.

Prompt: Insertion point:
Response: D1 {Figure 8-6}

Prompt: X-scale factor <1>/corner/XYZ:
Response: .0312↵

Prompt: Y-scale factor (default = x):
Response: ↵

Prompt: Rotation angle <0>:
Response: ↵

The floor plan should appear at a size that occupies most of the available drawing area on your C-size format. If you want the drawing to be smaller so there will be more room for dimensions, enter "U" from the keyboard to erase the drawing and reinsert it at a percentage of .0208 (¼″ = 1′). Now the appropriate scale may be placed in the title block and any other items in the title block may be changed to complete the drawing.

As stated in Chapter 7, all dimensioning of any drawing should be done at full-scale with DIMSCALE in effect so that dimensioning is very nearly automatic and reduction will not appreciably affect the size of dimensions and arrowheads. Any change in the size of arrowheads or text should be done on the full-size drawing.

To plot FP1 drawing:

Response: {Select} 3. Plot a drawing {from the Main Menu}.

Prompt: Enter NAME of drawing:
Response: FP1 ↵

Remember to precede the name of the drawing with the drive and directory if different from default drive.

Prompt: What to plot-Display, Extents, Limits, View, or Window:
Response: L ↵

The LIMITS response corresponds to the limits set when the plot was planned. The LIMITS setting is found on the SETTINGS Menu. Consult the AutoCAD manual chapters on plotting for an explanation of any of the other choices if they are not clear to you.

Prompt: Plot will NOT be written to a selected file.
Sizes are in Inches
Plot origin is at (0.00,0.00)
Plotting area is 15.75 wide by 11.20 high (MAX size)
Plot is NOT rotated 90 degrees
Pen width is 0.010
Area fill will be adjusted for pen width
Hidden lines will NOT be removed
Plot will be scaled to fit available area

Do you want to change anything? <N>:

Response: Y ↵

Prompt:

Entity Color	Pen No.	Line Type	Pen Speed	Entity Color	Pen No.	Line Type	Pen Speed
1 (red)	1	0	36	9	1	0	36
2 (yellow)	1	0	36	10	1	0	36
3 (green)	1	0	36	11	1	0	36
4 (cyan)	1	0	36	12	1	0	36
5 (blue)	1	0	36	13	1	0	36
6 (magenta)	1	0	36	14	1	0	36
7 (white)	1	0	36	15	1	0	36
8	1	0	36				

Line types
0 = continuous line
1 = ...
2 = ...
3 = ----------
4 = - - - - -

Do you want to change any of these parameters? <N>:

Response: Y ↵

Prompt:

Layer Color	Pen No.	Line Type	Pen Speed	
1 (red)	1	0	36	Pen Number <1>:

Response: C7 ↵

Prompt:

Layer Color	Pen No.	Line Type	Pen Speed	
7 (white)	1	0	36	Pen Number <1>:

Response: 2↵

Now all lines on all layers will be drawn with pen No. 1 except the lines on layer 7, which will be drawn with pen No. 2.

Note: *If you want to change the pen speed press* ↵ ↵.

Prompt:	Layer	Pen	Line	Pen	
	Color	No.	Type	Speed	
	7 (white)	2	0	36	Pen Number <1>:

Response: X ↵ {this allows you to exit from that sequence}

Prompt: Write the plot to a file? <N>:

Response: ↵ {no need to write it to a file}

Prompt: Size units (Inches or Millimeters) <I>:

Response: ↵ {the drawing was made in inches}

Prompt: Plot origin in Inches 0.00,0.00:

Response: ↵

The first 0.00 is the long side of the paper; the second 0.00 is the short side. You may have to play around with these numbers to make the plot fit your application. Usually –.5 to +.5 in both directions is the range for the plot origin.

Prompt: Standard values for plotting size

SIZE	WIDTH	HEIGHT
A	10.50	8.00
B	16.00	10.00
C	21.00	16.00
D	33.00	21.00
E	43.00	33.00
MAX	44.72	35.31
USER	8.00	11.00

These values may be abbreviated for your plotter.
Enter the Size or Width, Height (in units) <default>:

Response: 21,16 ↵ {or "C"—this produces a plot of a C-size sheet with a ½″ margin on all side}

Prompt: Rotate 2-D plots 90 degrees clockwise? <N>:

Response: ↵ {a response of Y would turn the plot 90°—a vertical C-size page}

Prompt: Pen width <0′ .010′ >: {this is used only on drawings which must be plotted very accurately—within .005″ or less}

Response: ↵

Prompt: Adjust area fill boundaries for pen width? <N>:

"No" is the correct response; "Yes" adjusts for the pen size entered in the response above.

Response: ↵

Prompt: Remove hidden lines? <N>:

This is used on 3-dimensional drawings.

Response: ↵

Prompt: Plotted Inches = Drawing Units or Fit or ? <F>:

Response: 1 = 1 {this will produce a full-size plot—F fits the plot into the plotting area and often results in a drawing not to scale; sometimes Fit is the appropriate response, which you can determine as the situation arises}

Prompt: Position paper in plotter.
Press RETURN to continue or S to Stop for hardware set up.

Load the paper and check the following to be sure that:

- the pens flow properly and are properly loaded in the carrousel,
- the carrousel is seated properly,
- settings on the plotter are set, and
- the switch box is set correctly if you have one.

Response: {Then press ↵ on the computer keyboard and the plot should proceed}

If the pens skip for any reason, leave the paper in the plotter and replot over the same plot after the pen problem is corrected.

EXERCISE 1

Create a horizontal A-size format and insert one of the drawings you created in Chapter 3 into it so it is well arranged in the center of the format. Change the information in the title block to:

    your school

    the current date

    Block Diagram No. 1 (for the title)

    your name in the "Drawn by" block

    any other changes requested by your instructor

EXERCISE 2

Create a C-size format. At a scale of $\frac{1}{4}'' = 1'$ insert one of the floor plans you created in Chapter 6. Place it in the center of the field of the drawing. Change the information in the title block to:

> your school
>
> the current date
>
> Floor Plan No. 1 (for the title)
>
> your name in the "Drawn by" block
>
> any other changes requested by your instructor

EXERCISE 3

Create a horizontal A-size format as shown in Figure 8-1.

- define variable attributes for title, drawing number, drawn by, next assembly, Rev, sheet __ of __, finish, material and company name (your school name should be the defualt value)
- WBLOCK the format using a name of your choice
- start a new drawing
- insert the new format and answer the prompts
- plot the drawing and submit it to your instructor

Test on Objectives—Chapter 8

Circle the correct answer.

1. Which of the following is *not* described as a standard sheet size by the AutoCAD Menu?
   a. $8\frac{1}{2} \times 11$ vertical
   b. $8\frac{1}{2} \times 11$ horizontal
   c. $8\frac{1}{2} \times 14$
   d. 11×17
   e. 17×22

2. Which of the following sheet sizes has both a vertical and horizontal format?
   a. $8\frac{1}{2} \times 11$
   b. 9×12
   c. $8\frac{1}{2} \times 14$
   d. 11×17
   e. 17×22

3. Why are the spaces in the format often filled in with x's or some other label that must be changed?

   a. changing is always faster than creating new text
   b. it ensures that labels are in the same place every time
   c. labels seldom require changes
   d. all of the above
   e. none of the above

4. Why was a single letter used for the format name?

   a. only one letter may be used for a format name
   b. less confusion results
   c. layers may be changed more easily
   d. less typing is required
   e. the title block has a single letter for the format size

5. To insert an existing drawing into a format on the screen, which of the following commands is used?

   a. INSERT
   b. BLOCK
   c. FORMAT
   d. DRAW
   e. CHANGE

6. Once a drawing is inserted into a format, which command must be used before the drawing can be changed?

   a. INSERT
   b. CHANGE
   c. EXPLODE
   d. MOVE
   e. ROTATE

7. When the drawing is inserted into a format labeled "C" and saved using a drawing number, the QUIT command is activated. What happens to the format drawing labeled "C"?

   a. it remains as it was before the drawing was inserted
   b. it remains as it was with the drawing in place
   c. both format and drawing are lost
   d. the format is lost
   e. none of the above

8. If a full-size drawing is to be inserted at a scale $\frac{1}{8}'' = 1'$, which of the following scale factors is used?

   a. .0104
   b. .0208
   c. .0312
   d. .0417
   e. .0625

9. If a full-size drawing is to be inserted at a scale of $1'' = 1'$, which of the following scale factors is used?
   a. .0104
   b. .0208
   c. .0312
   d. .0417
   e. .0833

10. After a drawing is inserted into a C-size format using a scale factor of $\frac{1}{4}'' = 1'$, which of the following is the correct *plotting* ratio?
    a. 1 = 48
    b. 48 = 1
    c. 1 = 24
    d. 24 = 1
    e. 1 = 1

11. List four standard sheet sizes.

    _____   _____

    _____   _____

12. List the command used to insert a drawing into the format.

    _____

13. List the command used to modify a block so that it may be changed.

    _____

14. Which scale factor should be used to insert a drawing at a scale of $\frac{1}{8}'' = 1'$?

    _____

15. Describe how a plotting ratio differs from an insert scale factor.

    _____

    _____

    _____

    _____

    _____

9

Sectional Drawings

Objectives

The student will use the HATCH command in conjunction with other draw and edit commands to produce:

■ sectional views of detail (single) parts

■ assemblies and walls

■ correctly answer questions regarding the use of the commands used to produce sectional views; these commands are:

HATCH	TRIM
BREAK	ARRAY
OSNAP	SCALE
ERASE	OFFSET
EXPLODE	STRETCH
COPY	SNAP (ROTATE)
EXTEND	

Use of Sectional Drawings

Sectional drawings are used to show the internal construction of parts (Figure 9-1), or external features that cannot be easily understood with external views (Figure 9-2). Sectional drawings are not only used to show someone how to make a part, but are also used to show someone how several parts function or how to assemble parts (Figure 9-3). The construction of sectional views is reviewed for your information in the following paragraphs. If you need further information regarding sectional views, consult any good technical drawing textbook.

Figure 9-1
Internal Construction

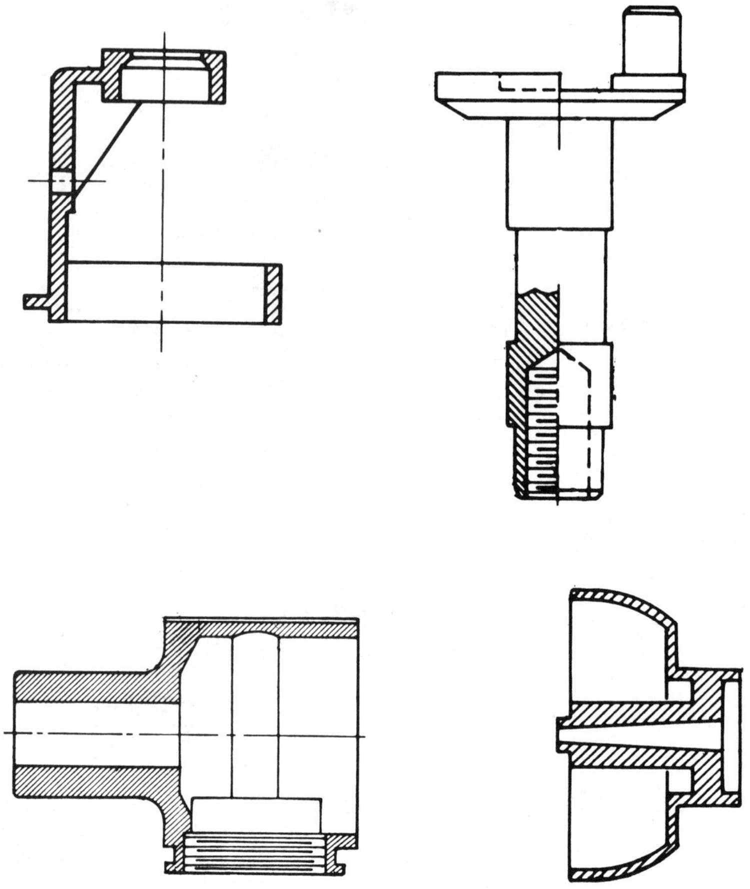

Figure 9-2
External Features
Shown in Section

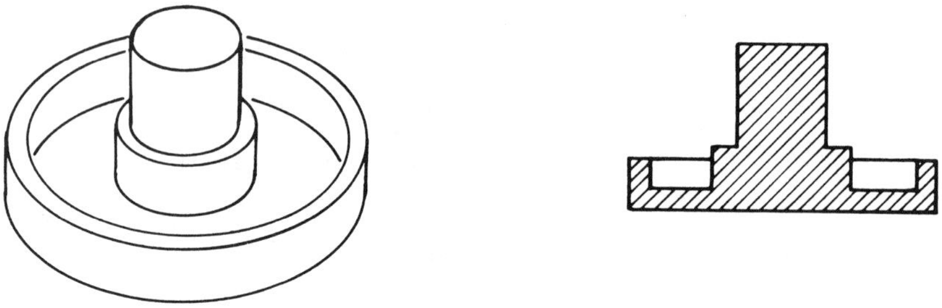

Constructing a Sectional View

Sectional views are easy to construct if you follow a simple series
of steps. These steps are shown in Figure 9-4. The object shown in
Figure 9-4 is a rather complex shape. Its features could be misunder-
stood if only external views were used. To clear up any misunderstand-
ing, a sectional view is chosen. To draw the sectional view:

Step 1. Decide which view would best show the hidden feature.
In your mind, cut off the part that is hiding the feature.

**Figure 9-3
Assembly Drawing**

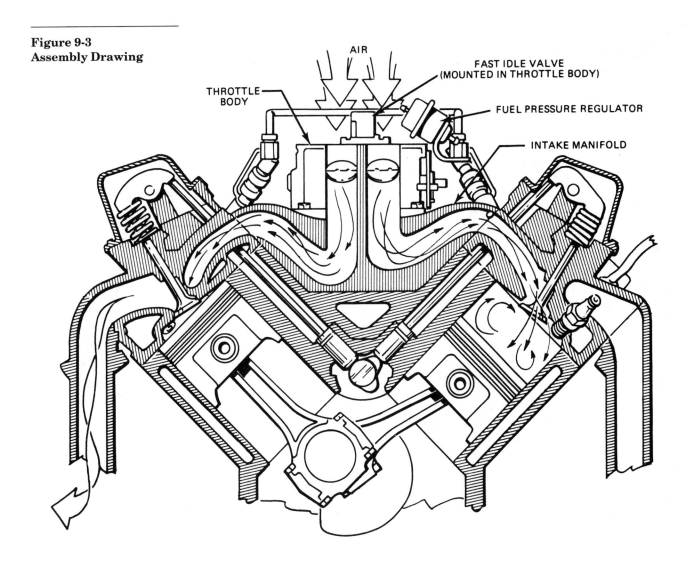

***Step 2. Throw away the part you cut off and do not think of it
again.***

Step 3. Look into the part that is left.

***Step 4. Draw the shape of what you see. Place the sectional view
in the standard view arrangement; for example, right side, left
side, top, bottom.***

   Occasionally, sections are placed away from the other views to
show details. Put section or crosshatch lines on the part that was cut.
You can think of putting saw marks on the part of the object that the
saw actually touched. Section lines are often drawn at a 45° angle and
are spaced approximately ⅙″ apart. They may be spaced wider apart

Figure 9-4
Constructing a
Sectional Drawing

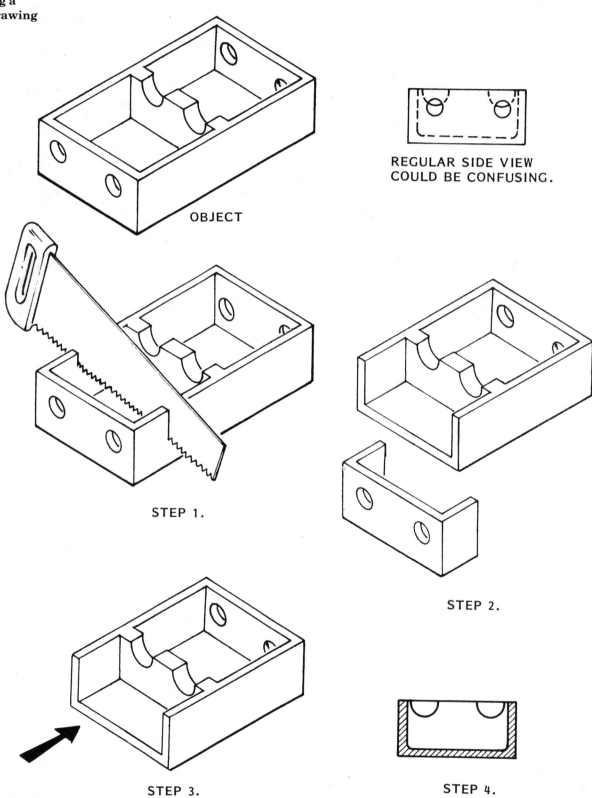

OBJECT

REGULAR SIDE VIEW
COULD BE CONFUSING.

STEP 1.

STEP 2.

STEP 3.

STEP 4.

Figure 9-5
Placing Hatch Patterns
on a Single Part

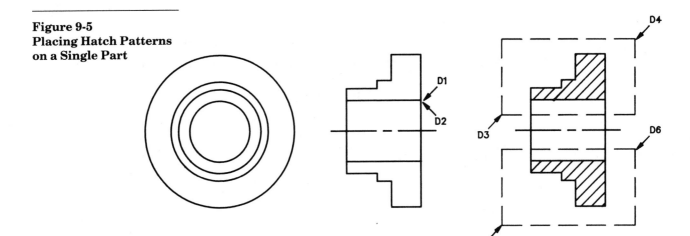

on very large drawings. Section lining in AutoCAD can take many forms. You will find these patterns in the *AutoCAD Reference Manual* index under "HATCH, Standard Patterns."

If you have Release 9, you will find slides showing the standard patterns under "?" on the pull-down HATCH Menu. In this chapter you will use these patterns:

U: the standard equally-spaced, solid lines

a curved line symbolizing wood

MUDST: a standard for symbolizing concrete

Begin by placing section lines on a single part. There are a few peculiarities of using the HATCH command that must be addressed. They will be covered as they occur.

To place hatch patterns on a single part:

The given drawing (Figure 9-5) contains a front view and a side view. The side view should be shown as a sectional view. (It will be to your advantage to place hatching on a different layer from the other lines of the drawing. Begin by creating a layer of another color of your choice and perform all hatching operations on that layer.) If the two views have already been drawn, it is often necessary to break some of the lines so the area to be hatched does not contain lines that extend outside of the area. To do this, use the BREAK command in this manner:

Prompt: Command:
Response: BREAK

Prompt: Select object:
Response: D1

Select the vertical line and the first point of the break. You may need to select the line at a point removed from the intersection, enter F, and then digitize both break points at the intersection.

Prompt: Enter second point (or F for first point):

Response: D2 {or select @ from the BREAK Menu—@ places the second point at the same place as the first point}

Be sure to perform the break on both vertical lines. After both areas to be hatched have been properly prepared, proceed as follows:

Prompt: Command:

Response: HATCH

Prompt: Pattern (? or Name/U, style)< >:

Response: U ↵

Prompt: Angle for crosshatch lines <0>:

Response: 45 ↵ {a 45° angle upward to the right}

Prompt: Spacing between lines <0>:

Response: .08 ↵ {a little less than 1/10″}

Prompt: Double hatch area? <N>:

Response: ↵ {or N if the default is Yes}

Prompt: Select objects:

Response: WINDOW {from the menu or W from the keyboard}

Prompt: First corner:

Response: D3

Prompt: Other corner:

Response: D4

The area forming the upper half of the view should be hatched now. Continue as follows:

Prompt: Command:

Response: ↵

This will activate the HATCH command again.

Prompt: Select objects:

Response: WINDOW

Prompt: First corner:

Response: D5

Prompt: Other corner:

Response: D6

Prompt: 8 found. Select objects:

Response: ⏎

Both top and bottom halves of the right side view should now be hatched to complete the figure. Now, place some of the same hatch pattern on an assembly section drawing, Figure 9-7.

To place hatch patterns on an assembly section drawing:

Step 1. Begin by breaking lines that will create patterns other than the ones required. Figure 9-6 shows the result of:

    a. not breaking either of the vertical lines 1 or 2 at the break point
    b. not breaking vertical line 1

Check all areas to be hatched as shown in Figure 9-7D. Each area to be hatched must be a complete boundary.

Note: *If you create a complex hatching, and a single line extends outside of the area, the hatch pattern may be exploded and the single hatch line may be erased or otherwise edited. The explode causes the hatch lines to take on the color white.*

You may change the color using the CHANGE command as follows:

Response: CHANGE

Prompt: Select objects:

Response: Select hatch pattern

Prompt: Properties/<Change Point>:

Response: {Select} COLOR {from the CHANGE Menu}

Prompt: New Color <BYBLOCK>:

Response: BYLAYER ⏎ ⏎

Then change hatch lines to the correct layer. Some examples of break points are shown at 9-7B.

Step 2. Place 45° hatch lines upward to the right.

Prompt: Command:

Response: HATCH

**Figure 9-6
Results of Lines
Extending Outside of the
Area to be Hatched**

**Figure 9-7
Placing Hatch Patterns
on an Assembly Section
Drawing**

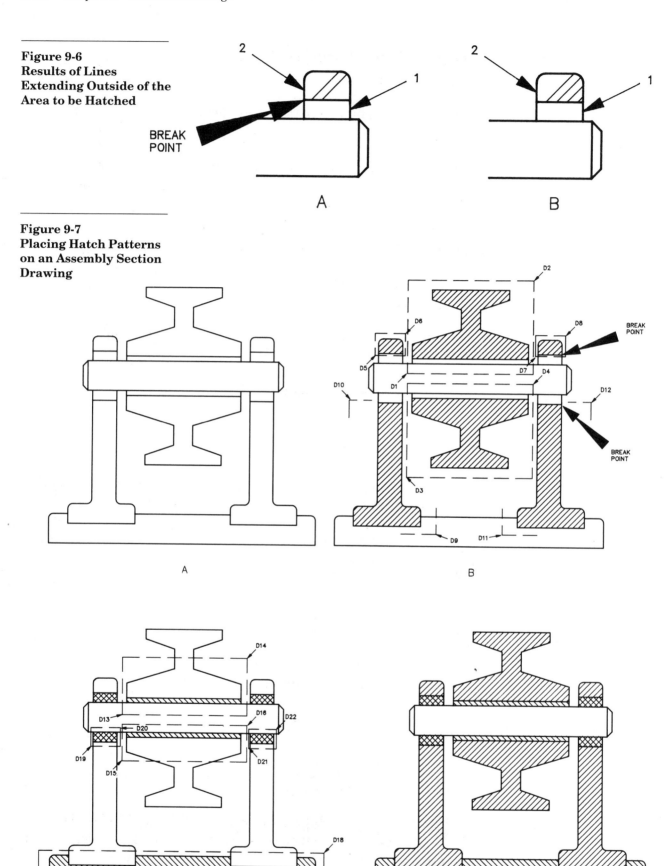

Prompt: Pattern (? or name/U, style) < >:
Response: U ↵

Prompt: Angle for crosshatch lines <45>:
Response: ↵ {or 45 if the default is other than 45}

Prompt: Spacing between lines <0.08>:
Response: ↵ {or .08 if the default is other than .08}

Prompt: Double hatch area? <N>:
Response: ↵ {or N if the default is Yes}

Prompt: Select objects:
Response: WINDOW

Prompt: First corner:
Response: D1

Prompt: Other corner:
Response: D2

Prompt: Select objects:
Response: W ↵

Prompt: First corner:
Response: D3

Prompt: Other corner:
Response: D4

Prompt: Select objects:
Response: WINDOW

Prompt: First corner:
Response: D5

Prompt: Other corner:
Response: D6

Prompt: Select objects:

Continue selecting objects with windows D7–D8, D9–D10, D11–D12. All hatching should appear as shown in Figure 9-7B. Now, hatch the parts shown in Figure 9-7C.

Step 3. Place 45° hatch lines upward to the left.

Prompt: Command:

Response: HATCH

Prompt: Pattern (? or name/U, style) <U>:

Response: ↵ {or U if U is not the default}

Prompt: Angle for crosshatch lines <45>:

Response: −45 {or 135}

Prompt: Spacing between lines (0.08):

Response: ↵ {or .08 if this spacing is not the default}

Prompt: Double hatch area? <N>:

Response: ↵

Prompt: Select objects:

Response: WINDOW

Prompt: First corner:

Response: D13

Prompt: Other corner:

Response: D14

Prompt: Select objects:

Response: WINDOW

Prompt: First corner:

Response: D15

Prompt: Other corner:

Response: D16

Prompt: Select objects:

Response: WINDOW

Prompt: First corner:

Response: D17

Prompt: Other corner:

Response: D18

Prompt: Select objects:

Response: ↵

Step 4. Place double hatch patterns on areas indicated in Figure 9-7C.

Prompt: Command:

Response: HATCH

Prompt: Pattern (? or name/U, style) (U):

Response: ↵

Prompt: Angle for crosshatch lines <135>:

Response: ↵

Prompt: Spacing between lines (0.08):

Response: ↵

Prompt: Double hatch area? <N>:

Response: Y {or yes from the menu}

Prompt: Select objects:

Response: WINDOW

Prompt: First corner:

Response: D19

Prompt: Other corner:

Response: D20

Prompt: Select objects:

Response: WINDOW

Prompt: First corner:

Response: D21

Prompt: Other corner:

Response: D22

Continue to select objects using windows for the other areas to be double-hatched.

The complete drawing should now appear with hatching as shown in Figure 9-7D. Now, make an architectural wall section as shown in Figure 9-8.

Figure 9-8
Wall Section

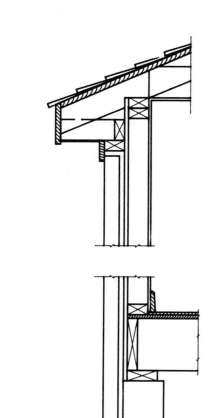

Figure 9-9
Measurements of the
Wall Section

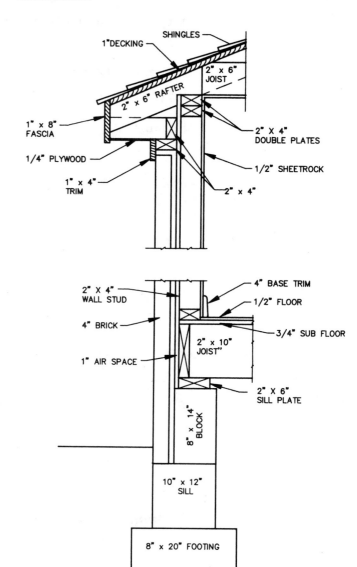

To draw a wall section (Figure 9-8):

Step 1. Draw the wall without hatching.

Wall sections are often drawn at a scale of 1″ = 1′. To do this, begin a new drawing and follow this sequence:

Prompt: Command:
Response: SETUP

Prompt: Select the units from the screen menu:
Response: Architectural

**Figure 9-10
Draw Some
Components
Separately**

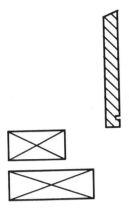

Prompt: Select the scale from the screen menu:

Response: 1″ = 1′

Prompt: Select the paper size from the screen menu:

Response: VERTICAL
8.5 × 11

Now you are ready to begin the drawing. Draw all of the wall section components using the dimensions shown in Figure 9-9. Drawing some of the components separately as shown in Figure 9-10, and copying or moving them into place will be helpful. You will have to approximate the length of some of the components. As long as the drawing looks the same as Figure 9-8 it will be fine for this exercise. After the drawing has been completed, begin hatching as shown in Figure 9-11.

Step 2. Hatch footing, sill, and the ground (Figure 9-11).

Begin hatching by making sure all lines extending outside of the area to be hatched are broken in the right spot. Then follow this sequence:

**Figure 9-11
MUDST Hatching**

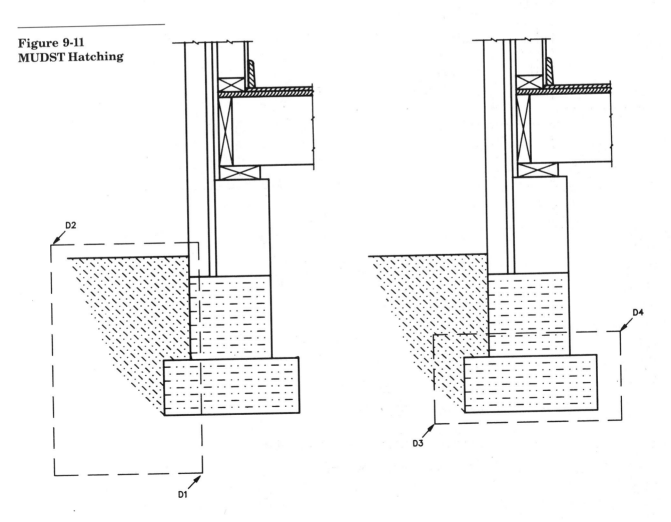

Prompt: Command:
Response: HATCH

Prompt: Pattern (? or name/U, Style (U):
Response: MUDST ↵

Prompt: Scale for pattern <1.0000>:
Response: 12 ↵ {because the scale is 1″ = 1′}

Prompt: Angle for pattern <0>:
Response: 135 ↵

Prompt: Select objects:
Response: WINDOW

Prompt: First corner:
Response: D1

Prompt: Second corner:
Response: D2

Prompt: Select objects:
Response: ↵

Prompt: Command:
Response: ↵

Prompt: Pattern (? or name/U, style (MUDST):
Response: ↵

Prompt: Scale for pattern <12.0000>:
Response: ↵

Prompt: Angle for pattern <135>:
Response: 0 ↵

Prompt: Select objects:
Response: WINDOW

Prompt: First corner:
Response: D3

Prompt: Other corner:
Response: D4

Figure 9-12
Creating a Wood Pattern

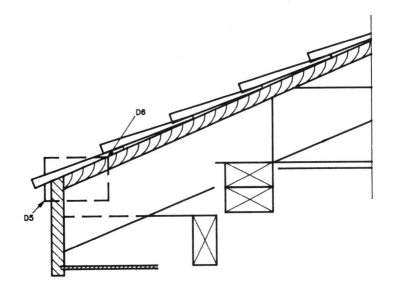

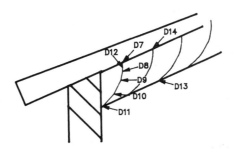

Prompt: Select objects:

Response: {Window the area labeled "10 × 12″ sill" above the footing to give it the same hatch pattern.}

Step 3. Hatch areas using the 45° "U" pattern.

The fascia, 1 × 4″ trim, 4″ base trim, floor, and subfloor may all be hatched using the standard 45° or 135° U pattern as shown in Figures 9-8, and 9-9. Use the same sequence of steps as you used to complete parts of Figure 9-7.

Step 4. Hatch the 1″ decking directly under the shingles (Figure 9-12).

Occasionally it may become necessary to create a different pattern from the standard ones available. Custom patterns may be created as described in the Appendix of the *AutoCAD Reference Manual*. These custom patterns must be made up of straight line segments, however. To create a wood grain such as the one shown in Figure 9-12 the PLINE command was used. The sequence is:

To enlarge an area for creating the pattern:

Prompt: Command:

Response: ZOOM

Prompt: All/Center/Dynamic/Extents/Left/Previous/Window/
<Scale(x)>:

Response: WINDOW

Prompt: First corner:

Response: D5

Prompt: Other corner:

Response: D6

Use PLINE to draw straight line segments.

Prompt: Command:

Response: PLINE {from the DRAW Menu}

Prompt: From point: {refer to Figure 9-12}

Response: D7

Prompt: Arc/Close/Halfwidth/Length/Undo/Width/
<Endpoint of line>:

Response: D8

Prompt: Arc/Close/Halfwidth/Length/Undo/Width/
<Endpoint of line>:

Response: D9

Prompt: Arc/Close/Halfwidth/Length/Undo/Width/
<Endpoint of line>:

Response: D10

Prompt: Arc/Close/Halfwidth/Length/Undo/Width/
<Endpoint of line>:

Response: D11

Prompt: Arc/Close/Halfwidth/Length/Undo/Width/
<Endpoint of line>:

Response: ↵

Prompt: Command:

Response: PEDIT {from the second display of the EDIT Menu}

Use PEDIT to make curved lines.

Prompt: Pedit select polyline:

Response: D12

Prompt: Close/Join/Width/Edit vertex/Fit curve/Decurve/Undo/ exit/<x>:

Response: Fit curve

Prompt: Close/Join/Width/Edit vertex/Fit curve/Decurve/Undo/ exit/<x>:

Response: ↵

Rotate the GRID to create an angular GRID.

Prompt: Command:

Response: SNAP {from the SETTINGS Menu second display}

Prompt: SNAP spacing or ON/OFF/Aspect/Rotate/style <0′–0¼″>:

Response: ROTATE

Prompt: Rotate Base point <----------->:

Response: D11 {again}

Prompt: Rotation angle <0>:

Response: D13

Prompt: Command:

Response: ARRAY {EDIT Menu}

Array the PLINE to form the wood pattern.

Prompt: Select objects:

Response: D12 {again}

Prompt: Rectangular or Polar array (R/P):

Response: R ↵

Prompt: Number of rows (---) <1>:

Response: ↵ {or 1 if the default is not 1}

Prompt: Number of columns (111) <1>:

Response: 30

This may be too many or too few, so choose the number of lines you think you need to fill the area. If you choose more than enough you can erase those you don't need.

Prompt: Distance between columns (111):
Response: D7 {again}

Prompt: Second point:
Response: D14

You should now have a wall section complete with hatching. These exercises and the *AutoCAD Reference Manual* will give you the information and skills you need to render any type of sectional view. Now complete the exercises and the quiz at the end of this chapter.

EXERCISE 1

Begin a new drawing and call it 9-1-(your initials). Measure the drawing from your book shown as Figure 9-5. Draw it twice-size on an $8\frac{1}{2} \times 11''$ horizontal format. Complete the title block:

Title: Pipe Flange
Drawing Number: 100324
NEXT ASSEMBLY NUMBER: 101352

Create the following layers (if they do not already exist on your drawing format):

O   White   for object lines-border and title block
Y   Yellow   for text (lettering in the title block)
D   Green   for section lines (hatching and center lines)

Hatch the drawing as described in Figure 9-5. Plot the drawing on a horizontal $11 \times 8.5''$ sheet.

EXERCISE 2

Begin a new drawing and call it 9-2-(your initials). Measure the drawing from your book shown as Figure 9-7A. Draw it twice-size on an $8\frac{1}{2} \times 11''$ horizontal format. Complete the title block:

Title: Shaft Support Assembly
DRAWING NUMBER: 10925
NEXT ASSEMBLY NUMBER: 200100

Create the following layers:

O   White   for object lines, border, and title

Y   Yellow   for text

G   Green   for section lines and center lines

Hatch the drawing as described in Figure 9-7. Plot the drawing on a horizontal 11 × 8.5″ sheet.

EXERCISE 3

Begin a new drawing and name it 9-3-(your initials). Using the information given in Figure 9-9, draw Figure 9-9 at a scale of 1″ = 1′. Draw this figure on a vertical 11 × 8.5″ sheet. Create the following layers:

O   White   for object lines

Y   Yellow   for text

G   Green   for hatching and any other thin lines

Hatch the drawing as described in Figures 9-9 through 9-12. Plot the drawing on a vertical 11 × 8.5″ sheet.

Exercise 4

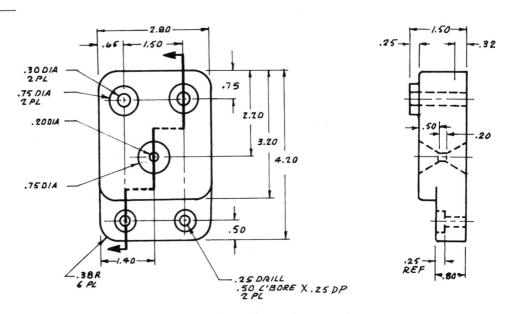

EXERCISE 4

Begin a new drawing and name it 9-4-(your initials). Draw the figure for this exercise full-size in an 11 × 8.5″ format. Draw a front view and a right side view. Make the right side a sectional view. Plot the drawing on a horizontal 11 × 8.5″ sheet.

Exercise 5

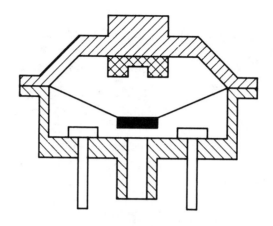

EXERCISE 5

Begin a new drawing and name it 9-5-(your initials). Measure the figure for this exercise and draw it twice-size on a vertical $11 \times 8.5''$ sheet. Use hatching as shown. Create the following layers:

O	White	for object
Y	Yellow	for text
G	Green	for hatching and leader lines

Plot the drawing on a vertical $11 \times 8.5''$ sheet.

EXERCISES 6, 7, AND 8

Double the dimensions given and make sectional drawings of the following figures. Draw all views and insert the drawing into your A-size horizontal format. Do not show dimensions. (Upper numbers are in inches; lower numbers are in millimeters.)

Exercise 6

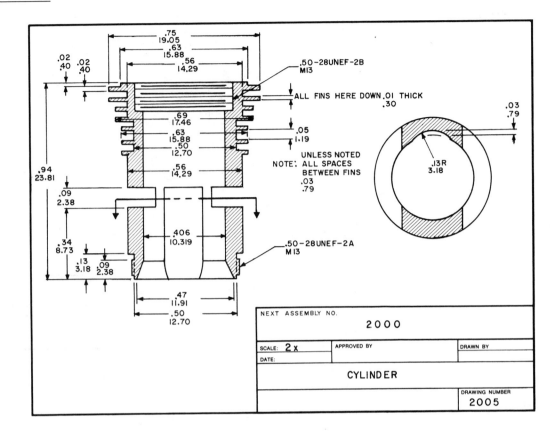

	NEXT ASSEMBLY NO.	
		2000

SCALE: 2x	APPROVED BY	DRAWN BY
DATE:		

CYLINDER

	DRAWING NUMBER
	2005

Exercise 7

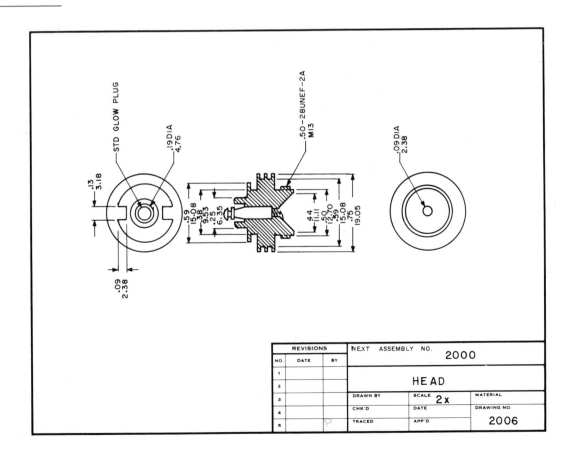

REVISIONS			NEXT ASSEMBLY NO.	2000
NO.	DATE	BY		
1				
2			HEAD	
3			DRAWN BY	SCALE 2x	MATERIAL
4			CHK'D	DATE	DRAWING NO.
5			TRACED	APP'D	2006

Exercise 8

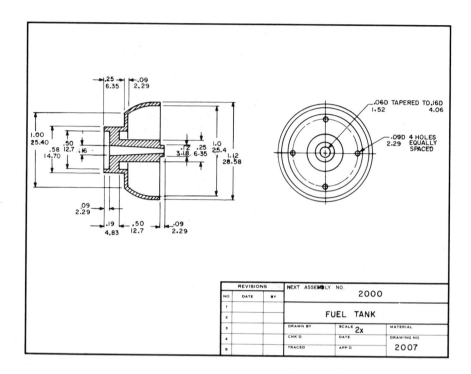

Exercise 9

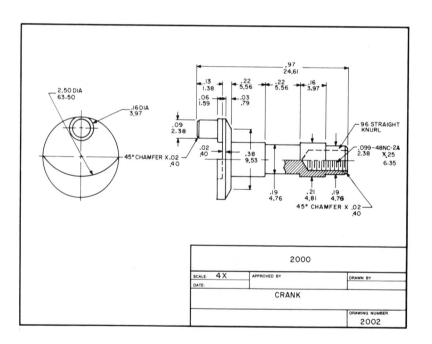

EXERCISE 9

Make a sectional drawing of the crank shown above. Draw all given views and insert the drawing into a horizontal A-size format. Make the drawing 4 times the dimensions shown. Do not show dimensions. (Upper numbers are in inches; lower numbers are in millimeters.)

Exercise 10

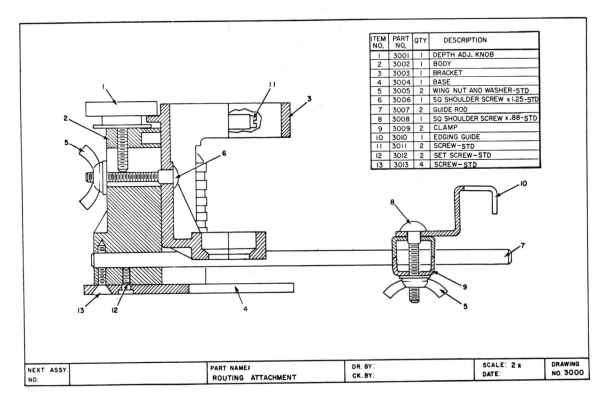

ITEM NO.	PART NO.	QTY	DESCRIPTION
1	3001	1	DEPTH ADJ. KNOB
2	3002	1	BODY
3	3003	1	BRACKET
4	3004	1	BASE
5	3005	2	WING NUT AND WASHER-STD
6	3006	1	SQ SHOULDER SCREW x 1.25-STD
7	3007	2	GUIDE ROD
8	3008	1	SQ SHOULDER SCREW x .88-STD
9	3009	2	CLAMP
10	3010	1	EDGING GUIDE
11	3011	2	SCREW-STD
12	3012	2	SET SCREW-STD
13	3013	4	SCREW-STD

NEXT ASSY. NO.		PART NAME: ROUTING ATTACHMENT	DR. BY: CK. BY:	SCALE: 2 x DATE:	DRAWING NO. 3000

EXERCISE 10

Make an AutoCAD drawing of the assembly section shown. Measure the drawing and make your drawing as near as possible to the same size. Show a parts list on the drawing and draw leaders and index numbers as shown. Your lettering should be simplex, .08″ high. Place it on a horizontal A-size format.

Exercise 11

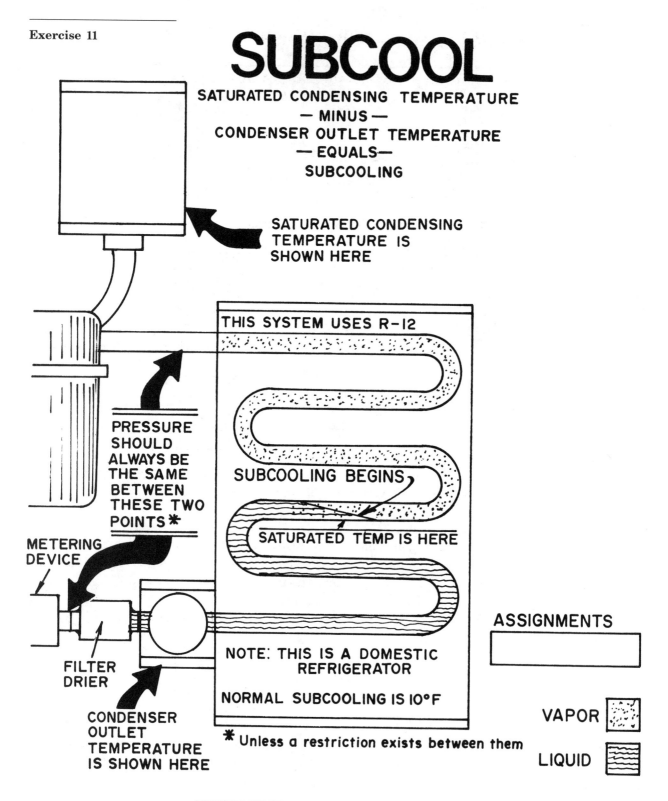

SUBCOOL

SATURATED CONDENSING TEMPERATURE
— MINUS —
CONDENSER OUTLET TEMPERATURE
—EQUALS—
SUBCOOLING

SATURATED CONDENSING
TEMPERATURE IS
SHOWN HERE

THIS SYSTEM USES R-12

PRESSURE
SHOULD
ALWAYS BE
THE SAME
BETWEEN
THESE TWO
POINTS *

SUBCOOLING BEGINS

SATURATED TEMP IS HERE

METERING
DEVICE

FILTER
DRIER

CONDENSER
OUTLET
TEMPERATURE
IS SHOWN HERE

NOTE: THIS IS A DOMESTIC
REFRIGERATOR

NORMAL SUBCOOLING IS 10°F

* Unless a restriction exists between them

ASSIGNMENTS

VAPOR

LIQUID

EXERCISE 11

Make an AutoCAD drawing of the diagram shown above. Use hatch
patterns that are similar to the shaded areas. Make lettering as near
as possible to the size shown. Place the drawing on a vertical A-size
sheet. Place your name in the lower right corner.

Test on Objectives—Chapter 9

1. Which of the following patterns produces continuous, evenly spaced lines?
   a. U
   b. MUDST
   c. PAT LINE
   d. U-LINE
   e. LINE

2. Which of the following angles produces the pattern shown below?
   a. 45
   b. 90
   c. 0
   d. 135
   e. 105

3. Which of the following angles produces the pattern shown below?
   a. 45
   b. 90
   c. 0
   d. 135
   e. 105

4. Which of the following commands can be used to correct an overlapping hatching pattern?
   a. ARRAY
   b. CHANGE
   c. MOVE
   d. TRIM
   e. BREAK

5. Which of the following describes the pattern shown below?
   a. X PAT
   b. 45, 145
   c. DOUBLE HATCH
   d. DOUBLE SECTION
   e. LINE - TWO

6. Which of the following responses to the "spacing between lines" prompt will produce HATCH lines ¼″ apart?
   a. 1-4
   b. .25
   c. 2.5
   d. 1,4
   e. 25

7. After a hatching command which spaced lines .10″ apart has been performed, what is the default response to the "spacing between lines:" prompt (original default was .08)?

    a. 0

    b. .10

    c. .08

    d. .125

    e. .06

8. Which of the following responses to the "spacing between lines" prompt will produce lines approximately $\frac{1}{12}$″ apart when the drawing is done at a scale of 1″ = 1′?

    a. 1-12

    b. $\frac{1}{12}$

    c. 1

    d. .085

    e. .12

9. Which of the following is used to make straight angular PLINES into a smooth curve?

    a. decurve

    b. edit vertex

    c. curve

    d. fit curve

    e. join

10. Which of the following SNAP responses will allow a Rectangular ARRAY to be produced at an angle?

    a. STYLE

    b. ROTATE

    c. ASPECT

    d. SPACING

    e. RECT – ANG

11. Write the correct name of the following pattern on the line beneath it.

_____

12. How may the standard patterns of the HATCH command be called up on the screen?

_____

_____

13. Correctly label the pattern below on the line beneath it showing pattern, angle, and spacing at full-scale.

Pattern _____ Angle _____ Spacing _____

14. Correctly label the pattern below on the line beneath it showing pattern, angle, and spacing at full-scale.

Pattern _____ Angle _____ Spacing _____

15. How may an overlapping hatch pattern be corrected?

_____

16. How may two lines of a 35 line hatch pattern be erased?

_____

17. How may all of the lines of a 35 line hatch pattern be erased?

_____

18. How may an array of a PLINE be produced at a 37° angle?

_____

19. Correctly list 7 modifiers for the PEDIT command.

_____   _____

_____   _____

_____   _____

_____

20. What HATCH spacing occurs when a response of .08 is given to "spacing between lines" if the drawing is being made at a scale of 1″ = 1′.

_____

10

Isometric Drawings and AutoCAD 3D

Objectives

The student will:

■ make isometric drawings to scale from two-dimensional drawings

■ correctly answer questions regarding the following commands:

ARRAY	CHANGE
POLYGON	EXPLODE
BLOCK	TOGGLE
ISOPLANE	ZOOM DYNAMIC
ELLIPSE	BREAK
SNAP STYLE	ELEVATION
OSNAP	VPOINT
LAYER SET	

■ produce three-dimensional drawings, which may be viewed from any angle

Isometric Drawing Settings

Isometric drawings can be done quickly and easily using AutoCAD software. Once the GRID and SNAP settings are properly made, the drawing itself proceeds with little difficulty. The three isometric axes are 30° right, 30° left, and vertical. All measurements are made full-scale on all three axes.

Preparation

We will begin with a simple rectangle so you become familiar with drawing lines on an isometric axis. With SNAP and GRID function keys ON, set the GRID and SNAP for isometric drawing as follows:

Prompt: Command:
Response: SNAP {from the SETTINGS Menu}

Prompt: Snap spacing or ON/OFF/Rotate/Style <0.0000>:
Response: S ↵ {from the keyboard or STYLE from the menu}

Prompt: Standard/Isometric <I>:
Response: I ↵ {from the keyboard or ISO from the menu}

Prompt: Iso vertical spacing <1.0000>:
Response: .125 ↵

This is a good SNAP spacing. You may choose to use .1 or another convenient SNAP spacing.

Prompt: Command:
Response: GRID

Prompt: GRID Spacing (X) or ON/OFF/Snap <0.1250>:
Response: .25 ↵

The isometric grid should appear. You may now get control of the plane (or surface) which you will be working. To do this press the "CONTROL" and the "E" keys on your keyboard simultaneously so that you "toggle" from the left, right, and top isometric planes. Now you are ready to draw the shape shown in Figure 10-1. With the cursor for the isometric plane in the position shown in Figure 10-1 follow this sequence:

To draw an isometric rectangle measuring 1″ × 2″ × 1″ (Figure 10-1):

Step 1. Draw the right plane.

Prompt: Command:
Response: LINE

Prompt: From point:
Response: D1

Figure 10-1
Isometric Rectangle

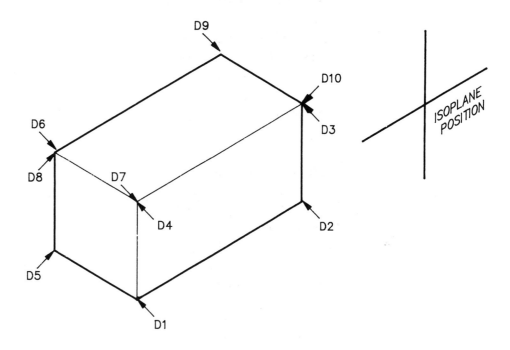

Prompt: To point:

Response: D2 {move eight .25 spaces upward to the right or @2<30↵ }

Prompt: To point:

Response: D3 {to move four .25 spaces upward or @1<90↵ }

Prompt: To point:

Response: D4 {move eight .25 spaces downward to the left or @2<210↵ }

Prompt: To point:

Response: C ↵ {from the keyboard}

You have drawn the right plane. You may leave the isometric plane the same to finish the rectangle, or you may toggle to the left plane.

Step 2. Draw the left plane.

Prompt: Command:

Response: LINE

Prompt: From point:

Response: ↵ {notice that the beginning point for this line is the endpoint of the last line you drew}

Prompt: To point:

Response: D5

Prompt: To point:

Response: D6

Prompt: To point:

Response: D7 ↵

Step 3. Draw the top plane.

Prompt: Command:

Response: ↵

Prompt: Line from point:

Response: D8

Prompt: To point:

Response: D9

Prompt: To point:

Response: D10 ↵

You have now drawn your first isometric rectangle on AutoCAD. To provide some variety in line weights, you may wish to change the inside lines to another layer, for example: a layer named G, color green. You may then use one pen to plot the outside lines and another thinner pen to plot the inside lines as Figure 10-1 shows. To do this make a new layer called G, color it green and use the change command to change the inside lines to the G layer.

The next problem is to draw an 1½″ isometric cube with a 1″ ellipse on each surface. This will introduce you to the standard isometric planes with which you must be very familiar to be successful with isometric drawing.

To draw a 1″ isometric cube with a 1″ ellipse on each surface (Figure 10-2):

Step 1. Draw the left plane (A).

Prompt: Command:

Response: LINE

Prompt: From point:

Response: D1

**Figure 10-2
Drawing the
Isometric Cube**

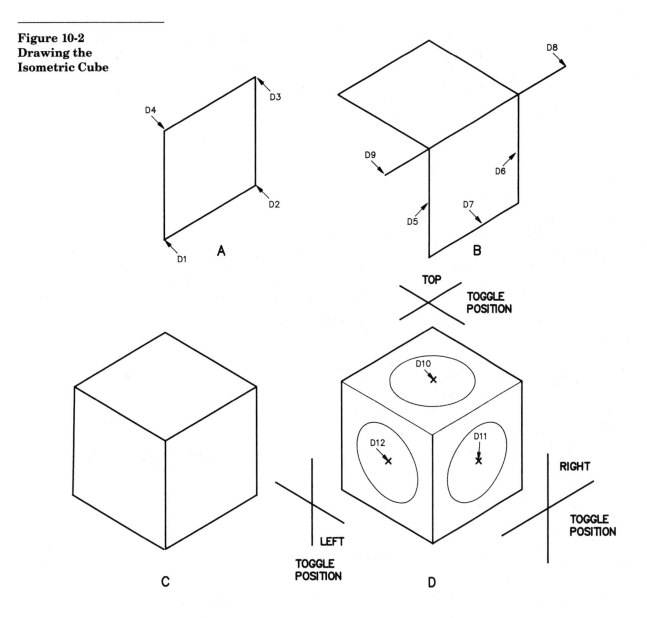

Prompt: To point:
Response: D2

Prompt: To point:
Response: D3

Prompt: To point:
Response: D4

Prompt: To point:
Response: C ↵

Step 2. Draw the top plane (B) and the left plane (C).

Now do something a little different.

Prompt: Command:
Response: MIRROR

Prompt: Select objects:
Response: D5, D6, D7 ↵

Prompt: First point of mirror line:
Response: D8

Prompt: Second point:
Response: D9

Prompt: Delete old objects: <N>
Response: ↵

You should have the figure shown at B in Figure 10-2. To draw the other face, you may use either MIRROR with a vertical mirror line or the LINE command.

Once you have the figure shown as C in Figure 10-2, you are ready to draw ellipses in these cube surfaces. To do this, use Ctrl-E to toggle to the top surface as shown at D. Follow these steps:

Step 3. Draw ellipses.

Prompt: Command:
Response: ELLIPSE

Prompt: <Axis endpoint 1>/Center/Isocircle:
Response: I ↵ {from the keyboard or ISO from the menu}

Prompt: Center of circle:
Response: D10

Prompt: <Circle radius>/Diameter:
Response: .5 ↵ {it defaults to radius}

Prompt: Command:

Now toggle using Ctrl-E to the right isometric plane.

Response: ELLIPSE

Prompt: <Axis endpoint 1>/Center/Isocircle:
Response: I ↵

Prompt: Center of circle:
Response: D11

Prompt: <Circle radius>/Diameter:
Response: .5 ↵

Prompt: Command:

Now toggle to the left isometric plane.

Response: ELLIPSE

Prompt: <Axis endpoint 1>/Center/Isocircle:
Response: I ↵

Prompt: Center of circle:
Response: D12

Prompt: <Circle radius>/Diameter:
Response: .5 ↵

Take a few minutes to study the position of the ellipses on the isometric planes. These positions are the same for all normal (perpendicular) surfaces and must not be rotated in any direction. Remember where Figure 10-2 is in case you need to return to it to refresh your memory later.

Now turn to Figure 10-3 and observe how to draw a slightly more complex part.

To draw an isometric view of a part from a two-dimensional drawing:

Be sure SNAP (F9) is ON, ORTHO is OFF, and the toggle and cursor are in the correct isometric plane (Figure 10-3).

Step 1. Draw the front surface (A).

Prompt: Command:
Response: LINE

Prompt: From point:
Response: D1

Figure 10-3
Drawing a Complex
Isometric Shape

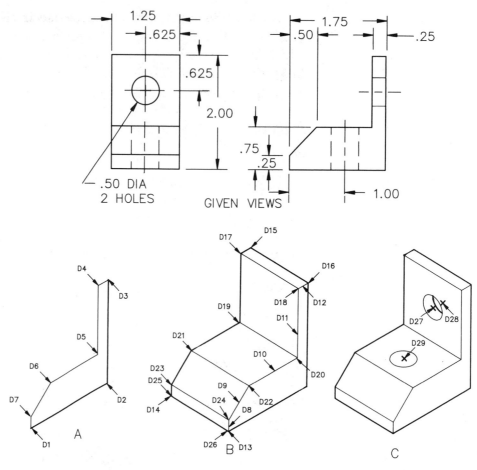

Prompt: To point:

Response: D2 {count seven ¼″ spaces (1.75 or 1¾″) on the 30°
isometric axis upward to the right or @1.75 < 30} ↵

Prompt: To point:

Response: D3 {count eight ¼″ spaces (2.00″) on the vertical axis or
@2 < 90} ↵

Prompt: To point:

Response: D4 {count one ¼″ space downward on the 30° isometric
axis to the left or @.25 < 210 (210 is 180 + 30)} ↵

Prompt: To point:

Response: D5 {count five ¼″ spaces downward on the vertical axis or
@1.25 < –90 (or 270)} ↵

Prompt: To point:

Response: D6 {count four ¼″ spaces downward on the 30 isometric
axis to the left or @1 < 210} ↵

Prompt: To point:

Response: D7

Now you have a problem because this angle cannot be identified easily on an isometric drawing; therefore, the other end of the angle, which is .25 upward on the vertical axis from D1, must be located. Find that point and D7. The angle can be identified by using LIST from the INQUIRY Menu, but you do not need that information now.

Prompt: To point:

Response: C ↵

Since you have already put some time into drawing the front surface, copy appears to be a good approach to drawing the identical back plane. To do this:

Step 2. Draw back surface (Figure 10-3 B).

Prompt: Command:

Response: COPY

Prompt: Select objects:

Response: D8 D9 D10 D11 D12 ↵ {or window the area}

Prompt: <Base point or displacement>/Multiple:

Response: D13

Prompt: Second point of displacement:

Response: D14
Count five ¼ ″ spaces on the 30° isometric axes upward to the left, or @1.25 < 150 ↵

Step 3. Connect the front and back surfaces.

With the SNAP ON (ORTHO OFF), lines will be cleanly drawn to the correct points so no cleanup is necessary.

Prompt: Command:

Response: LINE:

Prompt: From point:

Response: D15

Prompt: To point:

Response: D16 ↵

Prompt: Command:

Response: LINE

Repeat the above for lines D17–18, D19–20, D21–22, D23–24, and D25–26; or copy the line in four places using multiple.

Step 4. Draw the holes (Figure 10-3 C).

To complete this figure you must draw three ellipses, apply any finishing touches such as varying line weights, and clean up any excess lines. To draw the ellipses:

Prompt: Command:
Response: ELLIPSE

Prompt: <Axis endpoint 1>/Center/Isocircle:
Response: ISO

Be sure to toggle to the left isoplane.

Prompt: Center of circle:
Response: D27

Prompt: <Circle radius>/Diameter:
Response: .25 ↵ {the radius of the .5 diameter circles}

Prompt: Command:
Response: ELLIPSE

Prompt: <Axis endpoint 1> Center/Isocircle:
Response: ISO

Prompt: Center of circle:
Response: D28

Move one GRID space back on the 30° axis to the right.

Prompt: <Circle radius>/Diameter:
Response: .25 ↵

Prompt: Command:
Response: ELLIPSE

Prompt: <Axis endpoint1> Center/Isocircle:
Response: ISO

Be sure to toggle to the top isoplane.

Prompt: Center of circle:
Response: D29

Prompt: <Circle radius>/Diameter:
Response: .25 ↵

Figure 10-4
Drawing an Isometric
Hexagonal Head Bolt

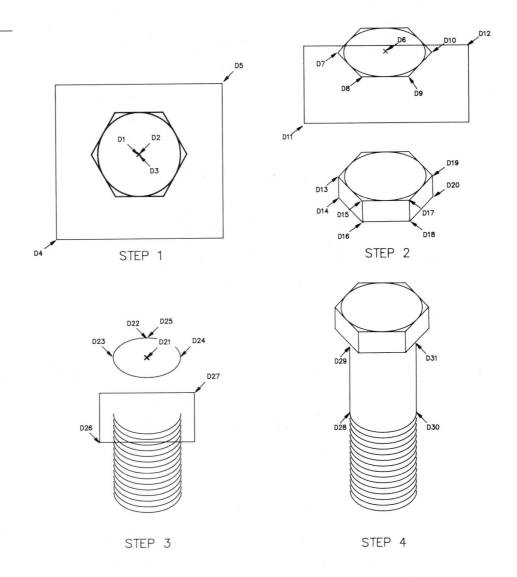

STEP 1

STEP 2

STEP 3

STEP 4

Prompt: Command:

Now use TRIM to get rid of the back part of the ellipse formed from the D28 digitize, select TRIM, crossing, window the entire area, press Enter, and select the unwanted portion. You may also wish to change the interior lines to a different layer from the outside lines as the last step in Figure 10-3 shows. Use the CHANGE command and digitize those lines you want to move to another layer. Then pick LAYER from the menu for property.

To draw an isometric hexagonal head bolt (Figure 10-4):

Some of the commonly used parts in many manufacturing firms are bolts, screws, and other threaded fasteners (Figure 10-4).

This part, once drawn, can be scaled up or down, modified, and rotated to fit into many different illustrations. The isometric hexagon on the top of the bolt is somewhat complicated by the fact that as a "block" it may not be exploded so that it may be changed. There is a way around that, however, which is described in the following paragraphs.

To allow this bolt to be drawn as simply as possible, make the threads of the bolt 1″ in diameter and the hexagonal head 1½″ (1.50) in diameter. Start with the hexagonal head.

Step 1. Draw the isometric hexagonal head.

Prompt: Command:
Response: POLYGON {from the DRAW Menu}

Prompt: Number of sides:
Response: 6 ↵

Prompt: Edge/<Center of polygon>:
Response: D1

Prompt: Inscribed in circle/Circumscribed about circle (I/C):
Response: C ↵ {from the keyboard or C-SCRIBE from the menu}

Prompt: Radius of circle:
Response: .75 ↵

Prompt: Command:
Response: CEN,RAD: {from the DRAW-CIRCLE Menu}

Prompt: Circle 3P/2P/TTR/<Center point>:
Response: D2 {same spot as D1}

Prompt: Diameter/<Radius>: DRAG
Response: .75 ↵

Step 2. Change the hexagonal head to isometric.

Now you have a hexagon circumscribed about a 1½″ diameter circle. You must now block it and bring it back into the drawing as an isometric hexagonal shape. Follow these steps:

Prompt: Command:
Response: BLOCK {from the BLOCKS Menu}

Prompt: Block name (or?):
Response: IH {or whatever you wish to name it using 8 characters or less with no spaces}

Keep all names (blocks, layers, colors, etc.) as short as possible to reduce the amount of typing required.

Prompt: Insertion base point:

Response: D3 {same spot as D1 and D2}

Prompt: Select objects:

Response: WINDOW {from the BLOCK Menu or W ↵ from the keyboard}

Prompt: First Corner:

Response: D4

Prompt: Other corner:

Response: D5

Prompt: 3 found-select objects:

Response: ↵

Prompt: Command:

Response: INSERT

Prompt: Block name (or?):

Response: IH ↵

Prompt: Insertion point:

Response: D6

Prompt: <SNAP ON> X-scale factor <1>/corner XYZ:

Response: ↵

Prompt: Y-scale factor (default = X):

Response: .58 ↵

This is a very close approximation of the isometric Y-axis scale factor.

Prompt: Rotation angle <0>:

Response: ↵

Now draw the bottom half of the hexagonal head. Because this block (IH) cannot be exploded, the bottom half of it cannot be copied; therefore, you must trace over the bottom half and then move those lines to form the bottom half of the hexagonal head.

Prompt: Command:

Response: LINE

Prompt: From point:

Response: D7

Prompt: To point:

Response: D8

Prompt: To point:

Response: D9

Prompt: To point:

Response: D10

Prompt: To point:

Response: ↵

Now move the lines you just drew to a location ⅜″ (.375) directly beneath the hexagonal head to form the bottom of the hex head.

Prompt: Command:

Response: MOVE

Prompt: Select objects:

Response: WINDOW {from the screen menu or W ↵ from the keyboard}

Prompt: First corner:

Response: D11

Prompt: Second corner:

Response: D12

Prompt: Select objects:

Response: ↵

Prompt: Base point or displacement:

Response: {press the HOME key your keyboard then ↵ or digitize a point on the horizontal line}

Prompt: Second point of displacement:

Response: @.375 < –90 ↵

Now, connect the top and bottom planes. To make sure you have accurately connected lines, use OSNAP in this manner.

Prompt: Command:

Response: OSNAP ↵ {type this from the keyboard}

Prompt: Object SNAP Modes:

Response: ENDPOINT ↵ {type this from the keyboard}

Now you will be able to use OSNAP-Endpoint without having to select endpoint each time. (You may also use other OSNAP modes such as CENter, while you are in the ENDpoint Mode by selecting them. After you use another mode OSNAP returns to the ENDpoint Mode.)

Prompt: Command:
Response: LINE

Prompt: From point:
Response: D13

Prompt: To point:
Response: D14 ↵

Prompt: Command:
Response: ↵

Prompt: Line from point:
Response: D15

Prompt: To point:
Response: D16

Prompt: Command:
Response: ↵

Prompt: Line from point:
Response: D17

Prompt: To point:
Response: D18 ↵

Prompt: Command:
Response: ↵

Prompt: Line from point:
Response: D19

Prompt: To point:
Response: D20 ↵

Prompt: Command:
Response: OSNAP ↵ {type this from the keyboard}

Prompt: Object SNAP modes:
Response: OFF {takes you out of the endpoint OSNAP mode}

The hexagonal head of the bolt is now complete. The next step is to draw the threads and connect them to the head to complete the drawing.

Step 3. Draw the threads.

Prompt: Command:
Response: ELLIPSE

Prompt: <Axis endpoint>/Center/Isocircle:
Response: ISO

Prompt: Center of circle:
Response: D21

Prompt: <Circle radius>/Diameter:
Response: .5 ↵ {the radius for a 1″ diameter circle}

The ellipse must now be broken in half to form the threads.

Prompt: Command:
Response: BREAK

Prompt: Select object:
Response: D22

Prompt: Enter second point or F for first point:
Response: D23

You may be able to perform the break with a single command, but it often takes two BREAK commands to do it.

Prompt: Command:
Response: BREAK

Prompt: Select object:
Response: D24

Prompt: Enter second point (or F for first point):
Response: D25

You should now have the bottom half of an isometric ellipse. Array it to form the screw threads.

Prompt: Command:
Response: ARRAY

Prompt: Select objects:

Response: WINDOW

Prompt: First corner:

Response: D26

Prompt: Other corner:

Response: D27

Prompt: Select objects:

Response: ↵

Prompt: Rectangular or Polar array (R/P):

Response: R ↵

Prompt: Number of rows (- - - -) <1>:

Response: 15 ↵ {could be more or less depending on how long the screw is}

Prompt: Number of columns (111) <1>:

Response: ↵

Prompt: Unit cell or distance between rows (- - - -):

Response: −.1 ↵ {one-tenth of an inch is a good space for this size thread}

Note: CAUTION: *be sure to make the distance negative so the array will be downward.*

Step 4. The threads must then be connected to the head to complete the bolt drawing.

Note: IMPORTANT: *toggle to left or right isoplane before drawing the vertical lines.*

Prompt: Command:

Response: LINE

Prompt: From point:

Response: OSNAP {from the screen menu **** or from ENDPOINT third key on the mouse} D28

Be sure ORTHO is ON so you will get a straight line.

Prompt: To point:

Response: D29

Prompt: Command:

Response: LINE

Prompt: From point:

Response: OSNAP-ENDPOINT-D30

Prompt: To point:

Response: D31 ↵

The bolt is now complete and you should now prepare for a quiz on isometric drawing with AutoCAD.

Note: *As this book is being printed, Release 10 of AutoCAD is being distributed. The 3-D package of Release 10 solves many of the earlier problems of AutoCAD 3D. It allows perspective objects to be drawn and rotated in space and allows holes to be created in vertical surfaces. The next edition of this book will contain a complete description of this function.*

AutoCAD 3D

This portion of the AutoCAD package allows objects to be drawn in three dimensions and viewed from any point in space. Although this software does not allow 3-D shapes to be drawn on vertical surfaces it can be appropriately applied to some types of drawings. In addition, an understanding of this part of the AutoCAD package will provide a background for more fully developed 3-D programs for personal computers.

This part of the AutoCAD package is simple, in that there are only three commands specific to 3-D, but using these commands in conjunction with the other AutoCAD requires some creative thought. The three commands are described by the procedures used to develop Figure 10-5. they are:

ELEV   This command allows you to set elevation and thickness for any entity.

VPOINT   This command sets the point from which the drawing may be viewed. It then regenerates the drawing so that it may be displayed and plotted from that view point.

HIDE   This command removes from the display any lines hidden by a surface in front of another surface. Some examples will explain how these commands may be used to create some 3-D pictures (Figure 10-5).

Figure 10-5

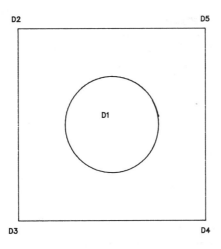

Drawing in 3-D

The object to be illustrated is an upright cylinder enclosed in a rectangular open box. The cylinder is 5 units high with a 2-unit diameter. The box is 2 units high and 4 units square.

To draw a cylinder in 3-D:

Step 1. Draw the object.

Set GRID and SNAP to .5.

Prompt: Command:
Response: {Select} ELEV {from the 3-D Menu}

Prompt: New current elevation <0.0000>:
Response: ↵

Prompt: New current thickness <0.0000>:
Response: 5 ↵

Now everything drawn until a new elevation and thickness are chosen will start at elevation 0 and will have a height (thickness) of 5.

Prompt: Command:
Response: {Digitize} CIRCLE RAD {on the DRAW Menu}

Prompt: 3P/2P/<Center point>:
Response: D1

Prompt: Diameter/<Radius>:
Response: 1 ↵

Figure 10-6

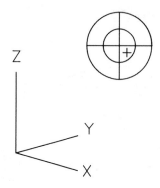

Prompt: Command:

Response: ELEV

Prompt: New current elevation <0.000>:

Response: ↵

Prompt: New current thickness <5.000>:

Response: 2 ↵

Now everything drawn will have an elevation of 0 and a height of 2.

Prompt: Command:

Response: {Select} LINE

Prompt: From point:

Response: D2, D3, D4, D5 {draw a 4-unit box around the circle}

Step 2. Set the viewpoint.

Prompt: Command:

Response: {Select} VPOINT {from the 3-D Menu}

Prompt: Enter view point <0,0,1>:

Response: ↵

The AutoCAD compass and axis tripod is displayed, Figure 10-6. Notice that the Z-axis is the height or thickness of the object.

The views obtained when the cursor is digitized in eight different positions is shown in Figure 10-7. Figure 10-8 describes the areas of the compass and the views obtained from each area. Select the position shown as 10-7A by digitizing the location shown. You should have a display similar to Figure 10-9.

Figure 10-7

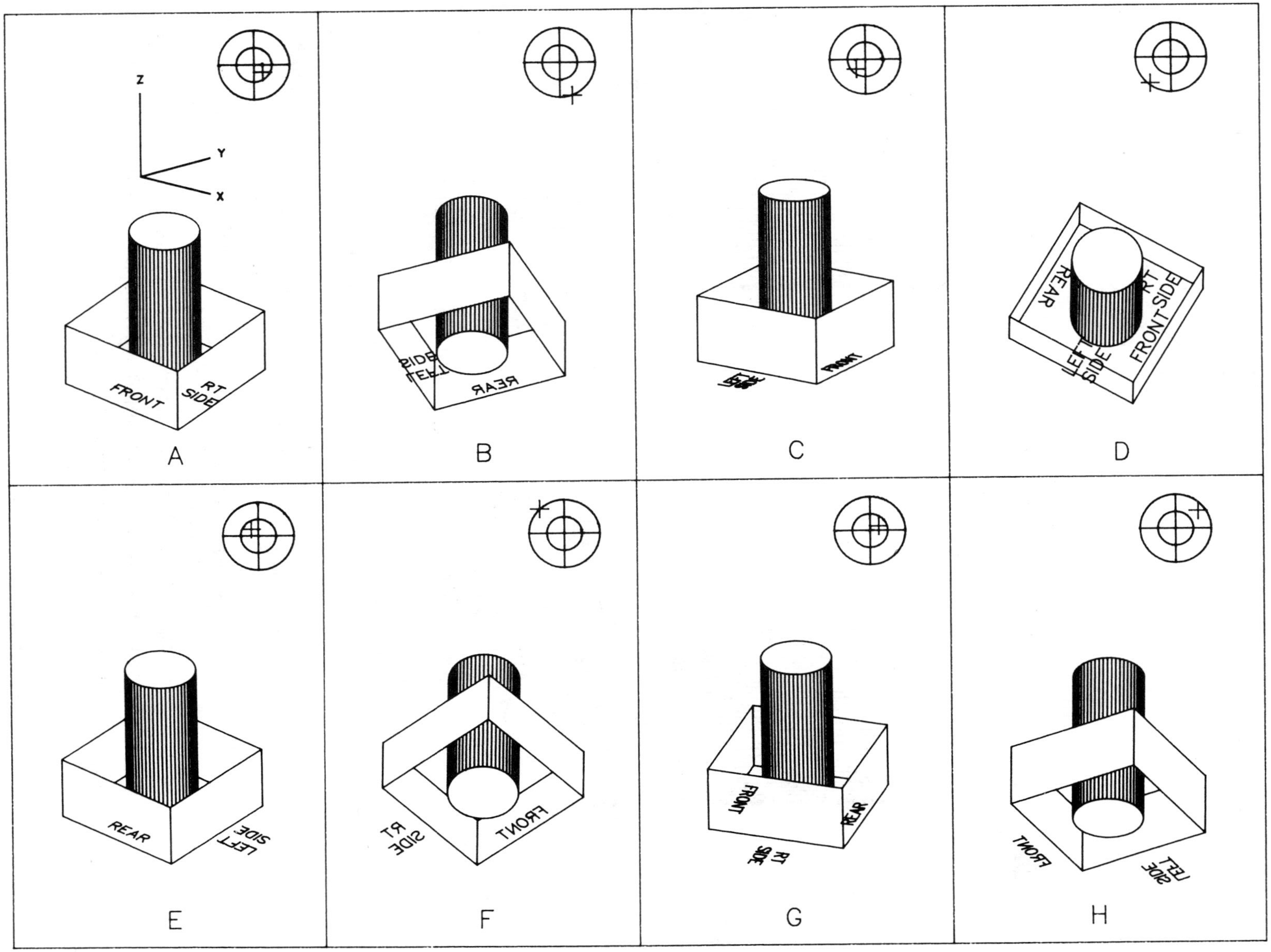
Z
Y
X
FRONT
RT SIDE
A
REAR
B
FRONT
C
REAR
RT FRONT-SIDE
LEFT SIDE
D
REAR
LEFT SIDE
E
RT SIDE
FRONT
F
FRONT
REAR
RT SIDE
G
FRONT
LEFT SIDE
H

Figure 10-8

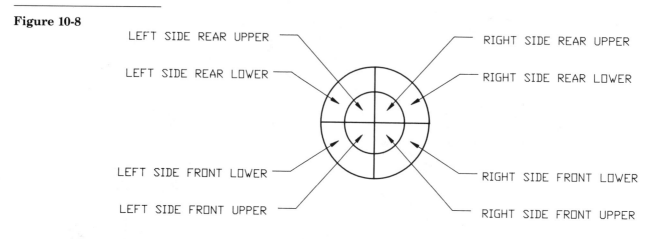

LEFT SIDE REAR UPPER

LEFT SIDE REAR LOWER

LEFT SIDE FRONT LOWER

LEFT SIDE FRONT UPPER

RIGHT SIDE REAR UPPER

RIGHT SIDE REAR LOWER

RIGHT SIDE FRONT LOWER

RIGHT SIDE FRONT UPPER

Figure 10-9

Figure 10-10

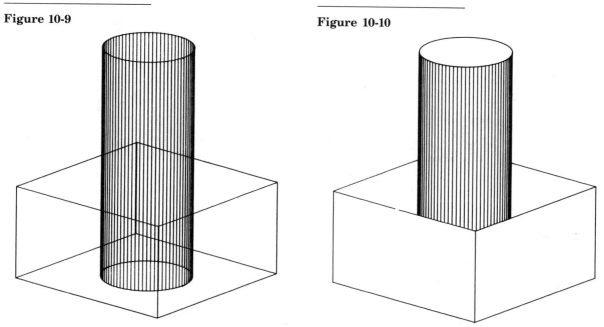

Step 3. Hide surfaces that are behind other surfaces.

Prompt: Command:

Response: {Select} HIDE {and} YES {from the 3-D Menu}

After a brief period, a display similar to Figure 10-10 should appear on your screen.

Step 4. Plot the drawing.

Select PLOT from the screen menu or END and select 3 from the Main Menu. Respond to all plot prompts as you would for a 2-D drawing except:

Prompt: Remove hidden lines? <N>:

Response: Y ↵ {to get a plot of Figure 10-10, hidden lines must be removed}

Figure 10-11

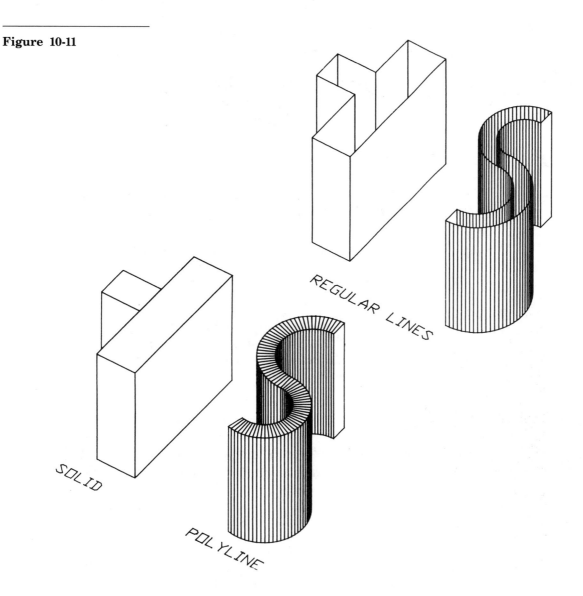

Other Information You Must Have to Draw in 3-D

Horizontal surfaces that you want to appear as solids must be drawn as solids, wide polylines or donuts (Figure 10-11).

To return to the 2-D view of any object:

Prompt: Command:

Response: {Select} VPOINT

Prompt: Enter view point <whatever your current viewpoint is>:

Response: {Select} PLAN {from the screen menu or type 0,0,1 which is the 2-D viewpoint}

EXERCISE 1

Reproduce Figures 10-1 through 10-4 on a horizontal 8½ × 11″ sheet and plot the drawing according to your teacher's instructions.

EXERCISE 2

Draw the figure for Exercise 2 approximately the size shown using the isometric method. Center the drawing in a horizontal 8½ × 11″ format. Plot as directed by your instructor.

EXERCISE 3

Draw the figure for Exercise 3 approximately the size shown using the isometric method. Center the drawing in a vertical 8½ × 11″ format. Plot as directed by your instructor.

EXERCISE 4

Make an isometric view from the orthographic views in the figure for Exercise 4. Center your drawing on an 8½ × 11″ horizontal format and plot it as your instructor directs.

EXERCISE 5

Make isometric drawings from the two-dimensional drawing shown in the figure for Exercise 5. Let the grid represent ¼″. Divide a horizontal A-size format into four equal spaces and place one drawing in each space. You will have two sheets when you finish. Complete the title block and title the drawing ISOMETRIC AUTOCAD SKETCHES.

EXERCISES 6, 7, 8, 9, 10, 11, 12

Make AutoCAD isometric drawings of the figures for these Exercises. Measure the drawings and make your drawings approximately the same size. Center each one in an 8½ × 11″ sheet. Make the lettering on Figure 10-12 simplex, .08″ high.

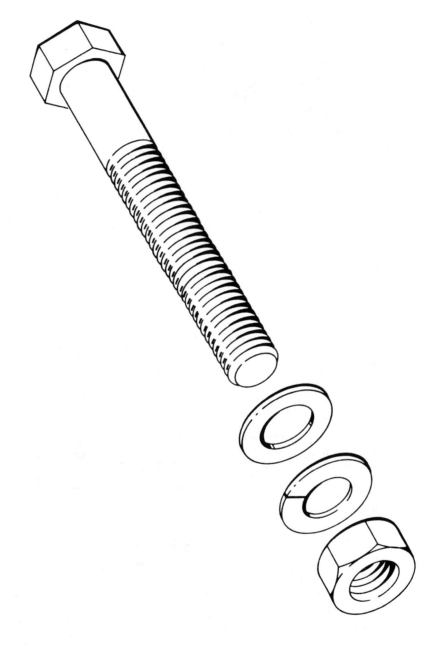

Exercise 3

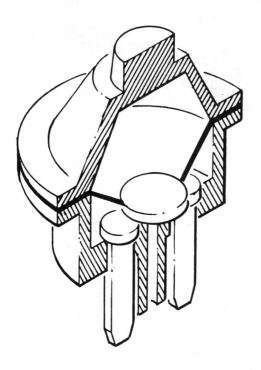

Exercise 4

DRAW FULL SCALE

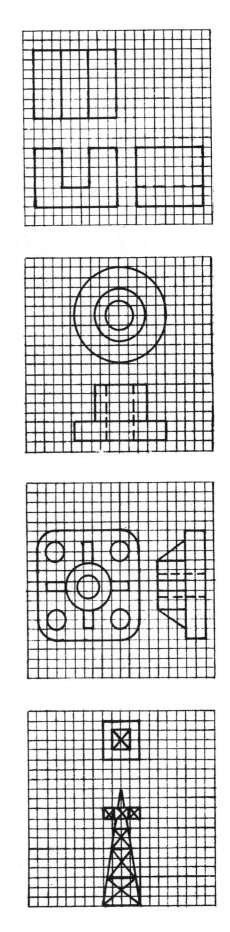

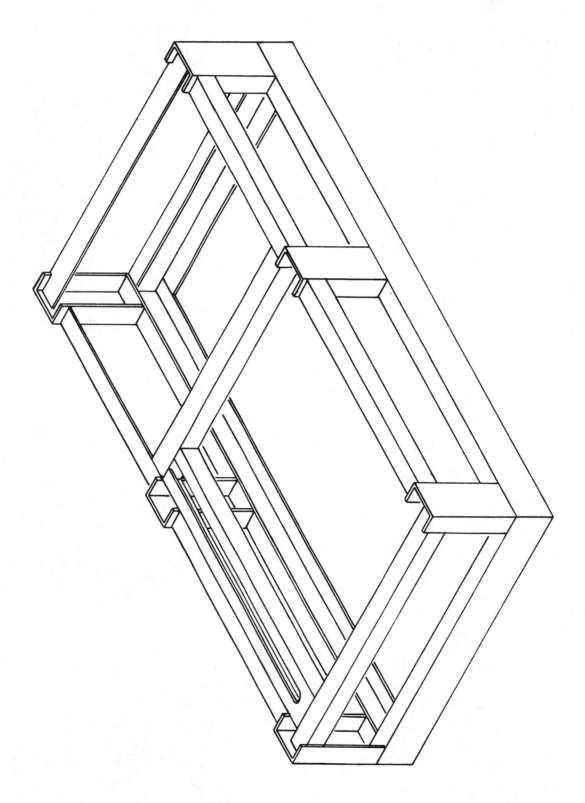

Exercise 7

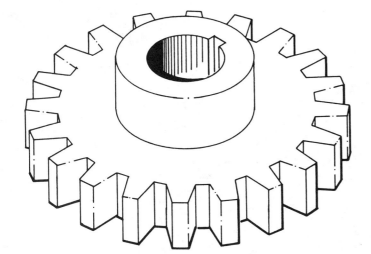

Exercise 8

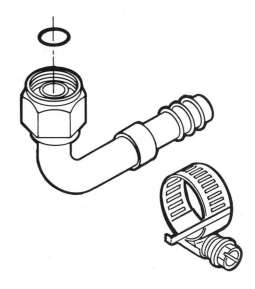

Exercise 9

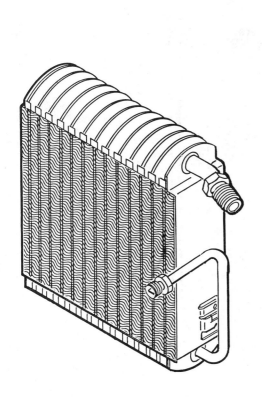

Exercise 10

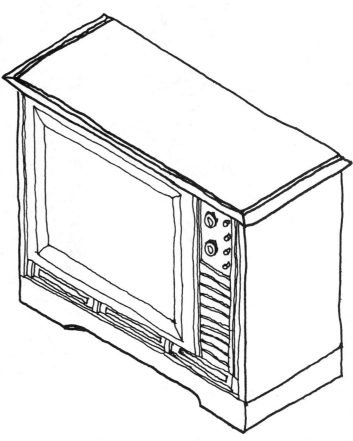

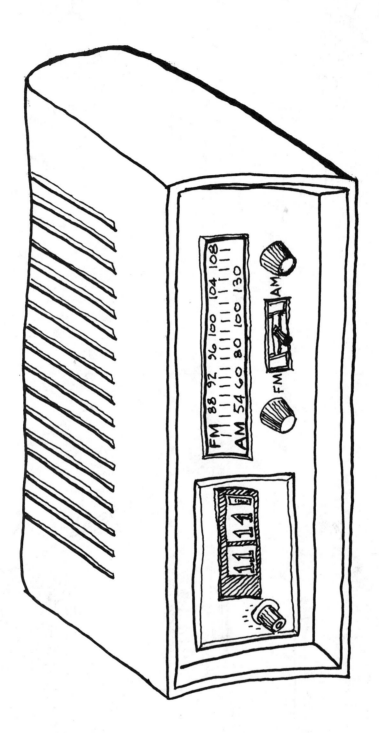

ITEM NO.	PART NO.	QTY	DESCRIPTION
I	3001	I	DEPTH ADJ. KNOB
2	3002	I	BODY
3	3003	I	BRACKET
4	3004	I	BASE
5	3005	2	WING NUT AND WASHER-STD
6	3006	I	SQ SHOULDER SCREW x 1.25-STD
7	3007	2	GUIDE ROD
8	3008	I	SQ SHOULDER SCREW x .88-STD
9	3009	2	CLAMP
10	3010	I	EDGING GUIDE
11	3011	2	SCREW-STD
12	3012	2	SET SCREW-STD
13	3013	4	SCREW-STD

Exercise 13

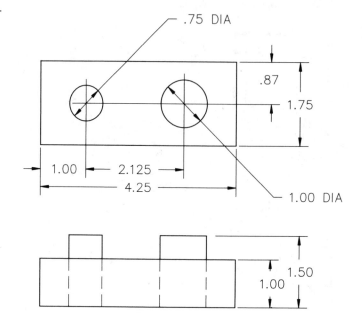

Exercise 14

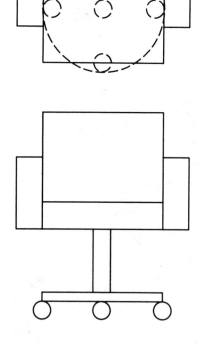

EXERCISES 13, 14, 15

Make AutoCAD 3D drawings (not isometric) of the following figures.
Plot them from two different view points, one from the upper front—
right side, the other from the upper rear—left side.

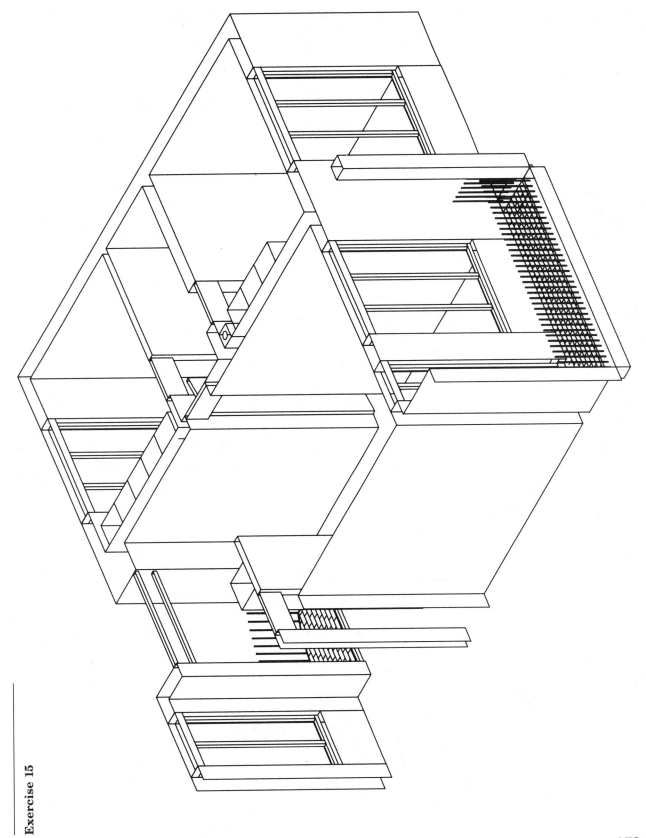

Test on Objectives—Chapter 10

It is suggested that the student complete this test at the computer after reproducing Figures 10-1 through 10-4.

1. The isometric grid is obtained from which of the following commands?

    a. ELEV
    b. LINE
    c. SNAP
    d. 3-D

2. Which of the following is used to toggle from one isoplane to another?

    a. F3
    b. Ctrl-E
    c. Ctrl-T
    d. Ctrl-P

3. What happens when the C key is struck as a response to the prompt: "to point"?

    a. the rectangle is copied
    b. the rectangle is changed to layer C
    c. the rectangle is opened
    d. the rectangle is closed

4. In response to the prompt: "Line: from point," which of the following starts a line from the endpoint of the last line drawn?

    a. Enter
    b. F6
    c. Ctrl-E
    d. REPEAT

5. Why use a single letter or number as a layer name?

    a. only one letter or number may be used for a layer name
    b. it requires fewer key strokes
    c. a single letter or number is selected from a list
    d. a single number or letter may not be used for a layer name

6. What is the maximum number of characters which may be used for a drawing name?

    a. four
    b. six
    c. eight
    d. ten

7. An ellipse that appears in the following position would have been drawn in?

    a. left Isoplane
    b. right Isoplane
    c. top Isoplane
    d. none of the above

8. An ellipse that appears in the following position would have been drawn in?

    a. left Isoplane
    b. right Isoplane
    c. top Isoplane
    d. none of the above

9. An ellipse that appears in the following position would have been drawn in?

    a. left Isoplane
    b. right Isoplane
    c. top Isoplane
    d. none of the above

10. Which of the following commands was used to produce the drawing at B from the drawing at A?

    a. FILLET
    b. EXTEND
    c. MIRROR
    d. CHANGE

11. Which of the following is the same as $-30°$?

    a. $60°$
    b. $150°$
    c. $210°$
    d. $330°$

12. Which of the following commands has a feature labeled "multiple"?

    a. COPY
    b. CHANGE
    c. LINE
    d. ARRAY

13. Which of the following commands is used to change lines from one layer to another?

    a. COLOR
    b. LAYER
    c. CHANGE
    d. BREAK

14. If you do not wish to break a line at the same point where you selected the line, which of the following keys must be struck?

    a. C
    b. F
    c. E
    d. F1

15. Which of the following is a reason for changing lines to another layer?

    a. so that lines weights may be varied during plotting
    b. so that the drawing will be more accurate
    c. so that circles may be drawn
    d. so that ellipses may be drawn

16. Which of the following isoplanes will not allow vertical lines to be drawn with a mouse when ORTHO is ON?

    a. left
    b. right
    c. top
    d. all will allow vertical lines to be drawn

17. A hexagon may be drawn most easily with which of the following commands?

    a. POLYGON
    b. LINE
    c. P LINE
    d. SHAPE

18. Which of the following can be used as a BLOCK name?

    a. ISOHEXAGON
    b. ISO HEX
    c. ISOHEX
    d. ISOM-HEXA

19. Inserting a polygon so that it appears correct in an isometric top plane requires a scale of _____ in the Y-Axis?

    a. .30
    b. .90
    c. .58
    d. .355

20. A hexagon inserted as a block so that it appears correct in an isometric top plane may not be exploded because?

    a. blocks cannot be exploded
    b. polygons cannot be exploded
    c. X, Y, and Z axes are not equal
    d. X, Y, and Z axes are equal

21. What response must be made to the "SNAP-style" prompt in order for an isometric grid to appear?

_____

22. Which function key is used to turn the isometric grid ON or OFF?

_____

23. Which keys are used to toggle from one isoplane to another?

_____

24. How are the three isoplanes labeled?

_____

_____

_____

25. Write the correct syntax (letters and numbers) to draw a line 5.25″ long at an angle 30° upward to the right.

_____

26. Write the correct sequence of keystrokes to draw the right side of the following isometric rectangle.

2.00

4.12

_____

_____

_____

_____

27. Why would the inside lines of a drawing be drawn in a different color than the outside lines?

_____

_____

_____

28. Which command is used to produce a mirror image of an object?

_____

29. What is the correct response to the prompt: "<Axis endpoint 1> /Center/Isocircle:" if an isometric ellipse is to be drawn?

_____

30. Why was it necessary to trace the bottom half of the isometric hexagon in order to draw the lower half of the hexagonal head in Figure 10-4.

_____

_____

11

Customizing Menus

Customizing menus is one of the most rewarding areas encountered in the AutoCAD software package. Learning to customize menus allows the user to exercise her/his creativity by rearranging standard menus and forming new commands that execute several commands with a single pick. AutoCAD may then be tailored to meet the needs of specific situations. Customizing menus can be used to reduce drawing time and increase productivity.

Customizing a menu is really quite easy, but remember to keep accurate notes containing the exact commands used. Commands must contain exactly the same spelling, punctuation and spacing every time.

Appearance of Screen and Tablet Menus

When reference is made to a screen menu, that menu is the list of commands appearing on the right side of the CRT screen when a drawing is active. They are the commands that may be selected with a pointing device.

The tablet menu list is a continuation of the screen menu list, but it does not appear on the screen. It is a list of commands that can be selected with a pointing device on a tablet (which takes the place of the mouse) after the tablet has been configured.

Both of these lists may be found and changed by the user. EDLIN, which is found on DOS disks, is a simple text editor, and is used in this chapter. Information on how to use EDLIN is presented later in this chapter.

The Tablet Overlay (Figure 11-1)

The tablet menu requires that an overlay be used to select commands. This overlay contains squares that are labeled with the names of

Figure 11-1
AutoCAD Tablet Overlay

commands. Some squares may have pictures on them describing the result of the command. For example, an arc could be drawn on one of the squares that would issue the ARC command.

Using tablet menus often allows drawings to be drawn faster. The tablet menu as well as the screen menu allows the use of MACRO commands. A MACRO command consists of several commands linked together. MACROs will be described in detail later in this chapter.

AutoCAD supplies a list of commands that may be selected from the tablet menu. This list includes some MACRO commands.

Before MACROs are described for the tablet, the tablet menu for AutoCAD must be set up. The following is a description of how to set up the tablet menu.

To set up the AutoCAD Tablet Menu (Figure 11-2):

Start a new drawing called MENTEST (select "1" on the Main Menu). Tape the menu overlay to the digitizing tablet and then follow these steps:

Prompt: Command:
Response: TABLET

Prompt: Option (ON/OFF/Cal/Cfg):
Response: CFG ↵

Prompt: Enter number of tablet menus desired (0–4) <1>
Response: 4 ↵

Prompt: Digitize upper left corner of menu area 1:
Response: D1 {Figure 11-2}

Prompt: Digitize lower left corner of menu area 1:
Response: D2

Prompt: Digitize lower right corner of menu area 1:
Response: D3

Prompt: Enter number of columns for menu area 1:
Response: 25 ↵

Prompt: Enter number of rows for menu area 1:
Response: 9 ↵

AutoCAD will continue to prompt you to digitize three corners each for the remaining three tablet menu areas. Refer to Figures 11-2 and 11-3 for the points to digitize and the number of columns and

Figure 11-2
Digitize Four Menu Areas

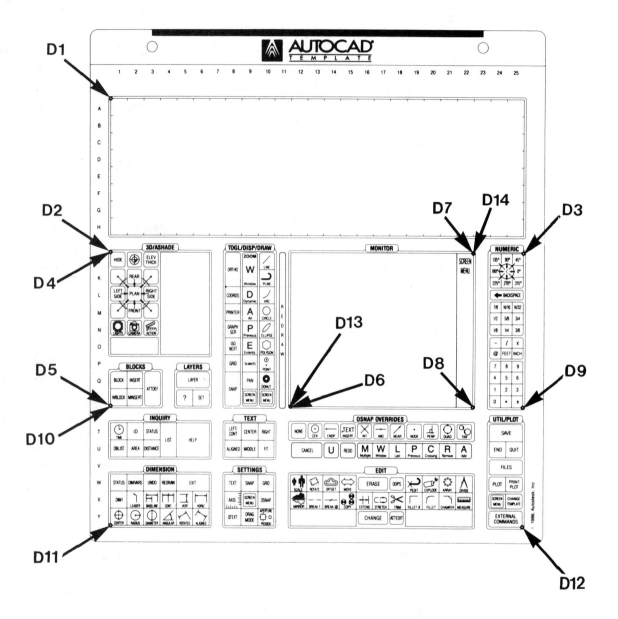

rows for each area. Use only the numbers of rows and columns given in Figure 11-3. Attempting to count the rows and columns on the menu overlay may result in errors.

AutoCAD will prompt for two points describing the lower left and upper right corners of the screen pointing area (points D13 and D14). Digitize these as they are shown in Figures 11-2 and 11-3.

Now that you have told AutoCAD which areas contain the ACAD.MNU, you should be able to touch the labeled rectangles in the menu overlay and see those commands appear at the bottom of the screen as if you had typed them.

Draw lines, arcs, and circles for awhile and experiment with mirroring, moving, etc. to get the feel of using the tablet menu. By now

Figure 11-3
Simplified Menu Area
Drawing with Row and
Column Information

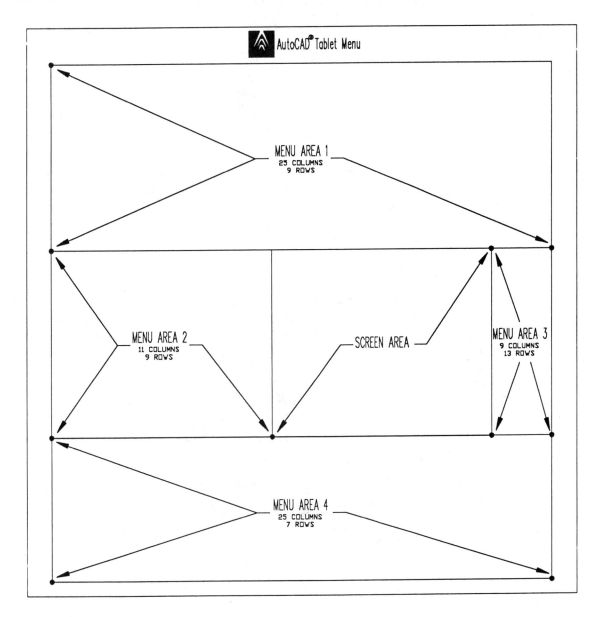

you have probably discovered that the first menu area that you digitized, tablet area 1, is not usable. This is the area to be customized. To do that, follow the procedure below:

To customize the AutoCAD Tablet Menu:

Prompt: Command:
Response: SHELL ↵

Prompt: DOS command:

Response: EDLIN ACAD.MNU ⏎

Prompt: End of input file:

If this command does not work, EDLIN is not in the working directory; therefore, you will have to copy the EDLIN.COM file from DOS to the ACAD directory. Consult the Appendix for information on copying files and creating directories. (EDLIN is awkward compared to many text editors and word processors. XTPRO is a text editor and file management system that is inexpensive and easier to use than EDLIN.)

You are now at the end of the ACAD.MNU file. You will have to learn to move around in this file. Notice the asterisk; it is waiting to move to some line in the file.

Prompt: *

Response: L ⏎

This takes you to the top of the file. Press the ⏎ key a few times. Notice that at one press the asterisk appears, and at the next press the number of the line, a colon, an asterisk, then symbols and letters or words appear.

Press ⏎ and hold it down a second or two. This moves you further into the file. The lines that are appearing are the commands that make up the ACAD.MNU screen menu. You will learn to customize parts of this list later in this chapter. Now the tablet menu area will be customized.

Press ⏎ until you again have the asterisk by itself with the cursor as below, then type as indicated.

Prompt: *

Response: L ⏎

This returns the prompt to the top of the list.

Prompt: * {returns the prompt}

Response: {Type} 1600 {and press Enter}

Your numbers may be as much as 200 to 300 different.

Prompt: * 1600

Notice that the prompt has moved to line 1600. Press ⏎ a few times and read what is on these lines. There are more commands from the ACAD.MNU screen menu. Press ↵ until your screen looks like this: 1625:****TABLET1 (or whatever your number for the tablet heading is).

Prompt: *1625:*

If you have difficulty locating the correct line, the search command may be used. To do this, follow this procedure from the single asterisk:

Response: {Type} 1, 10000 S***TABLET1 {1 to 10,000 is the number of the lines that will be searched, S means search, and *** TABLET1 is the item to be found}

This is the top of the ACAD.MNU tablet menu. The first asterisk is the one always provided by EDLIN and the three following are the ones that tell the computer this is the beginning of tablet area 1. If you accidentally go past this line, press the ↵ key until the single asterisk appears and type as follows:

Response: 1625 ↵

Prompt: *1625 {line 1625 will appear again} ↵↵
Response: 1626:*[T1-1] ↵

Prompt: 1626:*

The cursor is telling you that you can start typing. Whatever you type will replace what is on the top line. Let's start simply:

Prompt: 1626:*[T1-1]
Response: ↵

Prompt: 1626:
           *

Response: {Type} [T1-1]^C^CLINE;END\END\ ↵

The characters contained within the brackets will appear on the screen when the menu is compiled and activated. This is the label you are giving to the command. You should be back to the single blinking asterisk again and you have just created your first MACRO command.

Prompt: *E
Response: ↵

Prompt: Command:
Response: MENU ↵

Figure 11-4
Line-end-to-end
Macro Command

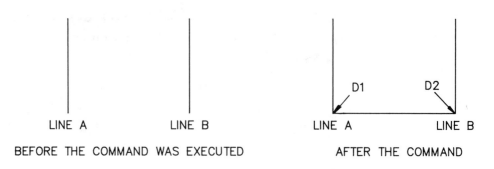

LINE A   LINE B   LINE A   LINE B

BEFORE THE COMMAND WAS EXECUTED   AFTER THE COMMAND

Prompt: MENU filename or . for none <ACAD>:

Response: ↵

The macro just created in EDLIN has been assigned to the first square of the top menu area on the ACAD Menu overlay.

Let us look at the structure of this MACRO command. This command will draw a line from the end of one line to the end of another line. The command will look like this in the EDLIN file:

^C^CLINE;END\END\

Each part of the MACRO command is described as follows:

^C^C   This has the same effect as pressing Ctrl-C (cancel) twice. (This is necessary to cancel a previous command and return AutoCAD to the command prompt.)

LINE   The AutoCAD LINE command.

        This has the same effect as pressing Enter (↵).

END\   The END has the same effect as the OSNAP END command. The backslash tells the computer to wait for the operator to digitize something that has an end, such as a line or arc.

END\   Again, the computer is being told to wait for the end of a line or arc to be digitized.

Figure 11-4 is an example of what this command will do. Label this command "Line from END to END." First, touch the square labeled "Line from END to END;" second, touch the end of line A; third, touch the end of line B. A line now joins the two ends that were touched. D1 and D2 indicate where lines A and B were digitized.

If the line was drawn to the ends of two lines by the standard method, the operator would have had to type or select LINE, press ↵, type or select END, END touch the end of line A, select END again, touch the end of line B, and then press ↵ again. By using the MACRO this line can be drawn much faster.

Now, create a second MACRO for the menu:

Prompt: Command:
Response: SHELL ↵

Prompt: DOS Command:
Response: EDLIN ACAD.MNU ↵

Prompt: End of input file:
Response: L ↵

Prompt: *
Response: 1627 ↵

Prompt: 1627:*
Response: [T1-2]^C^CCOPY;W; ↵

Prompt: *
Response: E ↵

The prompt is now back in the command mode. Notice that when a MACRO is created, the semicolon is used as a code for a ↵. When the line is finished the ↵ key is pressed. Now, go back to the ACAD Menu, which now contains a command called T1-2.

Prompt: Command:
Response: MENU ↵

Prompt: MENU filename or . for none <ACAD>:
Response: ↵

Note: *If your macro does not appear: END your drawing, EXIT from AutoCAD, then start AutoCAD again and recall your drawing.*

Draw some circles on the screen and use the COPY WINDOW MACRO, which is labeled T1-2.

These are simple MACROS used to get you started. Do not be afraid to experiment with MACROS. As you draw with AutoCAD, keep notes on a pad when you encounter tasks that are repetitive and that require several inputs. After you have identified a specific task calling for a MACRO, begin to experiment with automating these tasks.

Before you begin experimenting with changing the ACAD Menu, however, make several copies of the ACAD.MNU file under different names (such as MY.MNU, Your.MNU, etc.) and use these. If you make a mistake which makes the menu unusable, the original file will not be lost.

In addition, keep in mind that if you are at the single asterisk while in EDLIN, all you have to do if you have made a serious error is type:

Prompt: *

Response: Q ↵ {the Q is an abbreviation for QUIT}

Prompt: ABORT EDIT (Y/N):

Response: Y ↵

Any changes you have made will be discarded and the file will be the same as it was when you started. If you are on a numbered line and you want back out to the single asterisk, type Ctrl-C.

Response: 5:*Ctrl-C

Line five was used above as an example. You can return to the single asterisk from any line with this method. Now, to create an original custom menu.

Compiling a Custom Tablet Menu

Now that you have modified the ACAD.MNU and have become acquainted with using EDLIN, you are ready to create your own menu.

Although some planning is necessary to effectively arrange commands on the tablet menu, a loose arrangement which can be changed easily is preferred. If you wait until the apparently perfect overlay has been created before staring a menu, you will discover that it must be changed as an understanding of the tasks and the menu increases.

You will find that your ideas for new MACROS will come from having to make several picks to accomplish some frequent, repetitive task with AutoCAD. When this happens, consider possible MACRO commands that will automate the process. Have plenty of open squares to pick from on your menu. You may even want to replace some obsolete command or commands that have been rendered useless with a new MACRO.

As menus are created, be prepared for a lot of trial and error. Some of the most valuable MACROS are the simplest ones because they are the most frequently used.

**Figure 11-5
Custom Menu Overlay**

LINE END TO END	LINE FROM END	LINE	ARC	CIRCLE DIA	ELLIPSE
ERASE 1	ERASE L	ERASE W	ERASE	OOPS	REDRAW
SQUARE CORNER	FILLET R	ZOOM	ZOOM W	ZOOM P	ZOOM A
COPY	COPY W	ROTATE	MOVE	MOVE W	BREAK

Getting Started

Start a drawing called MNOVL. Begin with a simple menu, use Figure 11-5, for purposes of illustration. Draw and label this overlay on your computer. Make the squares 1 × 1″ so you will have enough room at first to described MACRO commands. You will be able to reduce the size of the squares on later menus as you learn to describe MACROS in more concise terms.

After you have finished this drawing, plot it on an A-size sheet and cut it out so it can be taped to your digitizing tablet. The usual size for squares on a tablet menu is ½ × ½″.

This simple menu is not meant to be a good working menu and is only used to demonstrate the relationship between the menu text file, the digitizer tablet, and the tablet overlay. It will also take you a little deeper into the creation of macros.

To create a Menu File:

Begin by creating the file you will need to activate this tablet menu. If your computer is currently in the AutoCAD program type END and exit AutoCAD by selecting "0" from the Main Menu. If your computer is set up with an AUTOEXEC.BAT file, this will take you to the Root directory. In order to get back into the ACAD directory, type:

Response: CD/ACAD ↵.

Prompt: C:>ACAD
Response: EDLIN FIRSTMEN.MNU ↵

Prompt: *_NEW FILE

Response: {Type} 1 ↵

Prompt: 1:*_

Response: 1:****TABLET1 ↵
2:*[T1-1]^C^CLINE;END\END\; ↵
3:*[T1-2]^C^CLINE;END\\; ↵
4:*[T1-3]^C^CLINE ↵
5:*[T1-4]^C^CARC ↵
6:*[T1-5]^C^CCIRCLE ↵
7:*[T1-6]^C^ELLIPSE ↵
8:*[T1-8]^C^CERASE;\;; ↵
9:*[T1-8]^C^CERASE;L;; ↵
10:8[T1-9]^C^CERASE;W ↵
11:*[T1-10]^C^CERASE ↵
12:*[T1-11]^C^COOPS ↵
13:*[T1-12]^C^CREDRAW ↵
14:*[T1-13]^C^CFILLET;R;O;FILLET ↵
15:*[T1-14]^C^CFILLET;R;\;FILLET ↵
16:*[T1-15]^C^CZOOM ↵
17:*[T1-16]^C^CZOOM;W; ↵
18:*[T1-17]^C^CZOOM;P; ↵
19:*[T1-18]^C^DZOOM;A; ↵
20:*[T1-19]^C^CCOPY ↵
21:*[T1-20]^C^CCOPY;W; ↵
22:*[T1-21]^C^CROTATE ↵
23:*[T1-22]^C^CMOVE ↵
24:*[T1-23]^C^CMOVE;W; ↵
25:*[T1-24]^C^CBREAK ↵
26:*PRESS Ctrl-C ↵

Prompt: *TYPE E ↵

Now go back to the first line and carefully check each line to be sure that each line is exactly as it should be. To do this:

Response: 1 ↵

Prompt: 1:****TABLET1

Response: ↵

Prompt: 1:*

Response: {If there are no changes or corrections press ↵ otherwise type the correct line}

Now return to the ACAD directory.

Prompt: C:>ACAD

Response: ACAD ↵

At this point you will be back at the Main Menu. Start a new drawing. Name this drawing: FIRSTMEN. Notice that the default menu that comes up is the ACAD.MNU. From the command prompt follow this sequence:

Prompt: Command:

Response: MENU ↵

Prompt: Name of the menu:

Response: FIRSTMEN ↵

Notice that you did not include the file extension—the portion that describes the type of file (in this case, .MNU). That is because you asked for a menu file when you typed MENU.

Your new menu is now ready to be activated and used. Tape the menu overlay securely to the tablet in a fashion that does not obscure any of the printing on it.

Prompt: Command:

Response: TABLET ↵

Prompt: Option (ON/OFF/Cal/Cfg):

Response: CFG ↵

The computer will ask you to enter the number of tablet menus desired. You may specify up to four, but for our purposes, choose one.

Response: 1 ↵

Now turn to Figure 11-6. The computer will tell you to digitize: first the upper left corner of menu area 1 (D1), second the lower left corner of menu area 1 (D2), and third the lower right corner of menu area 1 (D3). When you have done this, you will be asked to enter the number of columns and rows for menu area 1.

Prompt: Enter number of columns for menu area 1:

Response: 6 ↵

Prompt: Enter number of rows for menu area 1:

Response: 4 ↵

You will now be asked if you want to respecify the screen pointing area. AutoCAD now wants you to digitize the lower left corner of the drawing area, then the upper right corner. Pick a convenient rectan-

Figure 11-6
Digitize the New
Custom Menu Area

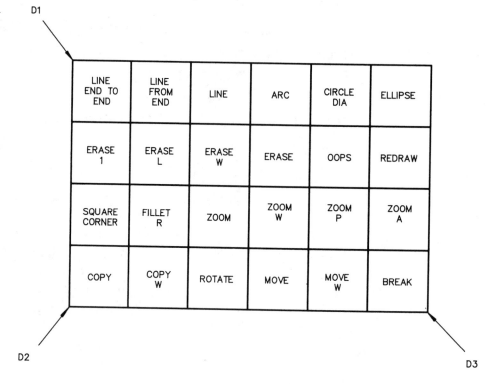

gle above the new menu area. An area approximately 5″ wide by 4″ tall should be sufficient. Digitize the lower left corner (D1) then the upper right corner of this drawing area (D2) as prompted. Now you are ready to execute commands from your first tablet menu.

Pick the line command and put several lines on the screen. Use the LINE END TO END command to put a line from the end of one line to the end of another. Use the FILLET R command and round a few corners. Use the SQUARE CORNER command to square a few corners.

Now you are ready to create a tablet menu with four areas. Look at Figure 11-2 for ideas on layout of a four area tablet menu.

Creating a Screen Menu

Now consider rearranging the AutoCAD screen menu and creating another screen menu for MACROS.

1. Make a list of what exists as opposed to what is used the most.

2. Make a new list of first and second pages of DRAW, EDIT, and SETTINGS menus.

3. Name your most commonly used blocks.

4. Rearrange the standard menu and add a command to take you to a newly created menu.

5. Add blocks to the block area on the DRAW Menu and define the blocks.

Begin with a list of edit commands.

Step 1. Make a list of what exists and another list of what is used the most.

The AutoCAD commands are arranged in alphabetical order. This often is not the best arrangement, so the program was made so these menus could be easily changed. The list of EDIT commands is used as an example.

Standard ACAD Edit Menu	Order which is Used the Most (this may not be your most commonly used order)
ARRAY	ARRAY
ATTEDIT	BREAK
BREAK	CHANGE
CHAMFER	COPY
COPY	ERASE
DIVIDE	EXPLODE
ERASE	MIRROR
EXPLODE	MOVE
EXTEND	ROTATE
FILLET	SCALE
MEASURE	STRETCH
MIRROR	TRIM
MOVE	ATTEDIT
PEDIT	PEDIT
ROTATE	CHAMFER
SCALE	FILLET
STRETCH	DIVIDE
TRIM	EXTEND
UNDO	

UNDO was left off because entry from the keyboard by pressing U is faster than picking UNDO from the screen.

There are some blank lines on most menu pages that can be used. There must be blank lines before and after "next." If these lines are filled, you will not be able to move to the second page of the EDIT Menu, so do not use those. Use only the obviously usable spaces. Each page of the screen menu will accept lines including the blank spaces, which are needed to activate other menus. Now make your new list for the first and second pages of the screen menu.

Step 2. Make a new list of the EDIT commands. Do the same for the DRAW and SETTINGS Menus later.

You may want to use the list of commands used the most in Step 1. Notice that there is room for two more commands on page one of this menu, so you may wish to move two more of the commands from page two to page one. After you have made your rearranged list of commands, think about six of the blocks you commonly use.

Step 3. Name six most commonly used blocks.

These names must be eight characters or less. They may identify arrowheads, standard notes, an architectural wall section, furniture, a commonly used organizational chart, a slot—anything that can be blocked. An example is the following list:

ARROW		BLOCK1
CHAIR		BLOCK2
WALL	*or*	BLOCK3
NOTES		BLOCK4
SLOT		BLOCK5
SYMBOL		BLOCK6

These names may then be placed in the blank spaces of the menu headed by the BLOCK command. They may then be selected from the screen menu instead of being typed from the keyboard when the block name is asked for. A list using BLOCKS1 through 6 may be more useful. The blocks may be redefined when they become outmoded for your use. A wall chart identifying the blocks will be needed if you do it that way.

Step 4. Rearrange the standard menu.

Begin by copying the ACAD.MNU file under a different name so that you may retrieve it easily if you create an unusable menu. To do this go to the Root directory of your hard drive and begin there. The procedure is:

Prompt: C>

Response: CD\ ↵

Prompt: C>

Response: COPY\ACAD\ACAD.MNU ACAD\NO1.MNU ↵

Prompt: C>

Response: EDLIN NO1.MNU ↵

If you get the response "*NEWFILE" you have not located the NO1.MNU file. You may have to list the directory in front of the filename, for example: EDLIN\ACAD\NO1.MNU. If you copy EDLIN.COM into the ACAD directory you will be able to use EDLIN from there. If NO1.MNU is in the SOURCE subdirectory under the ACAD directory, you will have to type EDLIN\ACAD\SOURCE \NO1.MNU as a filename after EDLIN.

Before you go any further, let us review what each character in the new line 116 below represents.

<BREAK>   This is the word that appears on the screen menu.

$S=X   The dollar sign in ACAD identifies the item. S indicates the screen menu. = X identifies whatever follows as a part of the screen menu and creates a blank screen before it moves to the part indicated.

$S=BREAK   Shows BREAK to be the identified part of the screen menu.

^C^C   Two cancels—the same as Ctrl-C from the keyboard twice. Two are needed: one to exit from a previous activity from within a previous command, and another to exit from the previous command itself.

BREAK   This is the command that will be activated when the bracketed command [BREAK] is picked.

Prompt: End of input file:
               *

Response: 115 ↵

Prompt: 115:*[ARRAY:]$S=X $S=ARRAY^C^CARRAY 115:*

Response: {You do not want to change this line; press ↵ until you get to 116}

Prompt: 116:* [ATTEDIT:] $S=X $S=ATTEDIT^C^CATTEDIT

Response: ↵

Prompt: 116:*

Response: [BREAK] $S=X $S=BREAK^C^CBREAK

You have now changed line 116, which was ATTEDIT on the Edit Menu to BREAK.

Continue through the EDIT Menu changing the appropriate lines as you go. Be careful to copy the command line exactly as it was before. To do this you will have to page through the edit commands and write them on a piece of paper exactly as they appear before you begin editing, or print them if you have a printer. If you pass up a line, type the line number from the "*" prompt. If you are using a text editor other than EDLIN you may be able to move lines easily from one position to another without retyping.

Prompt: 116:*

Response: ↵

Prompt: *

Response: 105 ↵

Prompt: 105:*[3DFACE:]$S=X $s=3DFACE^C^C3DFACE

After you finish arranging your EDIT Menu, add the blocks to your BLOCK Menu.

Step 5. Add block names to the BLOCK Menu.

Prompt: *

Response: 258 ↵

Prompt: *

Response: [BLOCK]^C^CINSERT;BLOCK1 ↵

Prompt: 259*

Find other open lines on the BLOCK Menu. You will find an open line under the ?, one after add and two after oops that can be used, the **** (OSNAP) line which can be changed to a block name, and the OOPS lines which can be changed to a block name. The OSNAP (****) line is not needed if you have OSNAP on the third button of your mouse and "U" or "OOPS" typed from the keyboard will replace the seldom used OOPS on this menu. Locate the line in the screen menu after line 258.

Response: {Press ↵ several times until you get to a blank line or another line which can be used for a block name, then add BLOCK2 as you did for BLOCK1}

Continue until you have inserted your six block names. After adding the block names to your BLOCK Menu, you are ready to test your new screen menu. Of course you will have to define the blocks from an ACAD drawing. (Draw some shapes and give them the names you have added to your menu. This can be done by using the

WBLOCK command. The block name you have written in your menu and the WBLOCK name must be exactly the same). Now to test the menu after your last entry:

Prompt: 116:* {or whatever your last line is}
Response: ↵

Prompt: *
Response: END ↵

Prompt: C>
Response: CD ACAD ↵

Start AutoCAD, call up a new drawing and type MENU ↵ from the command prompt. Then type "NO1" to enter your new menu. Flip to your new EDIT menu. Test your commands and correct any mistakes using EDLIN. Whenever the new menu is correct as you would like it, congratulate yourself. You are on the way to using AutoCAD in its most powerful capacity.

After you understand the screen menu, how it is arranged, and how it may be changed, you will want to add MACROS and arrange commands in perhaps another order. An excellent book for this is *The AutoCAD Productivity Book,* A. Ted Schaefer and James L. Brittain, Ventana Press, 1986.

Creating Icon Menus

Release 9 also allows you to change the pull-down icons or to add complete menus for pull-down use. It is very similar to arranging screen menus through the use of slides created in AutoCAD.

If you have Release 9 and want to modify any of the pop-down menus, use your word processor or EDLIN to add, modify or delete a line. If you want to add an icon (a picture representing a command or macro) or a series of icons, use the following procedure:

Step 1. Make a list of the commands you want on the pop-down menu and draw a simple sketch of what you want them to look like.

Each of the pop-down icon menus has room for 16 icons, 4 across and 4 down. If you use fewer than 16, each icon will be larger. Two icons will fill the entire page just as 16 icons do. The exit icon does not require a slide. The word "Exit" will appear in the icon menu because there is a space between "[" and "Exit" in the line "[Exit]^C^C" (Figure 11-8). This space instructs AutoCAD to use the text following instead of a slide menu.

Figure 11-7
Four-icon Menu Frame
Sketch

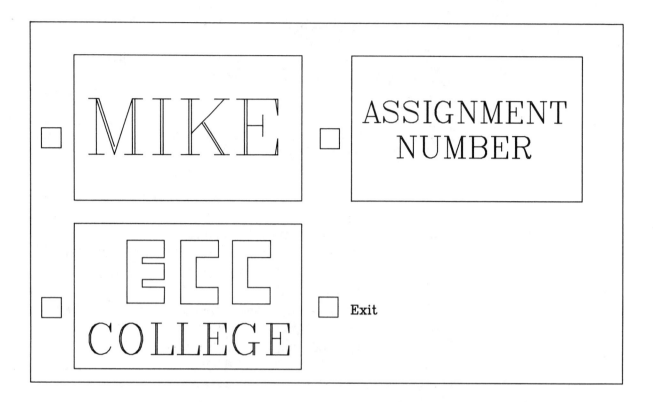

Step 2. Make a drawing of each icon and make a slide of each drawing.

In the example of Figure 11-7, the word "MIKE" was drawn in the center of the screen of a drawing named MIKE using DTEXT with a complex font. The word filled the entire screen as recommended by the *AutoCAD Reference Manual.* Then a slide was created and the drawing was saved so that it could be inserted when the icon is digitized. Two other drawings and slides were created, one for the school (ECC College) and one for the assignment number. Simple drawings could have been used instead of words for these icons. After the drawing MIKE was made, its slide was created and named MIKE as follows. With the drawing MIKE displayed so that it fills the screen:

Prompt: Command:

Response: MSLIDE {from the UTILITIES menu or type from the keyboard}

The screen will flash briefly and the slide is created.

Figure 11-8
POP8 Icon Menu File

```
***POP8
[POP8]
[NAME]^C^C$i=NAME $i=*

***icon
**as
[Select Ashade Command]
[acad(camera)]^C^C$S=X $S=CAMERA camera \\\$i=as $i=*
[acad(point)]^C^C$S=X $S=LIGHTS LIGHT \p \$i=as $i=*
[acad(directed)]^C^C$S=X $S=LIGHTS LIGHT \d \\$i=as $i=*
[acad(scene)]^C^C$S=X $S=ACTION scene
[acad(filmroll)]^C^C$S=X $S=ACTION filmroll
[ Exit]^c^c

**NAME
[Name]
[NAME]^C^Cinsert MIKE ; \;;;
[SCHOOL]^C^Cinsert SCHOOL ; \;;;
[ASSIGN]^C^CSTYLE ASGN;COMPLEX;.15;;;;;;DTEXT;C;\;;;
[ Exit]^c^c
```

Prompt: Slide name <MIKE>

Response: {Type} NAME ↵

Prompt: Command:

Response: END ↵

Create slides for your school icon and the assignment number in a similar manner. Name the school slide "SCHOOL" and the assignment number slide "ASSIGN."

Now you have three slides that will appear in your AutoCAD directory:

NAME.SLD

SCHOOL.SLD

ASSIGN.SLD

Step 3. Copy the ACAD.MNU file and name it (your initials). MNU.

Step 4. Find the ***POP7 part of the menu file and add ***POP8 after the end of that file just before the ***icon section as shown in Figure 11-8.

Figure 11-9
Pop-down Menu with
POP8 Added

Tools Draw Edit Display Modes Options File POP8
NAME

The line "[POP8]" will appear in the slot reserved for the eighth pop-down menu at the top of the screen (there are 10 slots), Figure 11-9. The line "[NAME^C^C$i=NAME $i=*" means this:

[NAME]	This is a label that will appear in the POP8 menu. When it is digitized the rest of the line will be activated.
^C^C	Cancels any previous commands.
$i=NAME	Instructs AutoCAD to load an icon labeled NAME.
$i=*	Instructs AutoCAD to display the icon.

Step 5. Insert the icon instructions in the icon section of the ACAD.MNU file.

The icon section will be identified with ***icon. You may place them before or after the **as (the autoshade icon files) section. Be sure to leave spaces above and below your NAME icon section as shown in Figure 11-8. The icon instructions in this figure mean:

**NAME   Identifies the icon menu labeled NAME.

[Name]   The label that appears on the icon menu shown in Figure 11-10.

[NAME]^C^Cinsert MIKE;\;;;
Tells AutoCAD to display the icon slide labeled NAME. When this slide is digitized, the previous command is canceled and the drawing named MIKE is inserted as a block. The \ asks for an operator response and the ;'s represent pressing the Enter key.

[SCHOOL]^C^Cinsert SCHOOL;;;;
This tells AutoCAD to display the icon slide labeled SCHOOL. When this slide is digitized the previous command is canceled and the drawing named SCHOOL is inserted as a block.

[ASSIGN]   Tells AutoCAD to display the icon slide labeled ASSIGN. When this slide is digitized it initiates a command to change the text style to ASGN with a font called COMPLEX with letter height of .15. The six ;'s are Enters for the other specifications for the STYLE command such as

Figure 11-10
NAME Icon Frame

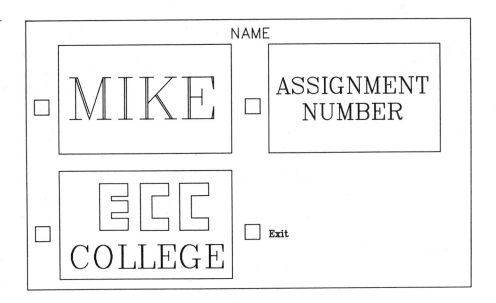

rotate, upside down, etc. The DTEXT command is then executed with "centered" as the location specification. The \ allows the operator to pick the location for the text and the ;'s are Enters for the remainder for the DTEXT specifications.

[Exit]^C^C Tells AutoCAD to display a word called Exit that allows you to exit from the NAME icon frame. The space between the "[" and "Exit" causes the text to be displayed without a slide (when that space does not exist, AutoCAD looks for a slide with the name "Exit").

Step 6. Save your MK.MNU file, exit from the text editor, and call up AutoCAD.

Step 7. Start a new drawing or edit an existing one.

Step 8. From the command prompt:

Prompt: Command:
Response: MENU

Prompt: Menu file name or . for none <ACAD>:
Response: (Your initials).MNU

The prompt line should state: "compiling (your initials).MNU."

Step 9. Test your menu, find out what is wrong with it, fix it, and test it again. If you get it right the first time you are very unusual.

EXERCISE 1

Create a tablet menu similar to the one described in Figure 11-6. Test and demonstrate your menu as your instructor requests.

EXERCISE 2

Modify the AutoCAD screen menu as described in this chapter. Test and demonstrate the menu as your instructor requests. Be sure to copy the ACAD.MNU file under another name before modifying it.

EXERCISE 3

Create a pull-down icon similar to the one shown in Figure 11-10. Use pictures instead of the text shown. You may create a working macro different from the one described for ASSIGNMENT NUMBER if you like. Test and demonstrate the menu per your instructor's request.

Test on Objectives—Chapter 11

Circle the most correct answer.

1. The text editor used in this chapter to add and change commands is:
   a. AutoCAD
   b. EDLIN
   c. WORD PERFECT
   d. MULTIMATE
   e. DOS

2. In the MACRO ^C^CLINE;END\END\ the ^C does which of the following?
   a. changes a line
   b. activates the line command
   c. activates the complete macro
   d. instructs AutoCAD that a change is forthcoming
   e. cancels a previous command

3. In the MACRO ^C^CLINE;END\END\ the semicolon does which of the following?
   a. cancels a previous command
   b. asks for an operator response
   c. acts as a return
   d. identifies an AutoCAD command
   e. identifies the end of a line or arc,

4. In the MACRO ^C^CLINE;END\END\ the backslash does which of the following?

   a. cancels a previous command

   b. asks for an operator response

   c. acts as a return

   d. identifies an AutoCAD command

   e. identifies the end of a line or arc,

5. In the MACRO ^C^CLINE;END\END\ a return occurs:

   a. between the first and second ^C.

   b. after\and the second END

   c. before each backslash

   d. between ^C and the command LINE.

   e. at the semicolon.

6. The command used to configure the AutoCAD tablet is:

   a. CFG

   b. TABLET

   c. CAL

   d. SETUP

   e. SETTINGS

7. Each of the tablet areas is identified to AutoCAD by:

   a. all four corners

   b. upper left, upper right, and lower left corners

   c. upper left, upper right, and lower right corners

   d. upper left, and lower right corners

   e. upper left, lower left, and lower right corners

8. Vertical lines of blocks on the AutoCAD tablet are identified as:

   a. rows

   b. columns

9. The area of the AutoCAD tablet menu that has been left blank so that other commands may be added is:

   a. area 1

   b. area 2

   c. area 3

   d. area 4

   e. area 5

10. To move from line 1607 to line 1601 in the ACAD.MNU file using the DOS text editor, which of the following is correct?

   a. backspace until line 1601 appears

   b. use the UP arrow on the keyboard

   c. type 1601 from the * and Press Enter

   d. type E 1601 from a numbered line and press Enter

   e. type L 1601 and press Enter and Ctrl-C

11. Write a MACRO command to draw a circle with a radius of .5. Label the MACRO CIR-R.5.

_____

12. Write a MACRO command to erase three items as they are digitized. Label the MACRO ERASE3.

_____

13. List the EDLIN response to the command EDLIN MENU1.MNU if MENU1.MNU is a new file.

_____

14. List the EDLIN response to the command EDLIN MENU1.MNU if MENU1.MNU is an existing file.

_____

15. List the operator inputs used to move from line 43 to line 1602 in EDLIN.

_____

_____

16. List the AutoCAD command, the prompts, and the operator responses used to configure area 1 on the AutoCAD tablet.

   Prompt: Command:
   Response:

   Prompt:
   Response:

   Prompt:
   Response:

   Prompt:
   Response:

   Prompt:
   Response:

   Prompt:
   Response:

   Prompt:
   Response:

17. List the response necessary to discard any changes you have made to a file and the prompt from which the response must be made.

_____

18. List the response necessary to end an editing session and keep all changes made to a file. List the prompt from which the response must be made.

_____

19. Describe a workable procedure for rearranging the standard AutoCAD Menu to be more efficient for a specific situation.

_____

_____

20. Describe what each set of characters in the following line does:

[MOVE]$S=X $S=MOVE ^C^CMOVE

[MOVE] _____

$S=X _____

$S=MOVE _____

^C _____

^C _____

MOVE _____

12

Common Problems and Solutions

Objectives

Problems occur occasionally during the use of AutoCAD. More of these problems occur when beginners use the system than when experienced AutoCAD users are at the keyboard. Most of the problems are easily remedied and are a result of not being familiar with the details necessary to ensure smooth functioning. Some of the problems, however, can result in a serious loss of time. This chapter will present the problems that commonly occur and one or more solutions for each of the problems. Cautions are presented for preventing the loss of time when problems do occur. We will begin with the CAUTIONS for preventing serious losses.

Cautions

Never Work for a Long Time Before Saving a Drawing

It is suggested that you use the SAVE command every hour so that no more than an hour's work will be lost in case:

- someone turns off a circuit breaker momentarily to check a circuit
- someone accidentally pulls the power cord to your computer out of the wall
- someone accidentally hits the ON/OFF switch on a power strip
- a power failure during a storm momentarily turns off your computer

Never Move the Computer Without Retracting (Locking or Parking) the Hard Disk

Serious damage to the hard disk can result with even a small movement of the computer; even one as minor as pulling the computer around to check the cables in the back. The damage can be serious enough to require replacement of the hard drive. To retract the hard disk, call up the Root directory of the hard drive and do the following:

Prompt: C:>

Response: PARK {or HDSIT or RETRACT depending on which command is in your DOS}

Always Save a Drawing File on More Than One Disk

If your computer has adequate space on the hard drive (usually the C drive), save the drawing on both the C drive and a floppy disk. If there is not adequate space on the C drive, save the drawing on two floppy disks and keep them separate in case one of the following happens:

■ someone writes on the floppy disk jacket with a ball point pen or another sharp writing instrument

■ someone leaves the floppy disk in a hot car and the disk warps

■ someone mangles the floppy disk

■ one of the disks is lost

■ someone exposes the floppy disk to a magnetic field

Always Make a Backup Copy of New Software Before You Install It

This will allow you to use the program even if one of the following happens:

■ someone mangles one of the original floppy disks

■ someone erases part or all of one of the original floppy disks

■ someone alters one or more of the files on one of the floppy disks

■ someone adds a file to one of the floppy disks which affects the operation of the software

Note: *The four precautions listed above are simple to observe and will prevent a serious loss of time and money. If they are not observed, serious losses can and will occur.*

Common Problems and Solutions

The common problems and their solutions have been divided into four groups. these groups are:

- hardware problems
- command problems that occur before the drawing is displayed
- problems that occur during drawing
- plotting problems

The first group to be presented is hardware problems.

Common Hardware Problems

Hardware Problem No. 1: System will not call up a drawing file from a floppy disk drive (example: Floppy Drive A).

Cause:

- Floppy drive is high-density and disk is double-density or vice versa.

Solution:

Copy drawing file to the hard drive and call it up from there. This will not always work—you may have to find a computer with both high- and double-density drives, and copy the drawing onto a disk of the correct density. To do that, go to the AutoCAD Main Menu and select "6. File utilities" and then select "5. Copy file."

Prompt: Enter name of source file:
Response: A: XXXXXXX.DWG {the drawing name}

Prompt: Enter name of destination file:
Response: C: XXXXX.DWG {or C:\ACAD\XXXXX.DWG if you have AutoCAD in a directory named ACAD}

The drawing will be copied from the floppy disk in the A drive to the hard disk, the C drive.

Hardware Problem No. 2: Mouse, tablet, printer or plotter does not respond.

Causes:

- Device is plugged into the wrong port (a port is a connector on the back of the computer).
- Mouse pad is turned in the wrong direction.
- System is improperly configured for the device used.
- Cables are not firmly plugged in.
- Device is defective or has lint obstructing the LED on the bottom of the mouse.

Solution 1:

Change ports for the device connector.

Solution 2:

Turn the pad to the correct orientation.

Solution 3:

Reconfigure AutoCAD (from the Main Menu).

Solution 4:

Plug in loose cables.

Solution 5:

Replace defective device or remove lint.

Hardware Problem No. 3: Visual display does not appear

Causes:

- Power or computer cable is not plugged in.
- Monitor power switch is off.
- Brightness control is not turned up.
- Defective visual display.

Solution 1:

Plug in power or computer cables.

Solution 2:

Turn on power switch.

Solution 3:

Turn up brightness.

Solution 4:

Replace or repair visual display.

Common Problems Involving Commands (DOS or AutoCAD) Before the Drawing is Displayed

Command Problem No. 1: Prompt shows: "DRAWING FILE NOT FOUND"

Causes:

- Drawing name is incorrect.
- Drawing is in a different directory.
- Drawing is on another disk.

Solution 1:

List drawing files on each disk and in each directory until the drawing is found. This may be done in at least three different ways.

Method A—Go to the AutoCAD file utilities on the Main Menu or, from the screen menu, select "1. List drawing files."

Prompt: Enter drive or directory:

Response: {Type the correct directory and drive–the directory is separated from the drive by a backward slash, Example: C:\ACAD, which would give a listing of all of the drawings in the ACAD directory on drive C}

Method B—

1. Exit AutoCAD and go to the drive that contains the DOS commands.

2. If DOS is on drive C (the hard drive in most cases), the prompt will read C: or C:>.

3. At the prompt C:, type the command DIR C:\ACAD*.DWG. This will give you a listing of all the drawing files (.DWG) in the ACAD directory on drive C.

If you want a listing of all of the backup files type the command: DIR C:\ACAD*.BAK. This will give you a listing of all the backup files (.BAK) in the ACAD directory on the C drive. (A backup file is created when you end a drawing; it will be the previous version of the drawing you are editing, or two versions of the same drawing if the drawing is new.)

Method C—

1. Activate a software program such as XTREE or XTPRO (if one is available on your system) and log onto the drive you wish to explore. These programs are inexpensive and are by far the easiest way to discover which directories and files have been created on any disk.

2. Once the location and the correct name of the drawing have been found, the drawing may be activated. Be sure to list the drive and the directory before the drawing name if the drawing is not in the ACAD directory. If the drawing is in the ACAD directory, the drive and the directory may be omitted.

      Example: C:\BOOK\DRAW-1
         (C drive, book directory, drawing named DRAW-1—drawing *not* in the ACAD directory)

      Example: DRAW-1
         (default to current drive (drive on which AutoCAD is located, ACAD directory), drawing named DRAW-1— drawing *is* in the ACAD directory)

Command Problem No. 2: AutoCAD will not call up a drawing from a floppy disk and displays a message that the disk is full.

Solution 1:

Delete unnecessary files from the floppy disk (such as .BAK files) and try again (see Command Problem No. 6).

Solution 2:

Copy the drawing to the hard disk and call it up from there.

Command Problem No. 3: The system will not boot up on the C drive (the hard drive) when ACAD and DOS have been installed on that drive.

Note: *You have to use a DOS disk in one of the floppy drives to* <u>*boot-up (start)*</u> *a software program.*

Cause:

■ The system program has not been transferred to the C drive.

Solution:

Go to the system prompt for the drive on which your active DOS exists—probably the A drive—the one in which you have your floppy disk.

Prompt: A:>

Response: SYS C: ↵

This transfers the initial system boot-up commands to the C drive. Turn the computer off and then back on to see if it will boot-up on the C drive. If this fails, re-boot the system from the A drive and copy everything stored on the C drive (the hard disk) onto floppy disks using a convenient software program or the BACKUP command from DOS. Then, with the DOS disk in drive A, reformat the hard disk and transfer the system (DOS) to the hard disk using the following command:

Prompt: A:>

Response: FORMAT C:/S ↵ {if C is the hard disk}

You will then be prompted with the following warning:

ALL INFORMATION ON THE HARD DRIVE WILL BE
    DESTROYED. DO YOU WANT TO PROCEED (Y/N)

Before you respond to the warning observe the following:

■ The FORMAT command erases everything on the hard drive.

■ You must have already copied all the files from the hard drive onto floppy disks *before* the FORMAT command is used; and be sure you have copied *all* the files from *every* directory and from *every* subdirectory.

■ Do *not* use the FORMAT command unless you have your instructor's permission to do so.

If you do not want to reformat the hard drive answer "N" to the warning prompt. If you do want to reformat the hard drive, answer "Y" to the warning prompt and, after the FORMAT has been completed, restore all software and files into the appropriate directories.

Command Problem No. 4: "Copy drawing file" command from the AutoCAD Main Menu did not work.

Causes:

■ The suffix ".DWG" was left off of the drawing name in response to either the "source" prompt or the "destination" prompt. In both cases, the drawing name must appear as: DRAW-1.DWG

■ The directory or the drive from which, or to which, the drawing was copied, was not properly typed.

Solution:

Redo the command using the correct drawing, directory, and disk names in the proper sequence.

For instance, if a drawing named DRAW1 is to be copied from a floppy disk in the A drive to a directory name BOOK on the C drive you would use the following procedure:

Prompt: Enter name of source file:
Response: A:DRAW1.DWG ↵

Prompt: Enter name of destination file:
Response: C:\BOOK\DRAW1.DWG ↵

Command Problem No. 5: Drawing file was lost and cannot be found.

Cause:

■ File was accidentally erased or deleted.

Solution 1:

Call for a listing of backup files. If the backup file for the last drawing exists, rename the backup file to make it the drawing file. To do this from the AutoCAD Menu, select SHELL from the UTILITIES Menu as shown below.

Prompt: Command:
Response: SHELL {or select SHELL from the Utility Menu}

Prompt: C:
Response: DIR\BOOK*.BAK ↵ {for a backup file named DRAW1.BAK in the BOOK directory on the C drive}

The listing will appear. If the backup file is located, press the F1 key (IBM AT/XT) to return to the AutoCAD Menu. Then continue as follows:

Prompt: Command:

Response: FILES

Prompt: Enter selection (0 to 5) <0>:

Response: 4 ↵ {rename files}

Prompt: Enter current filename:

Response: \BOOK\DRAW1.BAK ↵

Prompt: Enter new filename:

Response: \BOOK\DRAW1.DWG ↵

A new DRAW1.DWG file now exists, which was the previous version of the lost drawing file. The new drawing file may now be activated in the same manner as any drawing file.

Solution 2:

Recover the lost file using a program such as Norton Utilities.

Command Problem No. 6: System response time has become very slow.

Causes:

■ Hard disk is becoming full of unnecessary files and useless bytes that occur during computer use.

■ Drawing files may be unnecessarily large.

Solution 1:

Delete all backup (.BAK) drawing files from the ACAD directory. To do this:

Prompt: Command: {from the AutoCAD display}

Response: SELECT FILES

Prompt: Select 1-6:

Response: 3 {delete file}

Prompt: File name to delete:

Response: *.BAK ↵

All backup files will be erased from the ACAD directory. Repeat for all other directories by responding with:

Prompt: File name to delete:

Response: \DWG*.BAK ↵ {to delete all backup files in the DWG directory}

Solution 2:

Erase all useless bytes (called lost clusters).

Prompt: Command:

Response: SHELL ↵

Prompt: C: DOS command

Response: CHKDSK/F ↵

A file or files with the extension .CHK will be created, which may be identified and deleted.

Solution 3:

Purge all drawing files using the PURGE command (WBLOCK will often do a better job of purging than PURGE does). To use the PURGE command, call up each drawing file and immediately do the following:

Prompt: Command:

Response: PURGE {from the UTILITIES Menu}

Prompt: Purge unused Blocks/Layers/L Types/Shapes Styles/All:

Response: All ↵

Reply yes to all PURGE prompts unless you plan to use that feature on the drawing again. (If you purge a feature you want to use again, you will have to recreate it.)

Solution 4:

Copy all useful files from the hard disk to floppy disks using COPY or BACKUP, and FORMAT the hard disk again. To do this, go to the disk on which the DOS commands reside (in this case, the C drive) and, after copying all useful files to floppy disks, procede as follows:

Prompt: C:

Response: FORMAT/S ↵

Prompt: WARNING: ALL DATA WILL BE LOST(N)

Response: Y ↵

Solution 5:

Use the WBLOCK command in AutoCAD to reduce the size of each drawing file. (Drawing files that are WBLOCKED are often a fraction of the size of the original file.)

To do this: call up each drawing and be sure that anything you want to save on the drawing is displayed on the screen, activate the WBLOCK command, respond with the same drawing name as you originally used, window the entire drawing in response to the SELECT OBJECTS prompt, and then issue the QUIT command. Do *not* use the SAVE or END commands or you will save a blank screen.

Reload all software and drawing files and start a drawing file with a renewed hard disk.

Problems Occurring During Drawing

Drawing Problem No. 1: Command such as TRIM, BREAK, ERASE, CHANGE, and EXTEND do not work as they should.

Cause:

■ Display is not large enough to allow the commands to work correctly.

Solution:

ZOOM a window to make the lines larger and try the commands again.

Drawing Problem No. 2: Operator makes a mistake in editing (erasing, changing, etc.) or drawing.

Solution 1:

Press U on the keyboard to UNDO the mistake.

Solution 2:

If the mistake cannot be UNDONE, and it occurred before a great deal of work was done, type QUIT and call the drawing up again.

Drawing Problem No. 3: Operator uses UNDO by mistake.

Solution:

Type REDO or select REDO from the screen menu. (The UNDONE command sequence will be redone.)

Drawing Problem No. 4: OSNAP modifiers such as INTersection, PERPENdicular, ENDpoint, and MIDpoint do not work when used with EDITing and DRAW commands.

Causes:

- Lines are not quite as long as they appear to be.
- Lines or other entity selected is a block or polyline.

Solution 1:

ZOOM a very small window around the corner or other suspicious area and correct the problem.

Solution 2:

EXPLODE the block or polyline and try the command again.

Drawing Problem No. 5: Operator makes a mistake in typing or in digitizing before the command is activated.

Solution:

Use backspace (if appropriate) to correct a typing error or press Ctrl-C (the control key and the letter C at the same time) to cancel the command.

Drawing Problem No. 6: SOLID command will not fill (for two-dimensional drawings).

Causes:

- FILL setting is OFF.
- Solid shape was digitized in the wrong sequence.
- VPOINT incorrectly set.

Solution 1:

Set FILL to ON (FILL is found in the SETVAR Menu which is on the SETTINGS Menu).

Solution 2:

Digitize rectangles or squares in this sequence.

Prompt: Command:
Response: SOLID

Prompt: First point:
Response: D1

Prompt: Second point:
Response: D2

Prompt: Third point:
Response: D3

Prompt: Fourth point:
Response: D4

Prompt: Third point:
Response: ↵

Digitize triangles in this sequence:

Prompt: Command:
Response: SOLID

Prompt: First point:
Response: D1

Prompt: Second point:
Response: D2

Prompt: Third point
Response: D3

Prompt: Fourth point:
Response: ↵

Solution 3:

Reset VPOINT to 0,0,1 (this is the viewpoint for 2-D commands). To do this:

Prompt: Command:
Response: VPOINT {type or select from 3D Menu}

Prompt: Enter view point <X,X,X>:

Response: 0,0,1 ↵ {or select PLAN}

Drawing Problem No. 7: Hidden lines display solid (they will also plot solid), dimensioning arrowheads and text size are too small, dimensioning text is the incorrect value.

Cause:

■ LTSCALE and DIMSCALE have incorrect values for the drawing scale being used.

Solution:

Reset the LTSCALE and DIMSCALE values. To do this use the following procedure:

Prompt: Command:

Response: LTSCALE {from keyboard or SETTINGS Menu}

Prompt: New scale factor <1>:

Response: {Enter new scale factor—examples are shown below}

Scale or Units used in Drawing	Response to "new scale factor"
Drawing in millimeters	25.4
¼″ = 1″	.25
½″ = 1″	.5
1″ = 1″	1
¼″ = 1′	48
½″ = 1′	24
1″ = 1′	12
1″ = 10′	120
1″ = 100′	1200
1″ =1000′	12000

You may need to vary the scale up or down depending on the size of the drawing. Repeat for DIMSCALE (from the DIMVARS Menu on the DIM Menu).

Drawing Problem No. 8: ZOOM ALL places the drawing in one corner of the drawing with a great deal of open space on two sides.

Causes:

■ LIMITS incorrectly set.

■ Small line, point, or text in the open space.

■ A layer is off or frozen.

Solution 1:

Set LIMITS (on the SETTINGS Menu) correctly and then ZOOM ALL.

Solution 2.

Erase using WINDOW in the open spaces to eliminate the object and then ZOOM ALL.

Solution 3:

Turn ON all layers using LAYER then "ON" then "*" (for ALL). THAW all layers using LAYER then "THAW" then "*" (for ALL) and then ZOOM ALL.

Drawing Problem No. 9: System locks in OSNAP when typed from the keyboard.

Solution:

Press Ctrl-C (the control key and the letter C at the same time) and select OSNAP from the menu (or from the mouse if the right mouse key is so programmed).

Drawing Problem No. 10: PAN or ZOOM command displays only part of the drawing area selected.

Cause:

■ LIMITS incorrectly set.

Solution:

Set LIMITS correctly or turn LIMITS OFF.

Drawing Problem No. 11: Command prompt will not accept a decimal response (Example: .010).

Cause:

■ In some cases AutoCAD expects a zero before the decimal point.

Solution:

Place a zero before the decimal point (Example: 0.010).

Drawing Problem No. 12: Mirrored block cannot be exploded for editing.

Solution:

EXPLODE block before using the MIRROR command.

Drawing Problem No. 13: CHANGE (point or line) command does not work as expected.

Causes:

- ORTHO is ON (when it is not needed).
- CHANGE point on the line is more than half the length of the line.

Solution 1:

Turn ORTHO OFF (using the correct function key) and try again.

Solution 2:

CHANGE the line in more than one step or use another command such as TRIM or BREAK.

Drawing Problem No. 14: LINETYPE or COLOR does not change when the proper color is selected.

Cause:

- LINETYPE or COLOR was inadvertently set for all layers.

Solution:

Select LINETYPE or COLOR from the SETTINGS Menu (*not* from the LAYER Menu) and set them to BYLAYER. BYLAYER means that the colors and linetypes are determined by the layer on which the entity is drawn.

Drawing Problem No. 15: Dimensions are displayed as a block.

Note: *Extension lines, arrowheads, dimension lines and text must be exploded before they can be changed. This is OK in some situations, not OK in others.*

Cause:

- Dimensioning variable for associative dimensioning (DIMASO) is ON.

Solution:

Set DIMASO to OFF (go to DIMVARS on the DIM Menu and select DIMASO).

Common Plotting Problems

Plotting Problem No. 1: Plotted area turns out to be only a portion of the complete drawing.

Causes:

- LIMITS are incorrectly set.
- Plot is oriented incorrectly (vertical or horizontal).
- Plot scale is incorrectly set.
- Required layers are not ON.

Solution 1:

Call up drawing and set LIMITS to correspond to the page size, and position the drawing within the limits.

Solution 2:

Respond correctly to the plot prompt: "Rotate 2-D plots 90° clockwise <N> (yes) or (no)."

Solution 3:

Respond correctly to the plot prompt: "Plotted inches (or millimeters) = Drawing units or Fit or ? <1 = 1>." Some examples of correct responses are:

> 1=1   will produce a full-size drawing
> ¼″=1′ *or* 0.25=12 *or* 1=48 will produce a plot at a scale of ¼″=1′
> ⅛″=1′ *or* 0.125=12 *or* 1=96 will produce a plot a scale of ⅛″=1′

If millimeters was stated earlier in the unit plot prompt the scale prompt is:

Prompt: Plotted millimeters = Drawing Units or Fit or ? <1=1>

Response: 2.5 = 1 {will produce a plot of 2.5 millimeters = 1 drawing unit, if the drawing was done in meters 2.5mm would equal 1 meter}

Solution 4:

Call up the drawing and turn on the required layers.

Plotting Problem No. 2: Wet pens skip or fail to draw.

Causes:

- Pen is clogged.
- Pen is empty.
- Point is damaged.
- Ink is too thick.
- Paper is moist or oily.

Solution 1:

Clean pen.

Solution 2:

Fill pen with fresh ink.

Solution 3:

Replace point.

Solution 4:

Clean pen and refill with fresh ink.

Solution 5:

Replace paper and prepare the surface, if necessary, by rubbing with pounce and wiping the surface clean with tissue.

Solution 6:

Use disposable pens.

Plotting Problem No. 3: Drawing is not in the correct position on the sheet.

Cause:

- Plot origin is incorrectly set.

Solution:

Experiment with the origin until the correct setting is obtained. Check the drawing to be sure the lower left corner of the limits of the drawing are at 0,0. List the correct coordinates of the plot origin for A,B, and any other sheet sizes to be plotted. A chart of the correct origins for plotting placed next to the plotter will save many hours of plotting time. Begin the experiment by placing the origin at 0,0. Then move one of coordinates .5, then the other .5, until the correct setting is obtained.

Plotting Problem No. 4: Plotter apparently fails to respond.

Causes:

- Cables are loose.
- Switch box (if so equipped) is not in the correct position.
- Plotter paper is not loaded.
- Pen is not correctly positioned in its holder.
- Plotter switches are incorrectly set.
- Drawing limits are incorrectly set (plotter responded but there were no lines in the area requested).
- AutoCAD is not configured for the plotter used.

Solution 1:

Attach loose cables firmly.

Solution 2:

Place switch box in the correct position.

Solution 3:

Load paper.

Solution 4:

Check all pens and correctly position those out of place.

Solution 5:

Set plotter switches correctly.

Solution 6:

Call up drawing and set limits correctly.

Solution 7:

Configure AutoCAD (on Main Menu) for the plotter to be used.

Select 2—Configure ports and respond with "yes" when the prompt asks if you want to configure ports before you configure the plotter.

Select 5—Configure plotter.

Plotting Problem No. 5: Arrowheads plot smaller than drawn and do not touch the extension line.

Cause:

■ Area fill has been adjusted for the pen width. This is rarely necessary and requires careful planning as the drawing is created.

Solution:

Respond to the plot prompt as follows:

Prompt: Adjust area fill boundaries for pen width? <N>:
Response: ↵ {or N; do not respond with Y}

Test on Objectives—Chapter 12

Select the best of the possible choices.

1. SAVING a drawing should be done:
   a. only at the end of the drawing
   b. every hour
   c. only at the end of the every working day
   d. never

2. Which of the following can be the result of moving the computer without RETRACTing the hard disk?
   a. damage to the display
   b. damage to the hard disk
   c. damage to the floppy drive
   d. damage to the RAM memory
   e. RETRACTing has no effect

3. Which of the following can damage a floppy disk?
   a. writing on the jacket with a ball point pen
   b. a magnetic field
   c. excessive heat
   d. a scratch or thumb print on the exposed tracks
   e. all of the above

4. If the computer will not display a drawing that you know is on a disk in one of the floppy drives:
   a. a cable is loose
   b. the drawing limits are incorrectly set
   c. the floppy drive is high-density and the drawing is on a double-density disk
   d. the drawing file is lost
   e. none of the above

5. Which of the following is a solution to the problem in question 4?

    a. connect cables firmly

    b. reset drawing limits

    c. copy the drawing file to the hard disk and call it up from there

    d. rename the drawing backup file

    e. none of these is the correct solution

6. If the system will not call up a drawing file from a floppy disk in the A drive, which of the following is a possible cause?

    a. the floppy drive is high-density and the floppy disk is single-sided high-density

    b. the hard drive is incompatible with the floppy disk

    c. the hard drive is double-density and the floppy drive is high-density

    d. the hard disk is not the same density as the floppy disk

    e. the floppy disk in the A drive is full

7. Which of the following is a practical solution to the problem in question 6?

    a. rename the directory on the floppy disk

    b. redraw the drawing on the hard disk

    c. copy the drawing to the hard disk and call it up from there

    d. rename the drawing and call it up under another name

    e. copy the drawing to another floppy disk and call it up from there

8. If the mouse does not respond, which of the following is a possible cause?

    a. the mouse is defective

    b. the AutoCAD program is not properly configured

    c. the optical pad is turned in the wrong direction

    d. the mouse cable is not firmly plugged in

    e. all are possible causes

9. If the prompt shows: "Drawing file not found," which of the following is a possible cause?

    a. the drawing file is too big

    b. the disk is full

    c. the drawing name is incorrect

    d. the drawing file is too small

    e. all are possible causes

10. Which of the following is a possible solution to the problem in question 9?

    a. list drawing files and look for the correct name

    b. call it up again using the same name

    c. clean out backup files and call it up again

    d. purge the drawing file to reduce its size

    e. none of these are possible solutions

11. Which of the following will produce a listing of all of the drawing files on the A drive?

    a. A:DIR DWG
    b. :A DIR DWG.*
    c. DIR DWG A:
    d. DIR *.DWG A:
    e. DIR A:*.DWG

12. Which of the following is the correct extension for a backup file?

    a. .BAC
    b. .BAK
    c. .BACK
    d. .DWGB
    e. .DBK

13. To copy a drawing file named DRAW5 located in the ACAD directory using the AutoCAD file Utilities Menu, which of the following is the correct response to the prompt "Enter name of source file:" ?

    a. DWG.DRAW5
    b. DRAW5
    c. DRAW5.DWG
    d. DRAW5/C..DWG
    e. DRAW5. DWG/C/

14. Which of the following is a possible solution to recreating a drawing file which was accidentally erased?

    a. call the drawing file up as a block
    b. copy the lost file to the C drive and call it up from there
    c. format the floppy disk
    d. rename the backup file
    e. an erased drawing file cannot be recreated

15. Which of the following is most probably the correct solution when the CHANGE command does not work as it should?

    a. QUIT the drawing and call it up again
    b. change the current layer
    c. call a repairman
    d. type CHANGE instead of selecting it from the menu
    e. ZOOM a window to enlarge the area

16. Which of the following is most probably the correct solution for restoring an erased part of a drawing?

    a. SAVE the drawing and call it up again
    b. QUIT the drawing and call it up again
    c. END the drawing and call it up again
    d. PURGE the drawing and call it up again
    e. Do an INQUIRY on the drawing

17. Which of the following should be changed when hidden lines are displayed as solid?

    a. PDSIZE

    b. PDMODE

    c. LTSCALE

    d. LIMITS

    e. DIMVAR

18. Which of the following is the correct response to the prompt "New scale factor" for a scale of $\frac{1}{2}'' = 1'$?

    a. .5 = 1

    b. .5

    c. 1 = 12

    d. $\frac{1}{2}$ = 1

    e. 1 = 24

19. Which of the following is the best solution for exploding a mirrored block?

    a. explode the block before it is mirrored

    b. explode the block after it is mirrored

    c. explode the block before it is blocked

    d. rename the block

    e. avoid exploding the block

20. Which of the following is the best solution to a plotter's apparent failure to respond?

    a. reset LIMITS

    b. reset the computer

    c. repeat the same sequence you just tried

    d. set PDMODE correctly

    e. set DIMSCALE correctly

21. List two procedures that should *never* be done while using a computer for drawing.

    a. _____

    b. _____

22. List two procedures that should always be done while using a computer for drawing.

    a. _____

    b. _____

23. Describe a solution for calling up a drawing file from a double-density floppy disk if the computer has only a high-density floppy drive and a hard disk drive.

_____

24. Describe three ways to fix a mouse that fails to respond.

    a. _____

    b. _____

    c. _____

25. List three possible causes for the prompt "Drawing file not found."

    a. _____

    b. _____

    c. _____

26. Write the correct response to the prompt "Drawing Name" to call up an existing drawing named DRAW2 located in a directory labeled DWG on the C drive.

    _____

27. Write the correct syntax for source file and destination file to copy a drawing file labeled DRAW5 located on the A drive to a directory labeled BOOK on the C drive using the same name. ("Syntax" means all of the characters and punctuation in the correct order.)

    SOURCE FILE _____

    DESTINATION FILE _____

28. List two solutions for restoring several circles which were accidentally erased.

    a. _____

    b. _____

29. List two possible causes for OSNAP not working as it should.

    a. _____

    b. _____

30. List three possible causes for SOLID not filling correctly.

    a. _____

    b. _____

    c. _____

Appendix
DOS: The Disk Operating System

All microcomputers are controlled by a system of commands and functions known as the disk operating system. This Appendix contains the major commands and functions of the DOS system. The command is described first and then an example of how to use the command is presented. Before describing the commands, a brief look is necessary at how software systems on a microcomputer are structured.

System Structure

Disks and Drives

Most computers on which AutoCAD is used professionally have both hard (fixed) and floppy drives. These drives are used to operate disks on which files containing information reside. A common system has one or two floppy drives labeled "A" and "B" and a fixed drive labeled "C." The DOS system recognizes these drives by those letters. It is important to know on what drive the computer is operating so that the proper commands can be issued.

Directories

The disks in these drives contain files of drawings, functions, and commands that are often separated into directories. These directories, which you create, are simply groups of files that are more manageable and efficient as a result of being arranged in this order. Files may be moved from one directory to another as it becomes apparent that a different arrangement is better. The directories may also have sub-directories, which make for an even better system.

Directories are more commonly found on the hard disk because the hard disk has much more memory. Often floppy disks do not contain directories, and the files on floppy disks reside on the disk in no particular order.

A common directory structure for the hard disk (the C drive) is:

TITLE	DESCRIPTION
\Root directory	Root directory
ACAD	ACAD directory
ADWG	Drawing subdirectory (ACAD)
DRV	Driver subdirectory (ACAD)
DOS	DOS directory
WP	Word processor directory
DWG	drawing directory

Examples of how to make and use directories are explained later in this Appendix under the section on commands.

The System Prompt

The system prompt (or other similar mark) tells you that the computer is ready for a command and shows where the computer will look for program or data files (unless otherwise instructed).

Moving Around

Changing Directories

Let us say you are in the DOS directory and want to draw something using ACAD commands that you have placed in the ACAD directory. You must first change to the Root directory and then go to the ACAD directory. An example of how to do that is shown below. Depending on how you have your prompt set, you may or may not know which directory you are in; let us assume you do not know.

Prompt:　　C> {or C>DOS}

Response:　CD\ ↵ {this returns you to the Root directory—
　　　　　　　CD = Change directory; \ = Root directory}

Prompt:　　C> {you are now in the Root directory}

Response:　CD ACAD ↵ {to go to the ACAD directory}

Prompt: C> {or C> ACAD}

    You are now in the ACAD directory. If you had not returned to the Root directory, you would have seen displayed on the screen INVALID DIRECTORY.

Changing Drives

Moving from one drive to another is something that must be done often. To do this:

Prompt: C> {you are on the C drive}
Response: A: ↵ {to move to the A drive}

Prompt: A> {you are now on the A drive}
Response: B: ↵ {to move to the B drive}

Prompt: B>
Response: C: ↵ {to move to the C drive}

Prompt: C> {you are back on the C drive}

Changing Prompts

If you would like the prompt shown on the screen to show the directory as well as the drive, use the following procedure:

Prompt: C>
Response: PROMPT pg ↵ {to change the prompt}

Prompt: C:\ACAD> {if ACAD is the current directory}

    In this case, the "p" after the dollar sign indicates the current directory and the "g" after the dollar sign is asking for the character. Subdirectory branches, if there are any, are listed in this type of prompt. To return to the original prompt:

Prompt: C:\ACAD>
Response: PROMPT ng ↵

Prompt: C>

Other elements that may be used are:

$t	current time
$d	current date
$p	current directory
$n	default drive
$g	the > character
$L	the < character

Rebooting the System

Booting means to start the computer and the computer program. Rebooting or restarting is sometimes necessary when a mistake has been made that cannot be fixed easily.

Note: *Avoid rebooting when in AutoCAD or any other production program. This practice creates scattered bits of information on the hard disk, which will slow the ACAD response time. Always exit to the Root directory before rebooting. Save drawings often and backup files regularly to protect against losing work.*

To reboot the system (also known as a warm boot), hold these three keys down together:

Ctrl Alt Del

If this fails, turn off the computer and after waiting for the drives to come to a stop, turn it back on again. This is known as a cold boot. On some of the newer computers a reset switch as been added. If your computer is equipped with one, use it instead of turning the machine off. It is better for the machine's power supply and you do not have to wait for the hard drive to come to a stop.

DOS Commands

There are two types of DOS commands: external and internal. External commands must be listed as files on one of the disk drives to be activated. (You will not have to do this, the DOS disk is arranged in this manner.) Internal commands are a part of the COMMAND.COM file and do not need to be listed as separate files to be executed.

Four external commands commonly used are FORMAT, DISKCOPY, BACKUP, and RESTORE.

Note: USE OF THE FORMAT COMMAND CAN BE DANGEROUS
TO THE INFORMATION CONTAINED ON THE DRIVES.
*If the computer has a hard disk, backup all of the information
from the hard disk before starting (i.e., copy all of the information from the hard disk to floppy disks). Have a more experienced user help you the first time you work with these commands if one is available. If not, be careful, and use the
BACKUP command before you start. The BACKUP command
is described later in this Appendix.*

External Commands

FORMAT

The FORMAT command is used to prepare a disk to receive data.
Disks must usually be formatted before DOS will write anything on
them. Formatting sets up an index or directory where DOS puts the
names of files placed on the disk. Formatting automatically places
information on the disk that DOS uses to locate and keep track of
files. It also writes header information which DOS uses to recognize
the disk. Examples of the FORMAT command are shown below:

Prompt: C> {if you are on the C drive}

Response: FORMAT A: ↵ {be sure to put a space between FORMAT
and A}

Prompt: Insert new diskette for drive A: and strike ENTER when
ready.

Response: {Put a floppy disk in drive A, close the lock, and press ↵}

Prompt: Formatting . . .

The disk in drive A is now being prepared to accept data. In this
case, the FORMAT command was a success. Following are two cases
in which the FORMAT command was not located on the first try.

Prompt: C>

Response: FORMAT A: ↵

Prompt: Bad command or file name {you are in the wrong drive or
directory}

Response: CD\ ↵ {go to Root directory}

Prompt: C> {you are in the Root directory}

Response: FORMAT A: ↵

Prompt: Bad command or file name {the FORMAT command is in a directory named DOS, if it were on the Root directory, FORMAT would have worked}

Response: CD DOS ↵

Prompt: C> {you are in the DOS directory}

Response: FORMAT A: ↵

Prompt: Insert new diskettes for drive A: and strike ENTER when ready.

The FORMAT command was located on the C drive in a directory named DOS. Often the DOS system is in the Root directory and the additional step of changing to the DOS directory is not necessary.

This same procedure must be followed for all other DOS commands. Now, look at the FORMAT command which can wipe out all of the files on the hard drive if you are not careful.

Prompt: C>

Response: FORMAT ↵

Prompt: WARNING, ALL DATA ON NON-REMOVABLE DISK DRIVE C: WILL BE LOST! Proceed with FORMAT? (Y/N)

Response: N ↵ {unless you have everything you need from the hard drive on floppy disks}

Prompt: C> {no information was lost}

This example will illustrate the need to be on the correct drive and in the correct directory for any command to work.

Prompt: A> {you are on the A drive}

Response: FORMAT B: ↵

Prompt: Bad command or file name.

Response: {Place a floppy disk containing DOS in drive A}

Prompt: A>

Response: FORMAT B: ↵

Prompt: Insert new diskette for drive B: and strike ENTER when ready.

DISKCOPY

The DISKCOPY command is used to make a copy of one complete floppy disk to another floppy disk. Unlike the COPY command, DISKCOPY copies all of the subdirectories and all of the files within each subdirectory.

Note: *BOTH DISKS MUST BE OF THE SAME TYPE. If the original floppy disk is a double-sided, double-density disk, then the disk it is copied to must also be a double-sided, double-density disk. You cannot copy from a floppy disk to the hard drive with this command. An example follows:*

Prompt: C> {you are on the C drive and in the same directory as the DISKCOPY command}

Response: DISKCOPY A: B: ↵ {put a space between A: and B:}

Prompt: Insert SOURCE diskette in drive A:
Insert TARGET diskette in drive B:
Press any key when ready:

Response: {Place the disk to be copied in drive A and a blank disk in drive B and press ↵ (the new disk does not have to be formatted when using DISKCOPY)}

Prompt: Copying 40 tracks
9 sectors / track 2 side(s)
Copy another diskette (Y/N)?

The number of sectors, tracks, and sides shown in the prompt will vary according to the type of floppy disk drive you are using.

BACKUP

Although the COPY and DISKCOPY commands can be used to make backups of files, there are instances when a file is too large to fit on the floppy disk or disks onto which it is being copied. When this is the case, BACKUP.EXE will help.

Be sure to have several formatted disks ready to receive the files. Unlike the COPY command, if there is any information on the disk, it will be overwritten, so use empty disks only. The file must be restored in the same order in which it was backed up. To do this, number the disks to keep track of the information. After the file is backed up, it can be restored to the original drive or to another computer by using the RESTORE command. And example of the BACKUP command for a single file:

Prompt: C>

Response: BACKUP C> CHESS.BAS A: ↵ {you will copy the entire
file of the chess game file called CHESS.BAS from the C
drive to the A drive—substitute other file and drive names
to backup the file you wish to backup}

The BACKUP command can also be used to backup entire directories or the entire hard disk. In this situation, leaving out the filename.ext, and adding the /S option backs up all of the subdirectories. Other options are available, such as backing up only those files that have been changed since last use, backing up only those files created since a certain date, and adding files to the backup disk without erasing files currently there. See your DOS manual for these options.

To backup the hard disk (in this case the C drive):

Prompt: C>

Response: BACKUP C: /S ↵

RESTORE

The RESTORE command is used to restore files which have been removed to floppy disks using the BACKUP command. To restore all of the files from a hard disk, it is necessary to first create the same directories in which the files resided on the original disk. The RESTORE command insists on placing the files in the same directory from which they were taken. An example of the RESTORE command is:

Prompt: C> {you are on the C drive with your first backup disk in
the A drive}

Response: RESTORE A: C:\ ↵

The files will be restored in the order that they were copied using the BACKUP command. They are being restored from the A drive to the C drive.

With the exception of FORMAT and DISKCOPY, all of the commands in this Appendix can be used with subdirectory information included. For instance, to backup all of the files in the \ACAD\DWG subdirectory on the C drive to the A drive, this format would be used:

Response: BACKUP C:\ACAD\DWG*.* A: ↵

To restore all of the files, into the correct subdirectories the format is:

Prompt: C>

Response: RESTORE A: C: \ACAD\DWG ↵

If you have a file backed-up from a hard disk and you do not know the name of the subdirectory it came from, it is easy enough to find out by using the TYPE command to display the contents of the file on the screen, quickly pressing Ctrl-S to stop the flow of text. BACKUP writes information about the proper subdirectory near the top of the file where it should be easy to find.

Internal Commands

Some of the DOS manuals identify pages relating to internal and external commands with an I or an E. This section contains the I commands.

Files and filenames

Before discussing the individual commands, it is important to know how files are identified. A file is a drawing, a command, or other group of information used by a program. Filenames are used to identify the files. A filename is required for any information that is saved on a hard or a floppy disk. A filename may be from one to eight characters long and may contain no spaces (dashes are used instead). You may use either uppercase or lowercase letters when entering a filename, but DOS will convert all of the letters to uppercase. The filename must also be identified by drive and directory if it resides somewhere other than on the current drive and directory. The back-slash (\) is used to separate drives and directories. Examples of valid ACAD filenames are shown:

DRAWING1

> Resides on the default drive and directory, probably C:\ACAD.

B: DRAWING1

> On the disk in drive B.

C: \ACAD\DWG\DRAWING1

> In the DWG subdirectory of the ACAD directory located on the disk in the C drive.

\ACAD\DWG\DRAWING1

> In the DWG subdirectory of the ACAD directory located on the disk in the current working drive.

All of the filenames in ACAD are automatically given the extension .DWG when a new drawing is started. An extension identifies the file type and may be from 0 to 3 characters long. AutoCAD adds the appropriate extension for the task at hand but commands used outside of the ACAD directory often require a period and an extension after the filename:

C:\ACAD\DRAWING1.DWG

The characters allowed for filenames and extensions include:

A-Z 0-9 $ & # % ' ( ) @ ^ ' !

Several extensions are reserved for special use:

COM	command file programs
EXE	executable file programs
ASM	assembly language files
SYS	system files
BAK	backup files
BAS	BASIC files
BAT	batch file programs
AUX	reserved for serial port
PRN	reserved for printer port
CON	reserved for screen
NUL	reserved

Now for the commands:

DIRECTORY (DIR)

This command displays a list of the files stored on a disk. You may use this command in one of three ways:

Prompt: C:> {or whatever drive you examine}
Response: DIR ↵

Response: DIR/P ↵ {pauses when a full screen of information is displayed}

Response: DIR/W ↵ {a wide version of the directory, leaving out date and size information}

The DIR command displays the "total bytes free" at the bottom of the list. A 5¼-inch, double-sided, double-density disk holds 360K of information (1K = 1024 bytes; 1 byte = approximately 1 character). AT computers often have a 1.2M (1200K) floppy drive. Hard disks hold up to 80M or more of information. It is a good idea to leave some free space on a disk for editing files. If the total bytes free is less than 20,000 (20K) on a floppy disk, avoid storing any additional information there; either remove unnecessary files or start a new disk. Keep at least 1M available on a hard disk.

Wildcards

Wildcards are used in DOS to simplify the manner which filenames and their extensions are identified.

?	refers to any single character
*	refers to any character or group of characters

For example, assume that these files exist in a directory:

DRAWING1.DWG	COMMAND.COM
DRAWING2.DWG	MECH.MNU
AUTOEXEC.BAT	ACAD.MNX
INSTALL.BAT	INSTALL2.BAT
ACAD.MNU	DWG-321.DWG
MECH.DWG	MECH.MNX
NEW.MNU	NEW.MNX

The following demonstrates using a wildcard in a response, and shows the outcome of such use:

DIR *.* ↵   Displays a list of all of the files shown above. (The star to the left of the period calls for all filenames; the star to the right of the period calls for all extensions.)

DIR *.DWG ↵
  Displays a list of all of the files with the extension .DWG. In this case:

  DRAWING1.DWG

  DRAWING2.DWG

  DWG-321.DWG

  MECH.DWG

DIR DRAWING?.* ↵
> Displays the files:
>> DRAWING1.DWG
>>
>> DRAWING2.DWG

MECH.* ↵ Displays all files with the filename MECH:
>> MECH.DWG
>>
>> MECH.MNU
>>
>> MECH.MNX

DIR A: ↵   Lists all of the files in the disk in the A drive.

DIR\ACAD ↵
> Lists all files in the ACAD directory.

COPY (COPY)

This command allows individual files to be copied from one disk to another or from one filename to another. The FILES Menu in the AutoCAD program may also be used to copy files without exiting from AutoCAD. If the file is to be copied from DOS, however, the response is:

> COPY   A:DRAWING1.DWG   B:DRAWING1.DWG ↵

This copies a file with the name and extension DRAWING1.DWG from the A drive to the B drive.

The drawing name and extension may be left out if the name is to be the same. For example:

> COPY   A:DRAWING1.DWG   B: ↵

This will produce the same results as the previous response.

The following response copies the file under a different name.

> COPY   A:DRAWING1.DWG   B:DRAWING2.DWG ↵

This copies a file with the name and extension DRAWING1.DWG from the A drive to the B drive and gives the name DRAWING2.DWG to the new file on the B drive.

To copy DRAWING1.DWG from drive A to the filename DRAWING2.DWG on the same drive (when the default drive is the A drive) the response is:

COPY A:DRAWING1.DWG A:DRAWING2.DWG ↵

or

COPY DRAWING1.DWG DRAWING2.DWG ↵

The drive names can be left out because they are both the default drive.

To copy all files with the BAT extension from drive B to drive C when the default drive is B:

COPY B:*.BAT C:*.BAT ↵

or

COPY *.BAT C: ↵

A wildcard is used here to stand for all filenames with the BAT extension. The drive copied from is the default drive, so it does not need to be included in the command. The names will be the same on the C drive, so the filenames are not necessary.

DELETE (DEL) or ERASE (ERASE)

These two commands can be used to delete files from a disk—use them with care. If the wrong file is accidentally deleted, get help. It is possible to retrieve the file again as long as nothing is written over it. Norton Utilities is a popular software package that can be used to recover erased files. To delete a file, use either of the following:

DEL A:DRAWING1.DWG ↵

or

ERASE A:DRAWING1.DWG ↵

Both of these commands delete the file labeled DRAWING1.DWG from the disk in the A drive.

Note: *WARNING—the ERASE command will also erase the entire contents of a directory, so be extremely careful when using this command. It is suggested that you use the DELETE command rather than the ERASE command to remove files from your disks.*

TYPE (TYPE)

This command shows the information within a file. Only text or ASCII files will be in a form which can be viewed with the TYPE command. To see what is in the file ACAD.MSG (residing on the C drive) do the following:

TYPE C:ACAD.MSG ↵

Use the Ctrl-S key combination to stop the flow of text off the screen when the file has more than one screen of information. Type S to start the display again.

RENAME (REN)

This command is used to change the name of a file after it has been created. To do this the response is:

REN A:DRAWING1.DWG DRAWING2.DWG ↵

This changes the name of the file DRAWING1.DWG on the A drive to DRAWING2.DWG.

Directory Commands

Directories are used to break a hard disk into smaller and more manageable units or to group files into categories. Since the main directory will hold only a specific number of files (the number depends on the particular system, but is usually about 256), MS-DOS allows you to make subdirectories within directories and store files and programs in them. The main directory is often called the Root directory. (The words directory and subdirectory are often used interchangeably.)

d:\dirname \dir2name . . . \filename.ext

Filenames in a subdirectory look like this:

C:\ACAD\DWG\DRAWING1.DWG

This identifies the file DRAWING1.DWG that lies in a subdirectory, DWG, of the directory ACAD, which resides on the C drive.

MAKE DIRECTORY (MD)

This command is used to create a directory. The following forms are used:

MD C:MY-FILE ↵

This creates a directory called MY-FILE under the Root directory of the C drive (if you are on the C drive the C: may be left out).

MD C:\ACAD\MY-FILE ↵

This create a subdirectory called MY-FILE under the ACAD directory of the Root directory on the C drive.

The directory name may be from one to eight characters in length. No extension is required.

REMOVE DIRECTORY (RD)

This command is used to delete a directory. It can only be used after all of the files and subdirectories in that directory have been deleted. Some programs create hidden files or directories which can be removed only by programs such as Norton Utilities.

Other DOS commands may be found in MS-DOS users' manuals. Some of the manuals are not quite as clearly written as this Appendix because they must cover a very wide range of users. The commands in this Appendix will be a good start for you, however, and should make the DOS manuals easier to understand.

Activating Programs

External programs with the .COM, .EXE, or .BAT extensions can be activated by entering their names at the prompt. If the program is on a different drive from the default drive, the drive name must also be included. Because the computer recognizes programs, the extension does not need to be included. For example:

Prompt: C>
Response: A:CHESS ↵

This will start a video game named CHESS located on the A drive (the filename is CHESS.BAT). Another example:

Prompt: C>ACAD
Response: ACAD ↵

This will start the ACAD program, which lies in the ACAD directory on the C drive.

Printing Screens

To print data directly from the screen, Shift-PrtSc prints any text on the screen, and Ctrl-P prints any text that is sent to the screen until the next Ctrl-P.

Batch Files

You can create groups of commands to execute several commands in succession. If there is a file named AUTOEXEC.BAT in the Root directory it will run when you first turn on the computer. Many people set up the system to automatically go into the ACAD program.

AUTOEXEC.BAT File

To set up an AUTOEXEC.BAT file, which will run AutoCAD immediately after the computer is turned on (assume the AutoCAD software has been copied into the ACAD directory of the Root directory on the C drive) use the following procedure:

Prompt: C>

Response: COPY CON AUTOEXEC.BAT ↵

Prompt: –

Response: \ACAD\ACAD ↵

Prompt: –

Response: {Press F6 or press the Ctrl and Z keys simultaneously}

Prompt: ^Z

Response: ↵

Prompt: 1 File(s) copied
            C>

Response: {Turn the computer off, wait for the drives to stop, and turn it on again}

If all has been done correctly the AutoCAD message or the AutoCAD Menu should appear—depending on whether or not you have erased the ACAD.MSG file. If it did not, your AUTOEXEC.BAT file was incorrectly typed or is not in the Root directory. You may repeat the steps for creating the AUTOEXEC.BAT file without creating two files. You will replace the first one with the last one you create. To make sure you are in the Root directory of the C drive begin by doing:

Prompt: C>

Response: CD\ ↵

Prompt: C>

Now start with COPY CON AUTOEXEC.BAT and repeat the previous steps.

DOS References

Copeland, Cody T., and Bacon, Jonathan, *Understanding and Using MS-DOS/PC-DOS: A Complete Guide,* West Publishing Co., 1987.

Lewis, T. G., *Using the IBM Personal Computer,* Reston Publishing Co. Inc., 1983.

Pitter, Keido, *Application Software,* Mitchell Publishing Co., 1987.

Scanlon, Leo J., *The IBM PC Made Easy,* Prentice Hall Inc., 1984.

Glossary of Computer Terms

Baud rate See bps.

Bit (binary digit) The smallest unit of computer data.

Board (printed circuit board) Board onto which components are soldered and connected via etched circuits on the board.

Boot To turn the computer on and start a program.

bps (bits per second) A unit of transmission. Also called baud rate.

Busy lamp Indicator on the front of a disk drive that lights when the drive is writing or reading a disk.

Byte A group of eight bits.

Chip (integrated circuit) A miniature circuit made by etching electronic components on a silicon wafer.

Clock Electronic timer used to synchronize computer operations. A clock is an indication of the speed of the computer operations. A 10–20 MHz clock for AutoCAD is a good speed.

Cold boot Starting the computer by turning it off and then on again.

COM port A communications port allowing data to flow into and out of the computer. Most communication ports are serial ports. Digitizers and most plotters are connected to communication ports.

Command A word used to initiate a task.

Cursor An indicator on the display screen that shows where the next entered data will appear.

Directory Groups of files identified by a directory name.

Disk or diskette A thin, flexible platter coated with a magnetic material for storing information.

Disk or diskette drive A magnetic device that writes on and retrieves data from a disk.

Double-density Refers to how information is "packed" onto a disk. Information on double-density disks is packed at twice the density of that on single-density disks. A double-density disk has a storage capacity of 360K.

Drive A device used to read or write information on a disk or diskette.

Expansion slot Location inside the system unit for the connection of an optional printed circuit board. Expansion slots for optional boards are available in many computers.

Expansion option Add-on hardware that expands power and versatility.

File Information stored by a computer.

Formatting Preparing a disk to accept data.

Hard disk A rigid magnetic storage device that provides fast access to stored data.

Hardware The electronic and mechanical parts of a computer.

High-density The storage capacity of a disk or disk drive that uses high-capacity disks. A high-density disk drive uses a high-density disk with a storage capacity of 1.2 M.

Hz (Hertz) A unit of frequency equal to one cycle per second.

Interface A connection that allows two devices to communicate.

K (Kilobyte) 1024 bytes.

Load To enter a program into the computer's memory from a storage device.

Load lever Lever on the front of a disk drive that locks the disk in place.

M (Megabyte) One million bytes.

Memory An electronic part of a computer that stores information.

Menu A display of programs or tasks.

MHz (Megahertz) One thousand hertz.

Modem (modulator-demodulator) A device that links computers over a telephone.

Monochrome A video display that features different shades of a single color.

Motherboard The main printed circuit board in a computer to which all other boards are connected.

Overwrite Storing information at a location where information is already stored, thus destroying the original information.

Parallel interface Interface that communicates eight bits (or more on newer computers) at a time.

Parallel port A connector on the back of the computer that usually has holes rather than pins. This connector always has 25 connections. Most printers are connected to parallel ports.

Parallel printer A printer with a parallel interface.

Peripheral An input or output device not under direct computer control.

Pixels (picture elements) Tiny dots that make up a screen image.

Port A connection on a computer where a peripheral device can be connected.

Processor A computer on a chip.

RAM (random access memory) Temporary read/write memory that stores information only when the computer is on.

Read To extract data from a storage device such as a floppy disk or hard disk.

ROM (read-only memory) Permanent computer memory that cannot be written to.

RS-232C Standard interface cable for serial devices.

Serial interface An interface that communicates information one bit at a time.

Serial port A connector on the back of the computer that has pins rather than holes. This connector may have either 9 pins or 25 pins. Serial ports are often labeled COM1 or COM2 to identify them as communication ports.

Serial printer A printer with a serial interface (receives information one bit at a time).

Software Computer programs.

System board The main printed circuit board inside the system unit into which other boards are connected.

System unit The component that contains the computer parts, disk drives, and option boards.

Write To record or store information in a storage device.

Write-enable notch Slot on the side of a floppy disk that, when uncovered, permits the disk to be written on.

Write-protecting Covering a floppy disk write-enable notch, thus preventing writing on the disk.

Index

Exercise 4

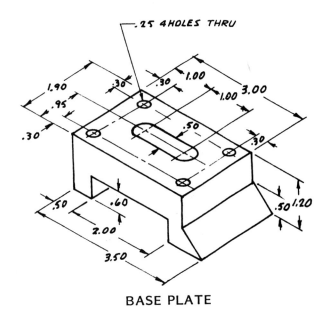

.25 4HOLES THRU

1.90
.95
.30
.30
.30
1.00
1.00 3.00
.50
.30
.50
.60
2.00
3.50
.50 1.20

BASE PLATE

EXERCISE 4

Draw three orthographic views of the object shown above using the following specifications:

> full-scale
> 17 × 11″ sheet of paper
> name in lower right corner
> object lines—thick
> all other lines and text—thin
> no dimensions

For Exercises 5-10, make AutoCAD drawings of the following figures. Use a scale that will allow each drawing to fit on a horizontal paper 11 × 8.5″. Place your name in the lower right corner. *Do not place any dimensions on any of these drawings.* Special instructions for each exercise are given below.

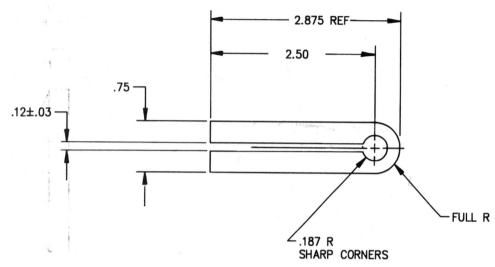

EXERCISE 5

Draw twice-size.

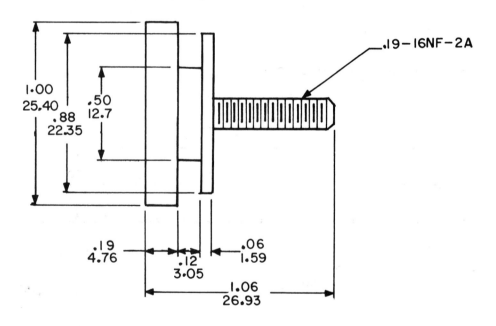

EXERCISE 6

Draw twice-size. Estimate the size of the chamfer and the screw thread symbol. The proportions should be approximately as shown.

Exercise 7

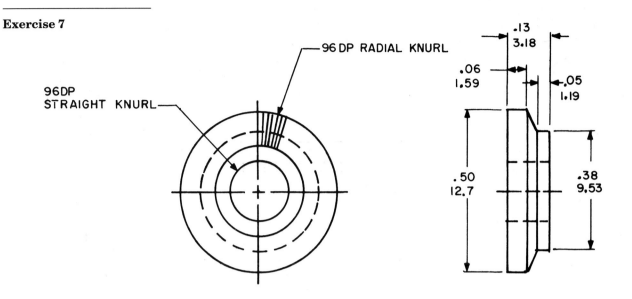

EXERCISE 7

Draw four-times-size. Draw the radial knurl all around the circular shape. Show 80 lines for the radial knurl.

Exercise 8

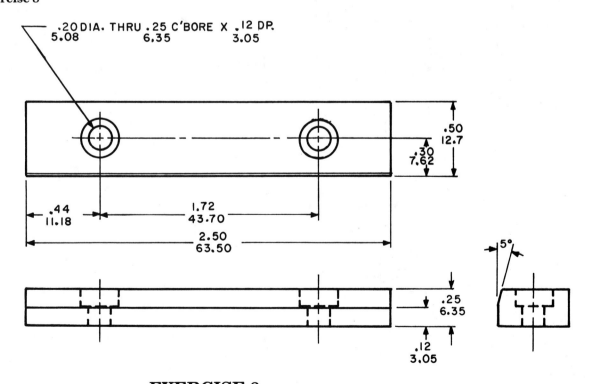

EXERCISE 8

Draw twice-size.

Exercise 9

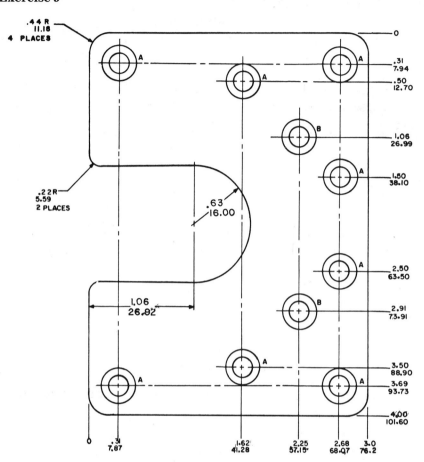

HOLE SCHEDULE		
	SIZE	NUMBER OF HOLES
A	.19 DIA -82°CSK TO .375	8
B	.19 DIA – C'BORE - .375 X .06 DP	2
A	4.83 DIA - 82°CSK TO 9.53	8
B	4.83 DIA–C'BORE 9.53 X 1.59 DP	2

MATERIAL: .125 STEEL PAINTED BLACK
3·18

EXERCISE 9

Draw full-size. Do not show the hole schedule that appears in the upper right corner.

Exercise 10

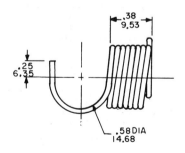

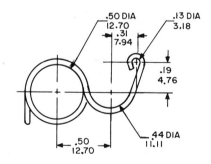

MATL: .03 SPRING WIRE
.79

EXERCISE 10

Draw twice-size. You will find PLINE and OFFSET helpful on this problem.